Libbin' (Living) In De (The) Billige (Village)

Sam Pitt (Sampit, Sampeet)

Lil Eff

Kingdom Builders Publications LLC

Libbin' (Living) **I**n **D**e (The) **B**illige (Village)

Sam **P**itt (Sampit, Sampeet)

In this awe inspiring photograph is **Zilcia Elizabeth Bryant** (Zilcie Bear), daughter of **Effson Chester Bryant** and **Queen Elizabeth Thomas Bryant** standing in front of the "**Sampit Community sign**" located off Saint Delights and Powell Road in Sampit, SC. Sampit is a small family friendly community in Georgetown County.
(Courtesy of the Lil Eff Affikan Cump'ny)

Libbin' (Living) In De (The) Billige (Village) Sam Pitt (Sampit, Sampeet)
Copyright@2017 Lil Eff Affikan Cump'ny
Kingdom Builders Publication

All rights reserved. No part of this book may be reproduced or transmitted in any form or by any means without written permission from the author.

Paperback ISBN: 978-0-692-83653-8
Library of Congress Control Number: 2017931782

Editing, Design, Production
Lil Eff Affikan Cump'ny

For all general information contact: Lil Eff Affikan Cump'ny

Contact Information
Daytime or Evening Phone: 318-518-5933
effson@bellsouth.net

FaceBook Page: Effson Bryant

Acknowledgements

Special thanks to all the **billiger**s (villagers), **Chu'ch's** (churches) of **Sam Pitt** (Sampit) and **North Santee** who shared their rich family stories, pictures, interviews, obituaries and historical knowledge. Thanks to **Loretta "Babe" Grayson**, AKA "Makeba" owner of Babe Creations for her inspiration, encouragement, enlightenment, support, and special love for the Gullah culture and story telling. I am very grateful and I t'engky' Gawd (thank God). **Effson Chester Bryant (Lil Eff)**

Table of Contents (Inflummashum) Information

De (The) Cover Page (The Bryants – Straight Outta Sam Pitt (Sampit)	1
De (The) Sam Pitt (Sampit) Community Sign - Zilcia Elizabeth Bryant	2
De (The) Editing, Design and Production	3
De (The) Acknowledgements	3
De (The) Table of Contents - Inflummashun (Information)	4-5
De (The) Eff and Bernice Jackson Bryant's Fambly (Family)	6
De (The) In Loving Memory of My Sistuh (Sister) Gladys Bryant Scott	7-8
De (The) Story of How Words Met Sound	9
De (The) Military	10
De (The) Introduction	11-14
De (The) Sam Pitt (Sampit)	15
De (The) Sam Pitt (Sampit) Ribbuh (River)	15
De (The) Waterways Map of Georgetown, South Carolina	16
De (The) Sam Pitt (Sampit)	17
De (The) South Carolina Parishes	18
De (The) Sam Pitt (Sampit) Plantesshun (Plantation)	19
De (The) Bighouse (Master's House)	20-21
De (The) Sam Pitt (Sampit) Black Turpentine Workers	21-22
Dis (This) Is Sullivan's Island	23
De (The) Slabes (Slave) Market	24
De (The) Mansfield Plantesshun (Plantation) - Chu'ch (Church)	24
De (The) Sam Pitt (Sampit) Sto's (Stores) - Bidness/Bidnfss (Business)	25-154
De (The) Gullah Museum - De (The) Gullah-Geechee Legend	155-161
De (The) Georgetown Outreach Ministries Inc. (GOMInc.)	162-168
De (The) Sam Pitt (Sampit) Masonic Lodge #409	169-171
De (The) Sam Pitt (Sampit) Gospel Singers	172-180
De (The) Sam Pitt (Sampit) – North Santee Eddycashun (Education)	181
De (The) Allen University, Columbia, South Carolina	182-197
De (The) Omega Phi Fraternity – Mu Sigma	198-201
De (The) Allen University Events/Activities	201-221
De (The) Oak Grove School	222
De (The) Cumberland African Methodist Episcopal Church ABC School	223
De (The) Oak Grove Colored School	224
De (The) Saint Paul African Methodist Episcopal ABC School	224-226
De (The) Sam Pitt (Sampit) Senior Citizens Center	227-232
De (The) Rosemary High School, Andrews, South Carolina	233-246
De (The) Ada Edith Brown Cokley (Mother)	247
De (The) Teacher Vera (Francis) Cokley	247
De (The) Reverend (Dr.) James H. Cokley	248-249
De (The) Mt. Zion African Methodist Church School, North Santee	250
De (The) Sam Pitt (Sampit) Elementary School	251-257
De (The) Sam Pitt (Sampit) New Elementary School	258-261
De (The) Staff Sergeant Leroy McDonald	262
De (The) Reverend Alphonso N. Scott	263
De (The) Claudia Sherald Wright, Teacher	264
De (The) Interdenominational Theological Center (ITC), Atlanta, GA	265-266

De (The) St. James – Santee Fambly (Family) Health Center	267-269
De (The) North Santee – Sam Pitt (Sampit) - Fambly (Family) Health Center	270-271
De (The) Pediatric Waiting Room – In Memory of Mr. Thomas J. Robinson	272
De (The) Mrs. Michelle LaVaughn Robinson Obama	273-274
De (The) Senator Barack Hussein Obama	275
De (The) Congressman James Enos "Jim" Clyburn	275
De (The) President Barack Hussein Obama – 44th President of the USA	276-277
De (The) Nine-Miles Curve Fiah (Fire) Station #2	278-280
De (The) Sam Pitt (Sampit) Cucumber Market (Shed)	281
De (The) Deputy Sheriff Leroy Gasque, Sr.	281
De (The) Deputy Sheriff Daniel Defoe Bryant	281-282
De (The) Gasque' Family (Pressley and Louise Gasque)	283-285
De (The) Caper's Family	286-287
De (The) Gasque Road	288-290
De (The) Bishop John Clifton Gasque (Bishop JC)	291-292
De (The) Confederate Pension Application for John Gasque	293
De (The) Elder Willie Gasque	294
De (The) John Wesley Gasque, Jr. and Carrie Lee Wilson Gasque	295
De (The) Sam Pitt (Sampit) Christ'mus (Christmas) Parade	296-299
De (The) Scribe With A Sam Pitt (Sampit) Root - a.k.a. Lula Mae (Stafford)	300
De (The) Franklin Sun (Franklin Stafford)	300-301
De (The) Sam Pitt (Sampit) Action Group	302
De (The) Sam Pitt (Sampit) Neighbor Clean Up Group	303-308
De (The) Vergie Tennison (Mrs. Vergie)	309-311
De (The) Sam Pitt (Sampit) Park	312-313
De (The) Sam Pitt (Sampit) Lookout Tower (Fire Lookout Tower)	313
De (The) Sam Pitt (Sampit) Recycle Center	314
De (The) Sam Pitt (Sampit) Hang (Heng) Man Tree (Tree V)	315
De (The) Brewington Eff Bryant and Zilcia Elizabeth Bryant	316
De (The) Bibliography (Effson Chester Bryant)	317

These set of rocking chairs were on my Mother, **Bernice's** front porch – her favorite place to relax, kick back and exhale! **(Courtesy of the Lil Eff Affikan Cump'ny)**

The Eff and Bernice Jackson Bryant's Fambly (Family)

This photograph are my **parents** and **siblings** standing in front of the old fashionable family home built in Sampit, South Carolina (Route 1 Box 303), Georgetown, South Carolina 29440 in 1952. **(Courtesy of the Lil Eff Affikan Cump'ny)**

(Left to Right)

Effson Chester (Lil' Eff or Beans), **Lou Emma** (Gogo) 9 July 1956 - 8 January 1982, **Daniel DeFoe** (Danny) 15 January 1971 - 13 March 2008, **Eff** (Buddy) 12 July 1914 - 19 May 1975, **Bernice** (Bern) 4 July 1933 - 23 June 2006, **Hughie Benjamin** (Huey), **Gladys** (November 20, 1954 – January 27, 2015) and **Wesley Michael Bryant** (Wes).

<u>Not pictured</u>: **Jack** (24 April 1961 - 27 April 1961) and **Jill** (24 April 1961 - 29 April 1961).

Photograph: The Eff and Bernice Jackson Bryant's Family (Sampit, South Carolina)
Photo by Effson Chester Bryant, Lil Eff Affikan (African) Cump'ny (Company)
(Courtesy of the Lil Eff Affikan Cump'ny)

"I'm Gonna Trust in the Lord Till I Die"
The Family Favorite Gospel Song

In Loving Memory of Gladys Bryant Scott, my Big Sister

Gladys Bryant

Gladys Bryant Scott and daughter, **Iesha Amanda Scott**

Pompey & **Gladys** marriage took place at **Saint Paul A.M.E. Church, Sampit, SC** on July 6, 1985. **Wedding Party**: Rev. Effson Bryant, Janice Davis, Freddie Stafford, Rev. Melvin Jenkins, Melissa Gasque and Harrison Bryant.

Gladys, Pompey (Scotty) and Iesha at The Olivet Church, Fayetteville, Georgia.
(Courtesy of the Lil Eff Affikan Cump'ny)

Gladys Bryant Scott

A Legacy Of Love & Laughter

November 20, 1953
January 27, 2015

Iesha Amanda Scott Brown & Ronald Charles Davis II - Wedding Day (May 24, 2015)

Iesha Amanda Scott　　　We Love and Honor You　　A Story of How Words Met Sound　　The Wedding Program

Officiant Sunni Patterson, Iesha Amanda Scott, Ronald Charles Davis II, Enid Brown, Maid of Honor, Hillary Carrere, Groomsman - Sunday, May 24, 2015 - The Georgia Railroad Freight Depot, Atlanta, GA.   At right is my beautiful niece, Iesha Scott Brown on her wedding day.

Pompey Scott, his daughter, Iesha S. David and son-in-law Ronald Davis. At right are Erin Labostrie, Jason Davis, Ronald Davis, Iesha S. Davis, Ronald's parents, Leo & Bari Jenks.
(Courtesy of the Lil Eff Affikan Cump'ny)

In January 2015, **Airman First Class** Zilcia Elizabeth Bryant followed the footsteps of her favorite Airmen, Chaplain, **Major Effson Chester Bryant** (Father) joining the United States Air Force.

Airman First Class Zilcia Elizabeth Bryant (left) once said, "I want to go into the military and be like my Aunt Gogo" - **Specialist (SPC)** Lou Emma Bryant Swayzer.
(Courtesy of the Lil Eff Affikan Cump'ny)

Introduction

Where is **Sam Pitt (Sampit)?** Is Sampit really on the map? How do I get to Sampit? Were you born there? These are some of the questions that people usually asked me about my hometown. **Sam Pitt (Sampit)** is a small rural, wooded, fishing, logging and farming community, once upon a time an **Indian village** (Sampas Indians). **Sampit** is off the old Kings Highway (Saint Delights), located in Georgetown County (Craven County), which was formerly the Prince George Parish.

The Prince George Winyah Parish was created in 1721. From the northwest part of St. James Santee Parish, a part of Craven County. The original church was near Brown's Ferry on the Black River (Dunbar), Georgetown, SC. In 1734 that building was given to the new Prince Frederick Parish, and a new church for Prince George Parish was constructed later in Georgetown, Georgetown, SC

Sampit is sandwiched between Georgetown to the east, North Santee to the south and Andrews to the west. The Gapway Bay, Little and Big Kilsock Bay, the Canon Bay, and the Winyah Bay surround it. The Sampit River called the "little river" by the Native Sampas Indians runs through it. The history of Sampit revolves around the "little river" that provided convenient transportation, abundant food, and several plantations along the way. This "billige" is where I grew up.

Sampit, my native home, is located some nine miles west of Georgetown and nine miles east of Andrews. **Sampit** is located on Highway 521, nine miles from the former Grave Station Train Depot, nowadays Grave Station to the Bethel Station Train Depot which was in Sampit. The Bethel Station was located some nine miles from the Rosemary Train Station, located in present day Andrews. The Bethel Station was located on the old Indian trail or cart road close to the former Oak Grove School (White school) or a few miles from Oak Grove Colored School, near Bethel United Methodist Church, off Andrews Highway. It is said that people from Sampit caught the Boll Weevil (passenger train) from the Bethel Station traveling to Rosemary Station in Andrews and Graves Station to Georgetown to shop or go to visit relatives. The "Bethel Station" in Sampit is similar to the Salters and Rosemary Stations, where passengers from Sampit caught the Boll Weevil (passenger train) to travel to Andrews and Graves Stations.

It was said that many **Sampit** residents were employed laying the tracks for the Bethel Station, Graves Station and Rosemary Station. The Old Cart road, which a portion is still visible today, led to the Sampit Station and was the main road leading to **Sampit**. Later on, the main roads to Sampit were moved about a mile to a place we called the "Nine Mile Curve". Why this location was called the "Nine Mile Curve?" It is said the "Nine Mile Curve" got its name because it was 9 miles from Andrews (Rosemary Station) to the Nine Miles Curve; and 9 miles from Georgetown (Graves Station) to the Nine Miles Curve. Long time ago, train stations or depots were built nine miles apart. Turn at the Nine Mile Curve to Highway 17 Alternate is the Sampit Township, named after the "Sam Pitt Indians" that lived and roamed around the Sampit River.

Sampit is my beloved hometown. It is the place where I was conceived, born and raised. Sampit is the genesis or beginning of my profound and exciting life as a historian. It served as the learning halls and educational village to which I was fully indoctrinated in my history. I learned about my past, rich history and stories of family there. Truly it took the whole "billige/village" to raise a child.

Sampit is very special and dear to me. This is where my family roots and ancestral lineage have their marvelous and historical beginnings. Many of them were slaves, working in the rice fields, indigo, and turpentine distillery that surrounded the Sampit River. It is the home of my paternal great-great grandparents, great grandparents, grandparents: my father, uncles, aunts, brothers, sisters, cousins and many other family members. Sampit is the burial ground for many of my honorable descendants whose sweat and tears, cultivated, cleared, planted and harvested the rice, indigo and turpentine that grew in the fields and trees surrounding the Sampit River.

Sampit is the hollow or holy ground in which many of my family got their first taste of life as slaves. Even though they have passed from this life to another glorious life, their spirits are very much alive. Their spirits bring meaning and hope to these holy grounds. We stand and live on these grounds today as proud descendants of a people of Africa.
Sampit will one day be my final resting-place and I will be home at last. There's no place like home!

The Bryant Family: This hand-drawing sketch is my Grandfather Robert, Grandmother Lula Louise, Uncle Whuie (Hughie), Uncle Joe, Uncle Wesley, Aunt Tisby, Aunt Sue, Father Eff, and Aunt Bessie Bryant

I have fond memories of my childhood days in the Saint Paul Section of Sampit, South Carolina. When I was child, daddy and momma used to tell stories and tales of Sampit Township, once an old Indian Village. The tales and stories were about the Sampits or Sampas Indians, white settlers, slave owners, white planters, plantations, rice fields, slaves, freemen, stores, schools, churches, songs, hangman tree, ghosts and hags, etc.

My parents told us about family tales and traditions that had been passed down to them from one generation to another generation. Many of the stories were told in a Gullah or Geechie, a language that has been used in a derogatory matter to or put down people from the Low country. A language the people spoke to communicate with each other. Some people say that we "talk funny" or cut in the syllable when we pronounced words. They said we don't speak "the king's English". It was said that the Gullah or Geechie language was the way slaves from different areas communicated with each other. Many of the slaves were brought from different areas of Africa, which created a communication gap. Struggling to bridge the communication gap, they borrowed words from different languages such as English, French, and their own dialect and came up with a language they could understand.

Dad and Mom had a saying, "In order to understand the future, one must have a vivid and keen understanding of the past." They also said, "The past is nothing to be ashamed of. They said we came from a line of great honorable people (Kings, Queens, Inventors, Scholars, Preachers, Teachers, etc.), who were taken away from the motherland of Africa and brought on slave ships with religious names to America. The captured slaves traveled for months in sardine-like positions, and bound in chains with prisoners on the chain gangs. They ended up at Sullivan Island where slaves were kept in warehouses until they were sold in slave markets like those in Georgetown and Charleston. These "ole time" stories, idioms and slang expressions have stuck with me throughout my life. Sampit carries many exciting stories of the past. What fun times we had listening to all those old time Sampit tales on Saturday nights!

In "**Libbin' in de Billige - Sam Pitt**" I want to recreate or bring to life some of the tales or stories I remembered hearing as a child of the soil through pictures. This unique book tell stories of the Sam Pitt Injuns (Indians), Slabes (Slaves), Sam Pitt Maussuh (Masters), Sam Pitt Ribbuh (River), Sam Pitt Big Roads, Sam Pitt Sto's (Stores), Tup'ntine (Turpentine), Sam Pitt Cump'ny's (Companies), Sam Pitt Bidness (Businesses), Eddycashun (Education), and Hang (Heng) Man Tree (Tree V).

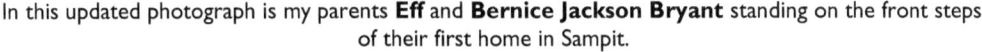

My father, **Eff Bryant**, who I am named after and my mother, **Bernice** were professional storytellers (African guru). I was captivated by their photographic memories of story times. They remembered every detail as they told their stories. They were like the griots or storytellers in Africa, who sat around in their villages and recalled tales that had been passed down to them from their ancestors.

In this updated photograph is my parents **Eff** and **Bernice Jackson Bryant** standing on the front steps of their first home in Sampit.

Daddy, not being able to read or write, had only a third grade education. He attended Saint Paul African Methodist Episcopal Church School known as the Saint Paul ABC School. They learned reading, writing, and arithmetic known as the three R's. It is unknown how long daddy attended school and what grade he completed. I think it was the first, second and third grade. Daddy only attended school for three to four months per year due to working the little family farm. Saturday and Sunday evening was story time at my house. It was a time when we talked about everything under the sun. The number one subject matter was on knowing the history of our past. It was show time at the Bryant's house. It was another great lesson in Black History. They were able to relive the stories of our descendants.

Daddy and **momma** took center stage and the **"Eff** and **Bernice"** show began. My brothers and sisters cheered them on! We imagined that we were sitting at one of the Grammy Awards Show. We sat around on handmade wooden benches in the front yard. One had to be careful how they sat on the old wooden benches due to the wood being rough and splinters were everywhere. Splinters really hurt; they will bring tears to your eyes. The front yard was always kept neat and clean. Rose bushes, three small oak trees covered with wild grapevines and a string of potted flowers adorned the front yard. Momma had a green thumb and she worked her magic, planting and growing flowers. I always remember momma giving away some of her plants to family members and friends that came to visit. We just couldn't wait for the grape season to start. My grandmother, Lula (nicknamed Jo Ma) had a large Muscadine grape harbor (we called black and white grape) on her property.

Sometimes **Daddy** on Saturday night would make "fried bread" for us to eat. We ate fried bread and homemade syrup as my parents told their stories. **Daddy** learned how to make fried bread while serving as a cook in the Army during World War II. The fried bread was made out of a white corn flour mix and stirred in water. The mixture was then put or cooked into a large black frying pan for several minutes on one side and then flipped to the other side. The finished product was a finger-licking piece of fried bread. My brothers and sisters often fought over who was going to get the first and last taste of the "fried bread." Occasionally daddy would save **Lou Emma**, the youngest girl in the family, nicknamed "**Gogo**", a piece of the fried bread from the table. We always looked forward to daddy cooking "fried bread."

I am indebted to my parents for telling me the stories of our people. Stories they'd learned from their parents and grandparents.

Both of them have transitioned from **Sampit** to a heavenly Billige/village with the Lord. The memories they shared live inside me. I am who I am today, because of my parents. They were my role models, teachers, protectors, providers, preachers, doctors, nurses, and breadwinners.

This classy old photograph is my parents, **Eff** (Buddy) and **Bernice** (Bern), baby brother **Wesley** (Wes) and nephew **Daniel** (Danny) **Bryant** standing in the front yard of **Uncle Joe** and **Aunt Hester Bryant's** home at 1236 Powell Road, Georgetown, South Carolina.
(Courtesy of the Lil Eff Affikan Cump'ny)

De (The) Sam Pitt 17-19

De (The) Sam Pitt Ribbuh (River)

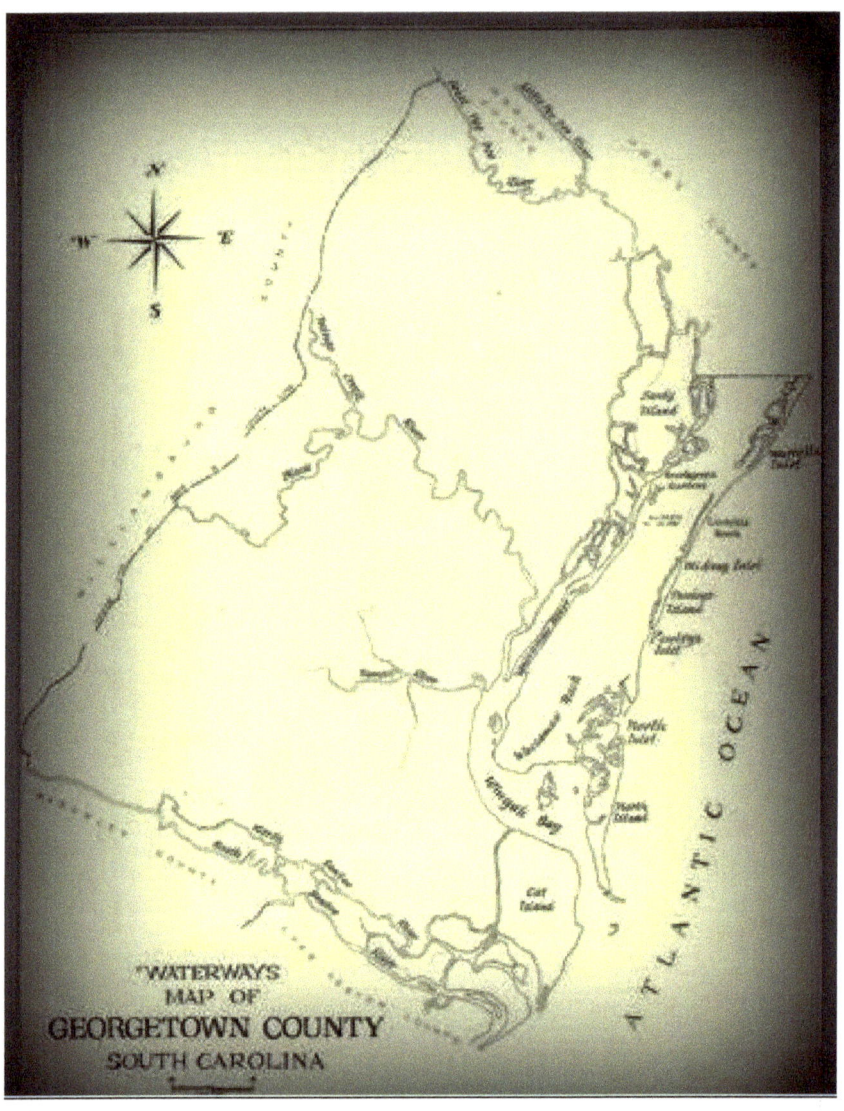

Waterways Map of Georgetown County, South Carolina
The Sampit River, called the "little river" by the Native Sampas Indians that lived in this area was the main waterway to travel by canoes and boats from **Samp**it to the city of **Georgetown.**
(Courtesy of the Lil Eff Affikan Cump'ny)

"**De Sampit**" is a phrase commonly heard for many reasons throughout the former **Craven County**, later called **Prince George Winyah Parish**, present-day Georgetown in the Low Country. Aesthetic beauty abounds throughout the natural environment that includes the vast piney wood, swampy swamp, deep gullies, backwoods and bottoms of **Sampit**. The meandering Sampit River, large majestic grand oaks with moss, tall pine trees, remnants of old rice fields, plantations, and the abundance of wildlife adds to the beauty of this old time Indian village. **(Courtesy of the Lil Eff Affikan Cump'ny)**

This **Sam Pitt Village** once was the home and happy hunting ground of the **Sampits**, or Sampas, Indian tribes. Little historical information exists about the Sampits or Sampas Indians.

The **Sampits** or **Sampas Indians** were one of the indigenous Indian tribes that made their home in Sampit. They belong to the Eastern Siouan family. They were once one of the major tribes that lived and roamed in and around Craven County, later called Prince George Winyah Parish, present-day Georgetown. The Sampits or Sampas tribe lived mainly in a wooded inland area around the Sampit River. The Sampit River, which means "Short River," is sandwiched between the Gapway Bay to the North, the little and Big Kilsock Bays to the South and the Canon Bay to the West and the Winyah Bay to the East. The Indians gave the river their own rich tribal name. The village "Sampit" is an Indian word meaning "Short River." It was consider "short" based on the fact that it was only a few miles from the "long" Winyah Bay. This "short river" served as a major canoeing waterway and used by the Sampeet tribe for fishing and trapping. The Sampit River was the Sampas River. The "short" river was plentiful with fish such as herring, shad, and red breast and used as an important dietary food for the Indians. They also use the river to travel to other Indian Territory to barter and to purchase goods. The Sampit River runs for miles, starting from Cedar Branch, off present day Andrews, runs into Boggy Swamp and Bond Swamp, dumps into the Sampit, empties into the Winyah Bay and flows in the Atlanta Ocean.
(Courtesy of the Lil Eff Affikan Cump'ny)

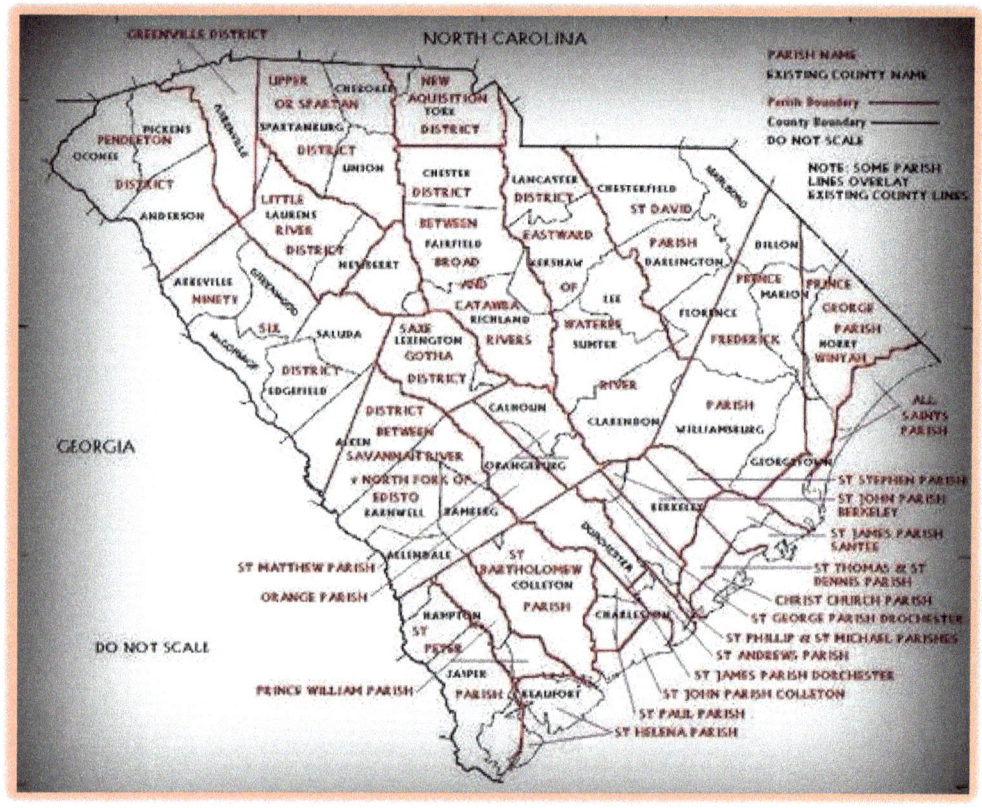

Map of South Carolina Parishes

Sam Pitt (Sampit) was located in the **Prince George Winyah Parish** that was created in 1721. Sampit today is a working history small town with many businesses, churches, cemeteries, barns, stores, and homes. **(Courtesy of the Lil Eff Affikan Cump'ny)**

De (The) Sam Pitt Plantesshun (Plantation)   21-26

    Dis (This) is Sullivan's Island

    De (The) Mansfield Plantesshun Chu'ch (Church)

Here are **Benjamin Oscar** and his wife; **Marian Levy Bourne** all dressed up sitting in chairs in their front yard of this large and spacious home. **(Courtesy of Herbert M. "Chip" Collins)**

Benjamin Oscar Bourne, affectionately known as **Pa Bourne**, grew up on the Sampit Plantation. At one time **Pa Bourne** was considered "well to do" and was considered to be one of the wealthiest men in Georgetown County. He was a successful businessman, entrepreneur, owned many businesses and known for his savvy business practices throughout Georgetown County.

Pa Bourne ran a large commissary - the only store of any size for miles around in Sampit. There was a shed built in front where horses and mules were protected from the weather. **"The Store",** as it was later called, included a grocery store, hardware store, farm implements, blacksmith shop, canning factory and a Millenary shop operated by a French milliner. Ladies from miles away drove over roads of deep ruts of sand to buy original French creations. He also built a Gristmill to grind corn into grits and cornmeal.

Pa Bourne also owned many acreages of land throughout Sampit, and, once upon a time owned most of North Santee. He was married to **Marian Levy Bourne** and they had seven children: **Amelia, Benjamin, Adlai, Edwin, Oscar, Gertrude,** and **Marian**.

The home that **Benjamin** and wife **Marian** lived in was made of lumber from the forest throughout Sampit. It was three stories with piazzas around three sides on the first floor. There were white rocking chairs for the grown-ups and a joggling board for the many children (a joggling board is a long pliable plank supported on each end by a frame with slots cut to prevent the plank from slipping). A long corridor - the entire length of the house - ended in the dining room and beyond that a kitchen with a long table down the middle of the room. Wide boards were used for the table and the floor and were scrubbed each day until they were almost white. The back door from the kitchen opened to an orchard and then a vegetable garden. To the left of the front door was a parlor that was opened only for very special guests and the preachers. Beyond that was a sitting room, which corresponds to the family room of today. On the other side were three bedrooms and upstairs were many bedrooms. On both floors a bathroom with so called running water, which worked only when the river was high and water was pumped by the "hands". The house also was called the "Big House or the Master's House." The Bourne's had house servants: **Lula the nurse**, her mother, **Mom Aimee**, the washwoman. Mom Aimee was brought over from Africa, and

Frank, the cook, and a succession of others for housework. We dearly loved Lula and Frank. They had cabins on the place. To keep us out of his cabin Frank told us he kept a snake under his pillow for company. It worked!

This two stories spacious Antebellum home belongs to **Benjamin Oscar** and **Marian Levy Bourne** of Sampit, SC. This home captured the lifestyle of a wealthy, rice-planting family. (Courtesy of Herbert M. "Chip" Collins)

Herbert M. "Chip" Collins is the great, great grandson of **Benjamin Oscar Bourne**. One of the sons of **B.B. Bourne** was named after him. He was born in 1873 and died in 1940. He graduated from Wofford College, Spartanburg, South Carolina and attended the School of Business Administration, Poughkeepsie, New York.

Bourne & Company of Sampit located west of Georgetown, operated a lumber railroad between Sampit and two plantation areas north of the town. The line terminated at Wee Nee Plantation at Johnson Corner and Marquis Bridge. This may well have been known locally as the **"Old Kilsock Tram."** The roadbed for this line is shown on maps of the Walker Farm block of Georgetown County and runs parallel to the newly built (1974) Seaboard Coast Line spur to the South Carolina Public Service Power Plant.

B.B. Bourne and **Company**, owner **Benjamin Oscar Bourne** was also the owner of the turpentine mill or distillery. Many black residents of Sampit worked in what was called "turpentine."

The 1880 census for Georgetown County shows the head of the household, names, age, sex, color, relationship to the head of the household, birthplace of the person name and especially the occupation.

The 1880 census shows that many blacks of Sampit worked in the **Turpentine** and worked as farmers, coopers, housekeeping, nurse, carpenter, ploughman, cook, merchant, wagoner, flat man, wood cutter, cabinet maker, laundresses and Ministers. The records also reveal that Sampit and Santee were part of Township No. 1. Some of the names listed:

Names	Age	Occupations
Philip Brown	35	Ploughman

Name	Age	Occupation
Samuel Bryant	35	Turpentine
Benjamin Cohen	33	Turpentine
Archie Davis, Sr.	50	Farmer
March Dobby	26	Turpentine
John Gasque	35	Turpentine
June Gasque	70	Farmer
William Gasque	27	Turpentine
Julius Grayson	26	Turpentine
Mary Green	51	Laundress
Rev. Saby Green	65	Minister
Thomas Holmes	55	Turpentine
Frank Humphrey	27	Cooper
Charles Keith	40	Farmer
Albert Marshall	25	Wagoner
Jeffrey Myers	75	Farmer
Peter Nowling	54	Turpentine
Robert Nowling, Jr.	47	Turpentine
Robert Nowling, Sr.	70	Carpenter
Quacoo Sanders	35	Farmer
Rev. March Singleton	46	Minister
William Smith	46	Turpentine
York Smith	36	Turpentine
London Stafford	50	Turpentine
Tony Swinton	50	Watchman
Henry Tompkins	28	Turpentine
Alexander Trappier	33	Cooper
Samuel Washington	22	Merchant
Abraham Williams	50	Turpentine

Turpentine was collected mostly from the long pine trees that grew plentiful throughout Sampit. The Turpentine business was lucrative and lasted for years. A large turpentine still was located at the foot of the **Sampit Bridge**. The workers collected the turpentine and put it in large containers, called **"stills."** The turpentine was hauled down to Sampit River on oxen or horse driven wagons, barreled and lashed to rafts and shipped to Georgetown for sale.

Sampit was once upon a time known for its long pine trees. After the rice and indigo businesses were decimated by hurricanes, many of the people of Sampit worked in the business of turpentine. Workers would go out and blaze the pine tree; put little small tin boxes or buckets to catch the slowly dripping turpentine.

After the tin boxes or buckets were full, it was then poured in large tin barrels. Once the barrels were filled, some of the workers went around in their oxen wagons, which held large barrels, and poured the turpentine into them. After all of the barrels were full, the turpentine was hauled to the Sampit River and sold to the mills.

The B. B. Bourne Company of **Sampit** had a very lucrative business in pulpwood that hired many blacks and whites from Sampit. The Company was a large landowner and had rights to acreages of land in Sampit. They owned property in and around the **New Hope Church** and **Alpha Holiness Church** areas. In March 1911, the membership of New Hope built their first church on two acres of land purchased from the **B. B. Bourne Company** for $5.00.

The **Company** also owned a tugboat and a Turpentine Mill at the Sampit River. The tugboat transported the turpentine barrels to Georgetown for sale. Most of the hired workers made about 50 cents per day. A story was told that **Mr. Bourne** had a very unorthodox way of paying his workers. He would put the money in a big hat and throw it up in the air. The workers then would fight and push each other to get a share of the money.

During the 1700s, thousands of Africans arrived in America and were sold as slave labor. For many, their first stop, primary disembarkation port or port of entry was Sullivan's Island, which was a sandy pit on the northeast edge of Charleston Harbor. According to several historians, anywhere from 50 to 60 percent of the Africans who were brought to America during the slave trade entered through this port in the Low country.

This **Historical Sign** was erected in 1999 by the S.C. Department of Archives and History, the Charleston Club of S.C. and the Avery Research Center, pursuant to a request from the South Carolina General Assembly as evidenced in concurrent Resolution S. 719, adopted June 3, 1998.

This Is Sullivan's Island

A place where… **Africans** were brought to this country under extreme conditions of human bondage and degradation. Tens of thousands of captives arrived on Sullivan's Island from the West African shores between 1700 and 1775. Those who remained in the Charleston community and those who passed through this site account for a significant number of African-American now residing in these United States. Only through God's blessings, a burning desire for justices, and persistent will to succeed against monumental odds, have African-Americans created a place for themselves in the American mosaic.

A place where…We commemorate this site as the entry of Africans who came and who contributed to the greatness of our country. The Africans who entered through this port have moved on to meet the challenges created by injustices, racial and economic discrimination, and withheld opportunities. Africans and African-Americans, through the sweat of their brow, have distinguished themselves in the Arts, Education, Medicines, Politics, Religion, Law, Athletics, Research, Artisans and Social Services.

A place where…This memorial rekindles the memory of a dismal time in American history, but it also serves as a reminder of a people who – despite injustice and intolerance-past and present, have retained the unique values, strengths and potential that flow form our West African culture which came to this nation through the middle passage.

(Courtesy of the Lil Eff Affikan Cump'ny)

The Georgetown Times (South Carolina's oldest Newspaper, established in 1798) confirmed through articles and advertisements that slave markets (Old Market circa 1841) in Georgetown participated in the selling and buying of human beings for the purpose of cheap labors and economic growth. The following quotation came from The Georgetown Times in 1798.

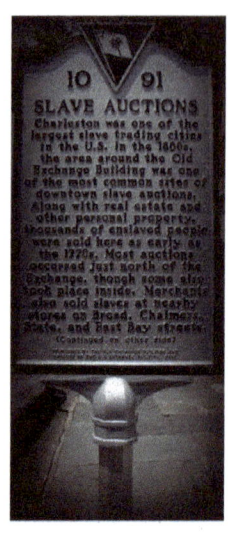

By Permission of Cornelius De Pre, Elq. Ordinary for Georgetown District will be sold at Public Auction, on Monday the Second Day of February next before the Market House in Georgetown, Six Negroes, And some Plantation Tools; Being the property of the estate of Henry Saultus, deceased. The conditions of sale – one third, cash, the remaining two thirds, credit, 1 and 2 years; the purchasers giving bond with approved security and paying for stamps. By order of David Swanson, Executor, Lizar Joseph. Georgetown, once upon a time, had one of the largest slave populations to work on more than 153 plantations that were strung along the waterways of Georgetown. The record also reveals that some of the white gentlemen, leading citizens, gentlemen of leisure, and holy clergymen of Georgetown were slaveholders. Many also fathered children whose ancestry is bonded in interracial blood mixing long before "legalized" interracial marriages were "legal." Others didn't want to tell that there is a black and white "family connection" in Sampit. Many of our black roots can be traced through some of those white families. At upper right is the **Slave Auction's** historical sign located at 122 East Bay Street at Broad Street – **Old Exchange** & **Provost Dungeon**, Charleston, SC. **(Courtesy of the Lil Eff Affikan Cump'ny)**

The **Mansfield Plantation** was established in 1718 on the banks of the Black River in historic **Georgetown**, the third oldest city in South Carolina. The slave village contains six slave cabins and a large slave chapel, wooden handmade pew, pulpit, tables, windows and church bell. Historical records reveal that over one hundred slaves lived and worked at the **Mansfield Plantation.** Mansfield Plantation's picturesque old wooden **Slave Chapel** documented the church were the slave master allowed his slaves to worship.
(Courtesy of the Lil Eff Affikan Cump'ny)

De (The) Sam Pitt (Sampit) Sto's (Stores) - De **Sam Pitt Cump'ny's** (Company) 30 - 185

De **Sam Pitt (Sampit) Bidness/Bidnfss** (Business)

De (The) Rufus Lambert's Store	27
De (The) Black Midwives - (Addie Bynum Berry)	27
De (The) Frances Davis (Midwife)	28
De (The) No. 2 Store	29-31
De (The) Edgar Cleveland Morris' Store	32-34
De (The) Miss Nell's Tour – The Real South Tour (Nell Cribb)	35-36
De (The) London Stafford - The Shop	37-38
De (The) Ross Stafford's Logging Business	39-43
De (The) Logger – Wesley Grayson	44-45
De (The) Richard Grayson, Sr.	46
De (The) Elizabeth Singleton Grayson	47-49
De (The) Dr. Antwon M. Sutton – Principal	50
De (The) Babe Creations, Anointed Quilts	50-51
De (The) Troy Gasque – Lena White Gasque	52
De (The) Jimmy's Place	53-55
De (The) Queen's Beauty & Hair Care	56
De (The) Gasque's Barber Shop	56
De (The) Wesley Bryant's Store	57-58
De (The) Green's Grocery	59-61
De (The) Keith's Grocery Store	62-65
De (The) David Smith's Grocery & Laundry	66-67
De (The) Logger Edward Wilson	68-70
De (The) Sampit Logging Company	71
De (The) Owner Vernon Smith	71
De (The) International Paper Company (IPC)	72
De (The) Quarter Century Society, Inc. – Eff Bryant	73
De (The) B. B. Smith's Grocery Store	74
De (The) McKnight & Frasier Funeral Homes	75-77
De (The) Deas' Logging Company	78-79
De (The) Joe Cooper's Logging Company	80
De (The) Luncheon Wragg Brick Work	81
De (The) Tricia's Beauty Salon	82
De (The) Bryant's Electric	82
De (The) Cuz Roland and Martha Pittman Bryant	83-88
De (The) Willie Green – Marie Brown Green	89-90
De (The) Jerome & Kimberly Houston Bryant	91
De (The) Patrice Bryant – Beatrice Bryant	92-93
De (The) Wesley Bryant's Shop	94-95
De (The) Holmes Electrical Building & Contractor	96-97
De (The) Smitty's Lawnmower Repair Shop	98-99
De (The) Linnie Knowlin's Transportation	100
De (The) Darby & Son Trucking Company	101-102
De (The) Sampit Monument Company	103-104
De (The) Ben Green's Courier	105
De (The) Sunset Inn Club	106-107

De (The) McKnight Professional Gardening & Cleaning Service	108
De (The) Bone's Radiation Shop	109
De (The) Smith General Merchandise & Store	110
De (The) The Beverage Depot	111
De (The) Lamar's Fish & Chip	112-113
De (The) Nurse Ethel Bolden Small	114
De (The) Maunie J. White & Son	115
De (The) Minnie Tax Service	116
De (The) Glen Stafford's Residential Electrical Business	116-121
De (The) Drayton's Auto Salvage	122-127
De (The) Keith Builders & Home Improvement	128
De (The) Henry H. Grant's Plumbing & Repair Service	128
De (The) D. J. Lord JAZZ	129-133
De (The) 30 Years of Love - George & Loretta Swayzer	134-135
De (The) Eve's Southern Café	136
De (The) James Thompson – Daisy Brown Thompson	137-139
De (The) Nurse Susan Brown Clark	140-141
De (The) Principal Edward Brown	142-145
De (The) Baker Welding Company	146-147
De (The) Nurse Roxie Sanders Giles	148-149
De (The) Becca's Gifts & Craft Shop	150-152
De (The) Luke Smith	153
De (The) Disnee Day Care	154
De (The) Gullah Museum & Gift Shop	155-161

This colorful artwork painting is a drawing of the old house "Home Sweet Home" I grew up in - drawn on the back of this old **cast iron frying pan** from my **grandparent's** home. It is believed that this cast iron frying pan is over 100 years old.
(Courtesy of the Lil Eff Affikan Cump'ny)

Rufus Lambert owned and operated the No. 1 Store. It was probably the first county store in Sampit. It was a large wooden store located down a dirt road behind the present day David Smith Store. The store sold mostly meats, grains, seeds and farming equipment. The county store served as the community post office, bank, pharmacy, grocery, hardware stores and filling stations (Fill 'er up). It sold every thing from "pills to petticoats to plows." Any item not available was as near as the mail-order catalog on the counter.

The store was also a news and social center where the "talk of the town" was discussed. When people came to pick up mail, get a telegraph, and buy groceries, they shared news, letters and newspapers with their neighbors. When news came, such as the death of a family member from another city, the family member usually met at community churches and rang the church bell. The sexton would ring the church bell; the community came together to get the news. One of the sextons who rang the bell (I remembered as a child) was **Troy Gasque**, who served as **Steward**, **Trustee** and **Sexton** at **St. Paul AME Church**.

Rufus was the only one that had a hand-crank telephone or a telegraph-messaging center in its store. Southern Bell Telephone and Telegraph Company installed the state's first telephones in Charleston in 1879. Most rural areas did not receive telephone service until the early 1950s. It is unknown the date of the telephone in the **No. 1 Store**. People had to go there to send and receive telephone calls. Most of the telephone messages sent and received were emergency messages such as death, illness or calling a doctor. Then a messenger or runner would go and fetch the family member to receive the message or telegraph.

It is said by many historians that **Dr. F. A. Bell's** medical practice or office was located at the No. 1 Store, which was located behind present day David Smith's Store. **Dr. F. A. Bell** was the first licensed doctor with practices in Sampit and the surrounding communities. He made many home calls riding in his horse-and-buggy or wagon to see the sick. He carried his doctor's black bag with medicine and medical items. He was the attending physician for most of the whites and made home calls to their homes. He delivered most of the white babies born in Sampit. He delivered only a few of the African American babies due to the fact that families could not afford to pay for medical care.

Midwives or "granny mid-wives" delivered many of the black babies from Sampit. They helped pregnant women through their labor and childbirth. Two of the well-known midwives were **Midwife Addie Bynum Berry** and **Midwife Francis Smalls Davis**.

Addie Bynum Berry (April 22, 1919 – August 22 1992) daughter of **Mary June** and **Esell Bynum**, born in Williamsburg County, South Carolina was a well-known mid-wife to many throughout the Sampit Community. She was joined in holy matrimony to **Deacon Charlie Berry, Sr**. (June 30, 1913 – November 20, 2000) a union that lasted fifty-four (54) years. At an early age, she joined St. Peter Baptist Church in the Sutton Community of Williamsburg County. After her marriage she joined the Greater Gethsemane Baptist Church, where she was a faithful member until her health failed. She served on the Usher Board, Deaconess Board, member of the Rising Sons and Daughters, the Eastern Star and the Will-Go Chorus. She started one of the first transportation routes to Myrtle Beach, South Carolina, insuring many citizens of Georgetown County a means of getting to work. **Courtesy of the Lil Eff Affikan Cump'ny)**

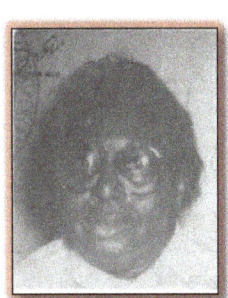

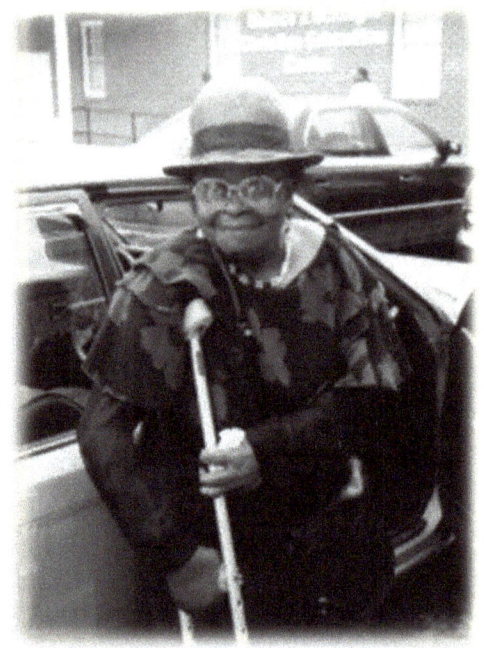

Another renowned midwife icon from Sampit was **Frances Smalls Davis** (July 2 1917 - February 15, 2005), daughter of **Elijah Smalls** and **Joanna Grant Smalls**. **Francis'** mother, **Joanna Grant Smalls** was also a "midwife" and **Francis** was a "chip off the old block" where her mother taught her the trade of bringing babies into the world. It was a practice within the African American community that the daughters learned the skills of their mothers.

Many babies from Sampit and surrounding communities were brought into this world by the hands of Frances who was a midwife for several decades. She stated that "when she was growing up in Sampit we didn't know what a doctor looked like." My mother and other midwives throughout Sampit were trained and when mothers went into labor, we went to their homes to deliver babies." She was the midwife for **Harold Thompson** (son of Roosevelt and Almeta Thompson) and **Angela Elizabeth Grant** (daughter of Lucius and Bertie Elizabeth Grant) born in the St. Paul section of Sampit. She lives to the ripe age of 88. **(Courtesy of the Lil Eff Affikan Cump'ny)**

On 24 July 1970 **Francis Davis** retired faithfully from her professional as a midwife. She received a Midwife Retirement Certificate from the South Carolina Board of Education/Division of Maternal and Child Health. The Certificate reads:

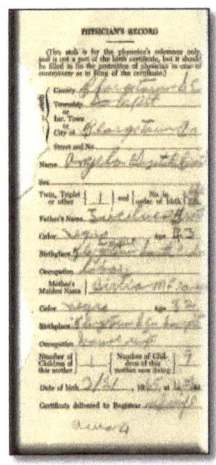

Above is copy of **Frances Davis** Physician's prorated record stub of birth certificate of **Angela Elizabeth Grant**.
(Courtesy of Frances Davis)

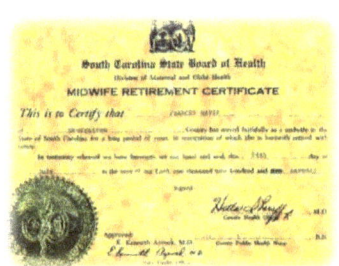

South Carolina Board of Education
Division of Maternal and Child Health
Midwife Retirement Certificate
This to certify that **Frances Davis** of Georgetown County has served faithfully as a midwife in State of South for a long period of years, in recognition of which she is herewith retired with honor in testimony whereof we have hereunto set our hand and seal, this 24th day of July in the year of our Lord, one thousand nine hundred and seventy.
Signed: Hilla Sheriff, MD   County Health Office
Approved: E. Kenneth Aycock, MD   State Health Officer
(Courtesy of Frances Davis)

The No. 2 Store was once located about 1/10 miles on the old main wagon or cart road from the present location. The old main cart or wagon road ran beside it. At one time, the store was known as the main grocery store in Saint Paul Section of Sampit. It is believed that **Ezekiel O. Boatwrights** (3 Oct 1887 – 11 Apr 1938) and **Laura Burgess Boatwrights** (9 Jun 1888 – 17 Jul 1964) were the first owners of the No. 2 Store. Other owners were **Walter Watts, Walter Roberts, Whites, Bourne, Ernest Cooper** and **Florence Virginia Lambert Cooper**, and now **Doris Cooper Gause**. No. 2 store has become a landmark for the Sampit community and is well over 100 years old. No. 2 is a breathtaking historical landmark that weaves together the tales of yesterday and today.
(Courtesy of the Lil Eff Affikan Cump'ny)

In this undated rusty photograph is one of the original signs displaying the name of the No. #2 store, **GEN (General) MSDE (Merchandise) Store** and the owner, **L. B. Boatwright** in Sampit. The store has weathered with time and basically it remains the same since its doors opened. The old kerosene pump (rusty) still sits on one end of the porch not too far from the wide double doors leading to the inside. As one enters the store, the old signs advertising Goody's headache powders for five cents are still visible. The old kerosene lamps that once provided lights are still hanging on the walls with nails.
(Courtesy of the Lil Eff Affikan Cump'ny)

These business makers **Ernest (Mr. Ernest) Cooper** and Florence Virginia Lambert **Cooper** (Mrs. Janie) brought the No. 2 Country Store in the 1940s. **Ernest** and **Florence** married on August 10, 1926 at the Clerk of Court Office in Georgetown - **Ben Frasier**, Clerk of Court, married them. **Mr. Ernest** and **Mrs. Janie** stated "that the Lord gave them the store after other people were looking to buy it. He blinded the other people and gave it to us. They didn't think it would be a good investment."
(Courtesy of Doris Cooper Gause)

This is the photograph of the original two-story wooden house built by the original owner of the No. 2 Store, **Ezekiel O. Boatwright** and **Laura Burgess Boatwright**. The house sits next door to the **No. 2 Store**. The house is probably one of the oldest built houses in Sampit and is well preserved. Not much have charged about the house since it was built. Today, **Doris Olivia Cooper Gause**, daughter of **Mr. Ernest** and **Mrs. Janie** lives in this two-story historical house. The large home is decorated with family pictures and old antiques from the past throughout. **(Courtesy of the Lil Eff Affikan Cump'ny)**

When the **Coopers** (**Mr. Ernest** and **Mrs. Janie**) brought the store in early 1940, the store was lit by kerosene lamps and heated by wood heaters. The store sold wrapped bologna, bacon, butt meats, sausage, neck bones, bananas, canned goods, sodas, candies, Teem (a lemon-like drink in a green bottle with a corn slogan that reads "Team up with Teem"), kerosene, gas, cigarettes, can stuff, Alka-Seltzer, grits and ice (large ice box). The ice for the handmade icebox was brought from the icehouse in the city of Georgetown. The ice was used to keep sodas cold and keep meat from spoiling. The ice was also sold to customers on a first come basis. Along with selling groceries, the **Coopers** stocked such items as cloth, thread, tablecloths, kerosene lamps, and medicine. Inside the store was a machine that ground corn into grits. Pictured above are the handmade wooden shelves, built by the hands of the people of Sampit, and are still stocked with a few items for sale. The handmade pine counter with the old cash register has seen the wear and tear of time.
(Courtesy of Doris Cooper Gause)

This 1930's **Ramon's Brownie Pills** Medicine Drug 21 Tin Thermometers "The Little Doctor" – Advertising Medical Kidneys Laxative. "The Little Doctor" carrying a doctor's bag. Advertising thermometer for Brownie Pills, a "Diuretic Stimulant to the Kidneys" and Pink Pills, which were "A Dependable Laxative." The bottom reads Ramon's Pink Pills a real laxative for adults. Great image of **"Brownie." (Courtesy of the Lil Eff Affikan Cump'ny)**

Today, **Doris Olivia Cooper Gause,** adopted daughter, of **Ernest** and **Janie Cooper** runs the **No. 2 Store**, along with her son, **Raymond Gause**. **Raymond** lives next door to the store. The store is open every day except Sunday for business. A **sign** made of cardboard hang on the door that reads **"Open! Blow horn!** I am at the house. **Doris**."

(Courtesy of the Lil Eff Affikan Cump'ny)

Here are **Reverend Ernest,** his wife **Mrs. Janie Cooper** and members of the **First Assembly of God Church** in **Kingstree,** South Carolina, the church he founded and became its first pastor serving for six years. Later Reverend Ernest left the Assembly of God congregation to plant the **First Pentecostal Church** of **Kingstree.** In 1943, **Mr. Ernest** and **Mrs. Janie** both got saved, (accepted Christ) as their personal Savior at the **Assembly Church** in Georgetown, South Carolina. After their religious experience the Lord first convicted **Mrs. Janie** about selling smoking products. And later, **Mr. Ernest** as he sat in the woods praying; no other smoking products were sold. Later **Mr. Ernest** was called into the ministry and founded the first **Assembly Church of Kingstree.** He served that church for six years. **(Courtesy of Doris Cooper Gause)**

This old **1948 Chevrolet (Fleet Master)** truck body – sort of "eye sore" for years was located behind the **No. 2 Store** on a short footpath leading to Columbus Road.
(Courtesy of the Lil Eff Affikan Cump'ny)

Edgar Cleveland Morris built this little country store in 1930. It also served as the office for his **saw-mill** (logging business) located in the **Britton Neck Section** of Sampit. The store/office consisted of three small rooms. A lucrative family business for many years, the sawmill was a facility where logs were cut into boards or lumber. Many people from **Sampit** brought the boards or lumber to build their houses, barns, outdoor toilets, smoke houses, and churches. The typical sawmill used a whipsaw, driven by a water wheel to cut the logs into boards. **(Courtesy of the Lil Eff Affikan Cump'ny)**

Photographed here is **Edgar Morris** and several of his employees cutting trees, and then transporting the trees to the sawmill at **Britton Neck**. **Edgar** employed many blacks and whites from the community to work at his small family business. Among the black employees were **Hallot Davis, Herman Davis, Eff Bryant (my father), Ross Stafford, Turner Stafford,** and **Moody Stafford, Sr.** **(Courtesy of Nell Cribb)**

This dateless photograph are **Edgar Morris** (April 30, 1891 – April 12, 1960) and **Dosia Trisvan Anderson Morris'** family of Sampit. Their children were: **Clifton, Dan, Rufus, Nell, Herbert, Jack, Ann, Marie, Lucille, Francis** and **Ida Bell**.
(Courtesy of Nell Cribb)

The Friendship United Methodist Church (part of the Sampit Circuit) was the family church of **Edgar Morris**, **Dosia Trisvan Anderson Morris** and family of Sampit. It is believed that the congregants who lived around the **Britton Neck** (Walker Road) section built this large wooden Church to accommodate the growing congregation consisting of farmers and businessmen. After the church membership dwindled, the church members and Conference voted to end worship service there. The church was torn down, and the materials were hauled on mules and wagons and used to help with the building of **Sampit United Methodist Church** on the Saint Delight Road some four miles away. Most of the membership then became active members at **Sampit United Methodist Church.**
(Courtesy of Doris Cooper Gause)

The **Oak Grove Grammar School** off of **Highway 521** was built in the early 1900s in the Oak Grove Section of Sampit for the white children only. As children, **Miss Nell** and her siblings attended Oak Grove Grammar School from first to sixth grades. Then in 7th and 8th grades they attended the Andrews High in Andrews. She graduated from Winyah High school in Georgetown in 1947. **Kate McConnell** was the school principal at this time. Some of the teachers were **Laura Boatwright** (co-owner of the No. 2 Store) and **Mrs. Joe Deal Smith**. **Miss Nell** worked for the Georgetown School District for 31 years and retired in 1988. She was secretary at Winyah High School for 29 years, and then transferred to the Georgetown District Office in the Assistant Superintendent's Office for the last 2 ½ years of her career. **(Courtesy of SC Historical Society)**

At left is a photo of **Miss Nell Cribb**, one of the daughters of **Edgar C. and Dosia A. Morris**. She was born January 12, 1931, the ninth of twelve children. Their large family consisted of six girls and six boys. **Dr. F. A. Bell,** who started his medical practice in **Number 1 Store**, Sampit (located behind where present day **David Smith Store**), was the attending physician and delivered most of the **Morris'** children. The **Morris** family owns family property in the Britton Neck section of Sampit, nowadays "**Village Road**." Their homes were located not too far from the **Friendship United Methodist Church**. They moved to a new home site on the Andrews Highway when **Mrs. Nell** was five years old. She stayed in that home until she left for high school. She married the late **Lloyd B. Cribb** and they had two daughters, **Cammie** and **Vickie**.
(Courtesy of the Lil Eff Affikan Cump'ny)

After **Miss Nell Cribb's** retirement, from the Georgetown School District, she began her own unique business; **Miss Nell's Tours - Walking Tour of Historical District of Georgetown**. She invites you to see "**The Real South**" in the Historical District of Georgetown. **Miss Nell** stated, "It is a pleasure to show off Georgetown to those locally, and, from near and far. It is a historical journey through the historical part of the town, yet for those on motor coaches, I act as a step-on guide and we do a riding tour." She is an active member of First Baptist Church in Georgetown and participates in various Church activities. She holds membership in: Georgetown County Historical Society, SC Historical Society, The Rice Museum, Georgetown Business & Professional Women's Club, The School District of Georgetown County (where she retired from after 31 years of service), Georgetown County Chamber of Commerce, and licensed by the City of Georgetown to do historical tours. **Miss Nell's** hobby is collecting Coca-Cola items and her home at 308 Front Street reflects this vast growing collection. The Georgetown Times on September 29, 2003 printed a "The Times EXTRA!" entitled "**It's The Real Thing**" showing Miss Nell's Coca-Cola collections. On Saturday, 5 December 2009, The Downtown Georgetown Christmas Festival took place with a street parade. The Georgetown's annual street parade featured Grand Marshall **Miss Nell Cribb**, known as "**The Coco-Cola Lady**," plus local high school bands, businesses, church groups and organizations, downs, **Santa** and **Mrs. Claus. (Courtesy of Miss Nell Cribb)**

This sign displaying "**Miss Nell's Tours -** invites you - to see The Real South Tours begins here" was located in the window of the Harbor walk Book Store at 723 Front Street. **(Courtesy of Mrs. Nell Cribb)**

London Stafford I, one of the most influential businessmen from Sampit came from North Carolina (January 10, 1876) to Santee Crossings near Lane, South Carolina. Once there, he found work as a logger and farmer. Settling in the "backwoods" area of Sampit, their family grew with the birth of sons, **London Stafford II** ("Grandpa") on January 10, 1876; **William, Eshmeil; Stiruffen; Ben**; and daughter **Sarah**. The family lived all their lives in the Sampit Community with all preceding London II to the grave. Eventually, he met and married **Rebecca Gatson** of Sampit, South Carolina. **London** is standing by his **1956 Chevrolet Bel-Air. (Courtesy of the Lil Eff Affikan Cump'ny)**

London Stafford II (Grand Pa) was married first to **Regina Darby**. **Regina** died shortly, **London** then married **Kiziah Gasque** (1883 – February 1, 1918) at left, the daughter of **William Gasque**. **Ross, Turner, London** and **Thomas** were their children. After the death of **Kiziah**, **London** married **Francis Sanders Stafford** (August 14, 1921 – April 12, 1998) at right. **(Courtesy of the Lil Eff Affikan Cump'ny)**

In addition to being a prominent landowner in the area, **London** founded the community's only African American grocery store business, started in 1944 known affectionately by all, as "**The Shop**." Next door to "**The Shop**" was a small wooden shed that held a gristmill to grind corn into grits and cornmeal. It is said that local farmers would bring wagons or truckloads of corn to the small building holding a gristmill to grind their corn into grits and cornmeal. After the cornmeal was made, it was placed into white or brown sacks. **London** is standing on the porch of the **Shop** and his 1948 Edsel is parked in front.
(**Courtesy of the Lil Eff Affikan Cump'ny**)

Standing in this undated photograph are devoted members and church leaders of **St. Paul African Methodist Episcopal Church; Peter Knowlin, Francis Stafford, London Stafford, Sarah Knowlin** and **Bertha Washington**.
(**Courtesy of the Lil Eff Affikan Cump'ny**)

Located on the Columbus Road is the "**old business office building**" used by **Ross Stafford** to transact his pulpwood business transactions. It was attached to a larger building that was used to store old equipment. **Ross** was one of the first blacks to contract with the International Paper Company for pulpwood business. **Ross** used this office to pay his employees, which took place on Friday evenings. Attached to the walls of the "**Shop**" with thumbtacks were his business licenses, notary papers, and a Certificate from the Governor. This photograph was taken on July 21, 1992. **(Courtesy of the Lil Eff Affikan Cump'ny)**

Ross Stafford (July 8, 1906 – September 26, 1997) the son of **London** and **Kiziah** or **Kuziah** Ross Stafford (July **Gasque** Stafford is pictured above. For over forty-four years, since 1935, Ross operated a successful pulpwood business that he inherited after the death of his father, **London.** As a businessman, organizer and negotiator he used his skills to help others and address many needs in the Sampit community. He was largely responsible for having the mail route extended far into Sampit and for the erection of mailboxes in front of individual homes. He was at the forefront of the movement to have paved roads throughout Sampit, south of the "**Nine Mile Curve.**" On a political level, he joined other leaders in the community in the organization and support of the Progressive Democratic Party and worked in voter registration efforts throughout his community. Serving as a Trustee of Allen University and worked hard to educate young people. **Ross** was marriage to the former **Emma Brewington** (May 16, 1909 – November 11 1986) from Andrews, South Carolina. Emma was a retired School Teacher at Rosemary Elementary School Andrews, South Carolina. **(Courtesy of the Lil Eff Affikan Cump'ny)**

In this updatable inspirational photograph is **Minnie Scott Brewington** and her trendy daughters; **Maggie B. Maze, Lucille B. Grant, Florie B. Legand**, and **Emma B. Stafford**. (Courtesy of Jackie Whitmore)

This religious maker and uniquely gifted preacher is **Reverend Levan "Van" Bruorton** (Brewington), husband of **Minnie Scott Brewington** and father of **Emma Brewington Stafford**. (Courtesy of Jackie Whitmore)

This old historical building is the **Maceo Lodge No. 55 F.A.M.**, Georgetown was established on December 11, 1901. **(Courtesy of the Lil Eff Affikan Cump'ny)**

Maceo Lodge No 50 F.A.M.
Established December 11, 1901
Dedicated - May 15, 1955 **W. J. Washington, W.M., J. J. Grant, S.W., E. P. Myers, J.W. Trustees:** W. S. Thompson, Sam Brown, B.C. Howard, Ross Stafford, and R.B. Anderson. **(Courtesy of the Lil Eff Affikan Cump'ny)**

Here is **Ross Stafford,** the civil right maker, churchmen and business icon with his wife, **Emma Brewington Stafford,** former teacher all dressed up for a evening of elegance. **(Courtesy of the Lil Eff Affikan Cump'ny)**

As one enter into the **Ross Stafford Conference Room,** located in the **Wallace J. McKnight Christian Education Building,** St. Paul AME Church, Sampit is a plaque on the outside door that reads "**Ross Stafford Conference Room**" in loving memory of **Ross Stafford** (1906 – 1997). **The Conference Room** is furnished with a large mahogany antique table and leather matching chairs. **(Courtesy of the Lil Eff Affikan Cump'ny)**

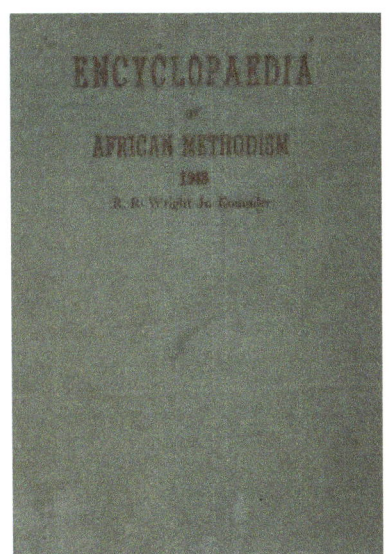 

This book, "**The Centennial Encyclopedia of the African Methodist Episcopal Church** written by **Richard Robert Wright, Jr., Compiler** in 1948. This unique history book containing principally the biographies of the men and women, both Ministers and Laymen, whose labors during a hundred years, helped make the A. M. E. Church what it is; Also short historical sketches of Annual Conferences, Educational Institutions, General Departments, Missionary Societies of the A. M. E. Church, and general information about African Methodism and the Christian Church in General; Being a literary contribution to the celebration of the One Hundredth Anniversary of the formation of the African Methodist Episcopal Church Denomination by **Richard Allen** and others, at Philadelphia, Pennsylvania in 1816. **(Courtesy of the Lil Eff Affikan Cump'ny)**

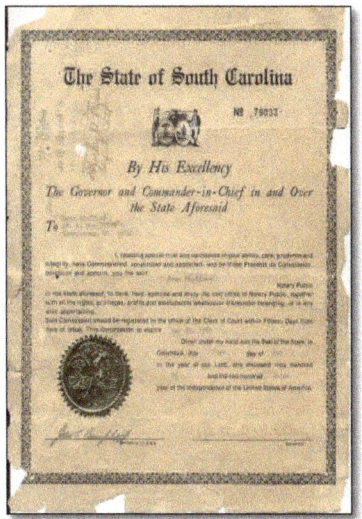

Displayed on the wall of Ross Stafford's old business office is his **Notary Public Certificate** dated May 23, 1989. **Jon T. Campbell** (Secretary of State) and **Richard W. Riley** (Governor). **(Courtesy of the Lil Eff Affikan Cump'ny)**

Many men of Sampit worked in pulpwood and were employed by the **Atlantic Coast Lumber Company**, Andrews, South Carolina. **The Atlantic Coast Lumber Company** (ACL) was formed in May 1899 in the West End section of Georgetown with an original capital of $1,000.000. The company owned the timber rights to 250,000 acres of land throughout South Carolina. In 1900, ACL hired over 4,585 blacks and whites to work in the work camps or company timber sites. They were hired to do jobs such as working in the machine shops, turpentine stills, car shops, foundries, pattern shops, boiler shops, blacksmith shops, and as loggers.
(Courtesy of the Lil Eff Affikan Cump'ny)

Wesley Grayson from North Santee was one of the dedicated employees of **Ross Stafford's** pulpwood business. In this family photo, **Wesley** is in the second row, fourth from left with hat on, standing with his wife, **Joanna Hamilton Grayson,** with white hat on and their children. Pictured from left to right, **Richard** (August 6, 1932 - July 25, 2014, **David Lee, Joe Lee, Wesley, Henry, Sammy, Matthew, Alfred, Maxine, Joanna, Elizabeth, Rose**, Idelle and **Mildred. (Courtesy of Loretta "Babe" Grayson)**

Standing on the front porch steps of their old county styled home in North Santee, SC are Wesley Grayson and his wife, Joanna Grayson. **Courtesy of Loretta "Babe" Grayson)**

These extremely rare undated pictures are **David** and **Phenie Ladson Grayson**, parents of **Wesley Grayson** from North Santee. **(Courtesy of the Lil Eff Affikan Cump'ny)**

Richard Grayson, Sr. (Sidney George, Duce-n-Berg) was born on Aug. 6, 1932 in Georgetown County to the marital union between **Henry Wesley Grayson** and **Joanna Hamilton Grayson**. **Richard**, age 82 died on July 25, 2014 at Tideland Hospice, Georgetown.

On September 10, 1951, he was joined in holy matrimony to the former **Elizabeth Singleton.** To this union seven children were born.

He was educated in the public schools of Georgetown County and worked for a number of years as a crane operator at Georgetown Steel Corporation.

Richard gave his life to Christ at Mt. Zion A.M.E. church. He was a faithful and longtime member having served as the church sexton and in other capacities as he was able.

Funeral services were held on Wed., July 29, 2014 at Mt. Zion AME Church, North Santee - conducted by **Rev. Alfred Darby, Pastor**. Pastor Darby also preached the "Words of Comfort." Burial followed at the Mt. Zion A.M.E. Church Cemetery.

Survivors include his wife of 63 years, **Elizabeth S. Grayson;** six daughters: **Delphine Sellers** of Columbia, **Patricia Mathis** of Stone Mountain, **Yvonne Sutton** of McClellanville, **Mary J. Benson** of Norcross, GA, **Loretta Gerald** of Tibwin, **Angeline Greene** of Jacksonville, FL, and **Marcetia Grayson** of Georgetown; one son, **Richard Grayson, Jr**. of Lithonia, GA; two granddaughter, who he reared, **Keywonda Williams**, Norcross, GA and **Be'auka Grayson**, Columbia, SC; dedicated uncle, **Railford Hamilton**; four brothers, **Elder David Lee Grayson, Henry Grayson, Sammy Grayson,** and **Matthew Grayson,** all of Georgetown; five sisters, **Mildred Knowlin, Maxine Geathers, Elizabeth Smith**, and **Idelle Deas,** all of Georgetown, and **Rose Moultrie** of New Jersey. **(Courtesy of Loretta "Babe" Grayson)**

Elizabeth Singleton Grayson was born in Georgetown, South Carolina on July 12, 1936 biologically to **Rose Manigault** and **Freddie Mitchell.** She was loved, parented and reared by **Henry** "Hackless" and **Maria Kennedy Singleton**.

Affectionately known by family members and friends as **"Lillie", "Lisbet"** and **"Sis. Ria Lizzie".**

She gave her life to Christ at an early age at Mt. Zion A.M.E. Church, where she was a faithful and longtime member having served as Women's Missionary Society (WMS), Trustee, Class Leader, Young People's Division Director (YPD), Sunday School Teacher, Gospel Choir member and sexton along with here husband, and in any other capacities as he was able and needed. She was also a member of the Order of Eastern Star.

Elizabeth's career path took her down various roads and included work with: Georgetown County Memorial Hospital in dietary service, Winyah High School in the cafeteria, and Winyah Nursing Home where she received training and served as a Nurse's Aide. She loved people and would care for them privately in their homes at the request of their family members.

Elizabeth died on March 30, 2016 in Florida. Funeral services were held on April 8, 2016 at Mt. Zion African Methodist Episcopal Church, **Rev. Phil Flowers,** Senior Pastor. **Rev. Alfred Darby,** Pastor of Nazareth A.M.E. Church and former Pastor of Mt. Zion A.M.E. Church delivered the eulogy.

Survivors include her children, **Patricia Mathis**, Stone Mountain, GA, **Yvonne Sutton**, McClellanville, SC, **Mary J. Benson**, Norcross, GA, **Loretta Gerald**, Tibwin, SC, **Angeline Greene**, Jacksonville, FL, **Marcetia Grayson**, Georgetown, SC, **Richard Grayson Jr.**, Lithonia, GA. Funeral services entrusted to Wilds Funeral Home, LLC. Interment was at the Mt. Zion A.M.E. Church Cemetery, North Santee.

Wearing these popular styles church hats are **Maria Kennedy Singleton**, nicknamed "**Danny**" and **Elizabeth Singleton Grayson. (Courtesy of Loretta "Babe" Grayson)**

This picture was taken at the fiftieth (50th) wedding anniversary of **Richard and Elizabeth Grayson**, (Sitting). Their children **Angeline, Yvonne, Loretta, Patricia, Mary, Marcetia** and **Richard Grayson, Jr**. are standing in the background.
(Courtesy of Loretta "Babe" Grayson)

Richard Grayson Sr. and **Elizabeth Singleton Grayson** celebrated their fifty (50th) wedding anniversary at **Elmore Williams Center, Mt. Zion African Methodist Episcopal Church**, North Santee. **(Courtesy of Loretta "Babe" Grayson)**

This kinfolks portrait is **Richard, Elizabeth, Delphine, Patricia, Yvonne, Mary, Loretta, Angeline**, and **Marcetia Grayson**. **(Courtesy of Loretta "Babe" Grayson)**

This adorable high school "babe" with afro or 'fro on left is Loretta **"Babe" Grayson's** 12th Grade photo taken at **Howard High School**, Georgetown, SC.
(Courtesy of Loretta "Babe" Grayson)

At right is **Dr. Antwon M. Sutton**, son of **Harry** and **Yvonne Grayson Sutton**, McClellanville and grandson of **Richard** and **Elizabeth Grayson**, North Santee. He attended Lincoln High School, McClellanville and graduated in 1998 as third in his class with full academic honors. He obtained his Bachelor of Science degree in business administration from Winthrop University and a masters of arts in teaching degree, in business and marketing education, also from Winthrop. He taught marketing, economics, and computer applications for three years, and was promoted to an assistant principal at Clover High School with over 2,000 students. While at Clover he was the first person to hold the title of Teacher of the Year and assistant principal at the same time. **Dr. Sutton** completed his doctoral program in Educational Leadership at South Carolina State University in May 2009. **Dr. Sutton** is now Principal at **Alcorn Middle School**, Columbia SC since 2013.
(Courtesy of the Lil Eff Affikan Cump'ny)

Loretta "Babe" Grayson of North Santee is Owner/CEO at **BABE Creations, Anointed Quilts** that started in 2000. Babe attended Atlanta College of Business and received her Associates Degree in Business. **Loretta** received an Interior Design license/certificate from Montgomery Ward Stores, Incorporated. She also did professional modeling in Atlanta for several years. **Loretta** has taught at Millie Lewis Modeling School in Charleston and appeared in television commercials, magazine ads and newspaper articles for various clients: Charleston Fashion Week, Charleston Place Hotel, Piggy Wiggly, Carolina Company and Charleston Harbor Innis fail Yacht to name a few. She received a Modeling Instructor Certificate from Barbizon Modeling School in Virginia Beach, worked at the largest full-service marketing, advertising, public relations and research firm in the coastal regions of the Carolinas and Georgia for 21 years. In 1999 she was honored with the TWIN Award from the YWCA of Greater Charleston for her managerial skills.
(Courtesy of Loretta "Babe" Grayson)

Loretta Grayson is an inspirational speaker, Gullah Storybook/Reader, Kwanzaa Awareness/Definition, caretaker for the elderly, emcee for various programs, and, of course, handmade quilt maker, seamstress, maker of African outfits and costumes. She is married and lives with her husband and three sons in the McClellanville area. **Loretta** has been moved by the Holy Spirit to make beautiful quilts. She says that these quilts are the First Fruits of her labor. She promised the First Fruits to her church for the renovations of Greater Joiner Temple. They are trying to raise $10,000. The quilts range from $750 to $2,500. You can e-mail Gerald at babe.grayson@gmail.com. **(Courtesy of the Loretta "Babe" Grayson)**

This fashion and stylish lady is **Loretta Grayson,** Owner/CEO of Babe Creations/Anointed Quilts. **(Courtesy of Loretta "Babe" Grayson)**

This stunning beautiful picture is **Loretta "Babe" Grayson,** the quilt maker, designer of these two African American Handmade Wall Hanging Quilts made **in 2016.** "**Bitter Fruit** and **Racial Crop and Systah"** are the names of these shocking pieces.
(Courtesy of Loretta "Babe" Grayson)

This aged picture is the large and spacious townhome of **Troy Gasque** (January 6, 1909 – April 4, 1988) and **Lena White Gasque, Nee** (May 3 1912 – July 23 1999) of Sampit. It is said that family and community members assisted with the building of this Gasque's home. **Leroy**, **Pressley**, **Rutha Mae** and **Oneil** were there beloved children.

This picture at left shows **Troy** and **Lena White Gasque** standing in front of the family car!

Here is the antique Vantage Wood Burning Cook Stove in the kitchen of **Troy** and **Lena White Gasque**. **Lena** was a well-known cook and known throughout Sampit for her "finger licking dinners and hot buttered biscuits.
(Courtesy of the Lil Eff Affikan Cump'ny)

Photographed at left are **Andrew White** (July 24, 1892 – March 3 1970) and his wife, **Sallie Grant White** standing in front of St. Paul AME Church after Sunday worship. They were the parents of **Lena White Gasque**. **Mr. Andrew**, as he was called by family members was a dedicated member and officer at St. Paul AME Church, favorite song **"I'm Gonna Walk that Milky White Way."** His **twin brother** was **James White**, (July 24, 1892 – January 1970) **married Lular Wilson on** February 16, 1916.
(Courtesy of the Lil Eff Affikan Cump'ny)

Today, the doors of **The Shop** are still opened for business and run by **Jimmy Leon Stafford**, the grandson of **Grandpa London** and nephew of **Ross Stafford**. In 1997, Jimmy opened "**Jimmy's Place**" formerly, **The Shop**, and is a very cozy place for Adults to go. The **Shop** is decorated with items of the past such as old weight scales, cash registers, soda machines, and working hand tools. **(Courtesy of the Lil Eff Affikan Cump'ny)**

Here pictured all decked up at the **Bryant-Stafford Family Reunion** are the children of **Thomas** and **Bessie Bryant Safford**. (Left to right) - **Thomas, Randolph, Jimmy, Edison, Cleo** and **Vernell**. Not pictured are **Franklin** (May 8, 1945 – May 15 1999) and **Suziah** (February 14, 1941 – July 26, 1990). **(Courtesy of the Lil Eff Affikan Cump'ny)**

This is a drawing of the modest home of **Thomas** (June 23, 1913 – March 7, 1953) and **Bessie Bryant Stafford** (September 14, 1916 – May 30, 1974). The home was a large wooden house, four bedrooms, large kitchen, back and front porch, wire fences surround the home, with several locked wooden gates. In the backyard was a large oak tree where we played: a small smokehouse, a small garden, and a large cornfield. Also, I remember a barn being there where the plows and garden equipment were kept.
(Courtesy of the Vernell Stafford Waye)

The home of **Thomas** and **Bessie Bryant Stafford** was enclosed within a wire fence. In order to get in and out their cozy home one had to come through the wooden gate called the "**Big Gate**". Pictured are their sons, **Franklin** and **Edison** sitting in a chair inside the wired fence. **(Courtesy of the Lil Eff Affikan Cump'ny)**

Here is **Bessie Bryant Stafford** (September 14, 1916 – May 30, 1974)), sitting all dressed up in the front yard outside of her cozy home on a warm and sunny day.
(Courtesy of the Lil Eff Affikan Cump'ny)

This handsome gentlemen is **Thomas Stafford** (June 23, 1913 – March 7, 1953), posing in this picture in the fenced in front yard, all dressed up with matching shoes, pant, shirt and tie. At right are three incredible poise sisters and my aunts, **Tisby Bryant** (November 25, 1911 – October 20, 1990), **Bessie** ((September 14, 1916 – May 30, 1974), and **Sue Bryant** (October 24, 1909 – February 8, 1993).
(Courtesy of Veronica Stafford Gasque)

Two of today's fasting growing businesses in the Sampit area is **Queen's Beauty** and **Hair Care Center** and **Gasque's Barbershop.** Both are located in the **Shop** owned by Jimmy L. Stafford. **Queen Elizabeth Smalls Stafford**, the queenly wife of Jimmy, owns the **Queen's Beauty** and **Hair Care Center**. The Hair Care Center was founded in 1991. **Queen** graduated from East High School in Rochester, New York. After that she moved back to South Carolina and attended Chris Logan Beauty School in 1989 and 1990. In 1995 through 1996 she attended the **Dudley Beauty College** in Greenville, South Carolina, founded by **Dr. Joe L. and Eunice M. Dudley** from Greensboro, North Carolina. In 1967, the Dudley's opened Fuller Products Distributorship in Greensboro, North Carolina. Most of the Dudley Beauty Schools and a chain of beauty stores were started in 1976 throughout the southeast. **(Courtesy of Queen Stafford)**

This Sampit born Barber is **Grover Gasque, Jr.;** the son of **Grover Gasque, Sr.** and **Jenette Gasque** is the owner of the **Gasque's Barber Shop** located in The Old Shop. **Grover Jr**. is the first professional, licensed barber in the Sampit Community. The barbershop is spacious with two barber chairs. **Grover Jr**. is a very active member of **Lighthouse Church,** Georgetown, where the **Bishop Floyd Knowlin** is the **Founder** and **Senior Pastor.** Sitting in barber chair is **Franklin Sanders**, aka "**Bigwheelz Sanders.**" **(Courtesy of the Lil Eff Affikan Cump'ny)**

This distinguished gentlemen and churchmen sitting down on small table posting for this image is **Wesley Bryant** (October 8, 1903 – March 13, 1962) locally owner and operator of the **Bryant's Grocery Store**. For many years he ran a small wooden grocery shop that sold items such as candies, Rock candies, Baby Ruth, bubble gums, and drinks. As one enters the small store-outer porch – the first thing you notice was the soda/drink/soda pop machine. It was really old but had the coldest drink in town. He also sold Root bear, Coke-a-cola, Pepsi, Doctor Pepper, RC Cola and Red Rock. After his death, the small shop was torn down.

Wesley is the oldest of the siblings of **Robert** (1884 – June 21, 1930) and **Lula Louise Smith Bryant** (February 2, 1886 – November 17, 1966). **Wesley** served as a Steward at the St. Paul African Methodist Episcopal Church, Sampit, and the family church. His nephew, **Wesley Michael Bryan**t takes on this distinguish and honorable name! **(Courtesy of the Lil Eff Affikan Cump'ny)**

This is the old long-standing wooden home of **Wesley** (October 8, 1903 – March 13, 1962) and **Rebecca Stafford Bryant** (May 6, 1904 – May 14, 1951). They married on April 24, 1924 in Sampit. **Rebec**ca was the daughter of **London Stafford Sr.** and **Kiziah Gasque Stafford** of Sampit. Their children were **Rollin, Ollin,** (January 16, 1927 – May 2, 1982) **Lucille** (May 5, 1928-December 23, 2015), **Mable** (January 30, 1931 – May 10, 1974), **Robert** (January 10, 1932- August 26, 1992) and **Lila Mae**. After the death of **Rebecca**, **Wesley** married his second wife, **Elizabeth Richardson** on November 10, 1951 in Sampit. **Elizabeth** (May 23, 1916 - February 3, 1982) was the daughter of **Ruthledge Richardson** and **Phoebie Davis**. **(Courtesy of the Lil Eff Affikan Cump'ny)**

In this 1990 picture are **Paul Bryant, Patricia Bryant, Christopher Bryant, Bernice J. Bryant** and **Tisby Bryant Holmes** standing in front of **Cecil and Tisby Holmes'** home on Powell Road. **(Courtesy of the Lil Eff Affikan Cump'ny)**

This "dressed to kill couple" at left is **Hughie (Whuie)** (September 16, 1905 – January 20, 1979) and **Elizabeth Johnson Bryant** (July 10, 1900 – June 2 1983).
(Courtesy of the Lil Eff Affikan Cump'ny)

(At Right) This picture dating July 1959 at right shows **Nicholas** (May 8, 1898 - July 22, 1987 and **Sue Elizabeth Bryant Dorsey (October 24, 1909 – February 3, 1993)** with their dog standing in the front yard of their home in **Mullins, SC. Nichols** and **Sue** were married on November 29, 1936. **(Courtesy of the Lil Eff Affikan Cump'ny)**

This old rustic sign on left stands in front of the **Green's Grocery Store** in the Cumberland Section of **Sampit** – On top is an advertisement sign - Mountain Dew (soda) for sale.
(Courtesy of the Lil Eff Affikan Cump'ny)

(At right) Carefully preserve, this early 1900's **Green's Grocery Store** was opened in the Cumberland Section of Sampit. In the background is the elegant home of the Green's painted in dark green and white trimming around the windows.
(Courtesy of the Lil Eff Affikan Cump'ny)

These history makers are **William Green, Sr.** (November 3, 1912 – May 13, 1995) and his wife, **Ida Holmes Green** (October 28, 1910 – February 9, 2002).
(Courtesy of Augustus Green Jr.)

This large picturesque weathered old storage barn with metal rooftop belongs to **William Green** of the Cumberland Section of Sampit. (**Courtesy of the Lil Eff Affikan Cump'ny**)

These two images are **Reverend William Green, Sr.** (November 3, 1912 – May 13, 1995) and his wife, **Ida Holmes Green** (October 28, 1910 – February 9, 2002) from the Cumberland Section of Sampit. **Reverend Williams Green, Jr.,** was a **Local Elder** (Ordained) at Cumberland A.M.E. Church, the family church. He was the son **Reverend Augustus Green** (April 10, 1881 – October 30, 1974), known as the Community Historian and **Charity Green** (July 28, 1888 – September 22, 1967). **Reverend Green** served as assistant pastor, Sunday School teacher, Class Leader, and Trustee at Cumberland AME Church. He was actively in the Home Charity Lodge, Home of Ruth, Order of Eastern Star New Hope **Chapter # 343, Masonic Lodge #429, NAACP, and was a certified Public Notary.** The Green's (Reverend William Green, Sr., and Ida Holmes Green) married in 1936. **(Courtesy of Augustus Green, Jr.)**

Standing in front of the **William** and **Ida Green's** beautiful and traditional county styled home are **Doris Green,** her brother, **Samuel "S.J," Green** and their cousin, **Ida Mae Green. (Courtesy of the Lil Eff Affikan Cump'ny)**

At left is **Maude Ernestine Gary Green** (September 30, 1907 – May 25, 2004) from the Cumberland community. She was born to **Reverend Ambrose Gary** and **Rosa Lee Peguese Gary**. She was reared and educated in the Suttons Community of Williamsburg County.

"**Miss Maude,**" as she was lovely called, began her religious experience at Nazareth A.M.E. Church in Suttons, SC. She later transferred her membership to Cumberland A.M.E. Church after her marriage to **Reverend Samuel Green** in 1939. At Cumberland she served faithfully in many capacities: Class Leader, sang on the Senior Choir, member of the Stewardess Board, Women's Missionary Society (WMS), Willing Workers Club and Church School.

"**Miss Maude,**" was also a member of Home Charity Lodge No. 20 and Order of the Eastern Star Chapter 343.

Reverend Samuel Green and **Maude Green** was blessed with two children, **Samuel "S.J.,"** and **Doris**.

"**Miss Maude,**" died early morning on May 25, 2004. Homegoing Celebration was held on Friday, May 28, 2004, Cumberland A.M.E. Church at 3:00 P.M. where **Reverend Thomas Habersham** served at Pastor. **Pastor Habersham** preached the eulogy, committal and benediction was at the Cumberland A.M.E. Church Cemetery.
(Courtesy of the Lil Eff Affikan Cump'ny)

The original **Keith's Grocery Store** was started in 1952 in the small garden spot next to the home of the late **Reverend Sam** (Reverend Sam I) and **Creola Grant Sanders**. **Ezekiel Sanders**, the father of **Reverend Sam** was the landowner that gave the shop away to **Nathaniel Lee** and **Edith Sanders Keith**. **Nathaniel Keith**, called **Mr. Nathaniel** was born in the Cumberland Section of Sampit on December 17, 1920 – January 28, 2009). The shop served the community well for many years. Customers to the store shopped daily and many times charged things on "**credit**." Crediting is a process where the customers brought items and promised to pay at a later time. **Nathaniel** stated that "crediting" was bad for business because only a few people came back to pay their bills.
(Courtesy of the Lil Eff Affikan Cump'ny)

Siblings **Gertrude, Helen, Herbert, Lila, Vermel, Inez,** and **Nathaniel Keith** posing for a family shot after the funeral service of their brother **Robert Keith** in Columbia, South Carolina. **(Courtesy of Ingera Reown)**

This old and undated photograph is **Ezekiel** (died April 10, 1962) and his wife, **Rock Humphrey Sanders** (December 12, 1886 – May 13, 1970), the parents of **Edith, Sam, Jim, Tom, Dodie, Bernice, Rosa, Francis, Lillian,** and **Teresa Sanders**. **(Courtesy of Roxie Sanders Giles)**

After **Nathaniel Keith's** three years in the United States Army, he returned home at Cumberland. Three years later on February 12, 1946 he married the former **Edith Sanders** from the St. Paul Section at the Georgetown Court House, Georgetown, SC. In 1947 the newlywed couple started building their home in the Cumberland Section of Sampit. **Tom Hughes** from the Cumberland section built the original home. Later the house was torn down and moved to the present location off Columbus Road in the St Paul Section.

For many years **Nathaniel** worked at the **International Paper Company (IPC)** in Georgetown as a laborer. He left the company after given a job that was hazardous to his health, unsafe, and dangerous. He then worked for the Waterfront as a longshoreman loading craft paper where he retired. **Nathaniel** and **Edith** are the proud parents of **Geraldine** and **Nathaniel Keith**. **(Courtesy of Edith Sanders Keith)**

Mrs. Edith Keith, the matriarch of the family celebrated her **ninety-first** (91st) birthday party with loving and adoring family members. In this celebration family photo are her two children, **Nathaniel, Geraldine** and almost all of her grandchildren and great grandchildren in attendance. **(Courtesy of Geraldine Keith)**

Mrs. Edith Keith (left) and daughter, **Geraldine Keith** (right) posing in these two fashionable look a like pictures. **(Courtesy of the Lil Eff Affikan Cump'ny)**

The Youngs Chapel AME Church, Irmo, SC celebrated 128th years of African Methodism in Irmo, SC on October 25, 2015! (Left to Right**)** **Beulah Bristow** (84), **Edith Keith** (91), Mother **Agnes Bell** (95), **Decmist Inez Scott** (92), and **Lillie Corley** (89). How rich the worship experience to have **Mrs. Edith Keith** with us. **(STRAIGHT OUTTA SAM PITT) (Courtesy of the Lil Eff Affikan Cump'ny)**

This outfitted lady with matching dress, hat and accessory worn together is **Mrs. Edith Keith** standing in the vestibule at Bethel AME Church, Columbia, SC!
(Courtesy of the Lil Eff Affikan Cump'ny)

Two of the most profound, charitable and well-known business partnership of Sampit was **David Samuel** (October 15, 1925 – February 4, 1996) and **Pearline William Smith** (December 21, 1925 – July 17, 2013). They were owners of the **David Smith's Grocery and Laundry**. **David** was the son of **Reverend David William Smith** (January 6, 1878 – November 13, 1940) and **Mary Bertha Duncan Smith**. **David** married the former, **Pearline Williams,** of the Trinity Section of Sampit on July 25, 1942. **Pearline** was the daughter of **Sollie** and **Daisy Williams**. She was a former member the Trinity A.M.E. Church, Trinity Section. After their marriage, **Pearline** transferred her membership from Trinity A.M.E. Church to St. Paul A.M.E. Church. **David** served his country valiantly in the United States Army and was honorably discharged on February 5, 1946.
(Courtesy of the Lil Eff Affikan Cump'ny)

In the early 1964, the **Smiths** bought the property where **Rufus Lambert's Store** stood for years and later renamed it "**David Smith's Grocery**". Later, **David** added a kerosene pump, gas pumps, laundry mat, and renamed the store **"David Smith's Grocery and Laundry." (Courtesy of the Lil Eff Affikan Cump'ny)**

In this four (4) generational family photo are **Creola Sanders** (Mother), **Mary Alice Grant** (Daughter) **Glendale Grant**, (Granddaughter), and **Joey A. Grant Sr.** (Great grandson) **(Courtesy of Glendale Grant)**

At left is **Shirley Smith** (October 3, 1950 – February 21, 2012), the daughter of **Glennie** and **Dorothy S. Grant** and raided in the home of **David** and **Pearline Smith**. She was an active member of St. Paul A.M.E Church. She held membership with the Sisterhood of the United Orders of Tents, Ruth Tent No. 149. For years **Shirley** worked at the office of the Georgetown County Clerk and as Secretary for Sampit Logging Company. **Shirley** was known to be an outgoing person with a great sense of humor.

This #1 Dallas Cowboys Fan is **Sherman Omar Smith** (October 31, 1967 – December 11, 2014) of Sampit. He was the son of Shirley Smith and adopted and reared by **David** and **Pearline W. Smith**. He was committed **Dallas Cowboys fan**, and never hesitated to say **"What about them boys."** He had a smile for all whom came in contact with him. He was a fun, loving and caring young man with a great sense of humor. His sense of family will always be remembered. He was married to **Wilma Spann Smith** and he has one son, **Dominique Middleton**. **(Courtesy of Glendale Grant)**

David and **Pearline Smith** opened and operated the **David S. Smith Logging Company** of Sampit for many years. Mr. David hired many men from Sampit to work in his logging business. Some of his hired men were **Vernon Smith, Edward Wilson, Franklin Grant,** and **Bernie Washington**. Both of the Smith's business enterprises were profitable to the community for many years. **The Smith's**, David and Pearline was known throughout Sampit for their "kindness to strangers". They were very generous and always the first ones to step forward to give monies and items from their store for community events and activities. David was equally active and committed to the growth and development of the Sampit Community. He gave many years and much energy to the management of the Sampit Community baseball team. He donated the land for the "**Ball Diamond**" where the Sampit Baseball Team played against other baseball teams from many surrounding communities. David was very instrumental in starting the Sampit Community Center, with other community leaders. He donated the land, which now houses the **Senior Citizens Group** and **Sampit Headstart** program. **(Courtesy of the Lil Eff Affikan Cump'ny)**

(Courtesy of the Lil Eff Affikan Cump'ny)

One of the most faithful employees for **David S. Smith Logging Company** was **Edward Wilson** (October 14, 1933 – February 6, 1989), son of **William** and **Carrie Moyd Wilson**. He was an active member of the St. Paul AME Church. There he served as Class Leader for Class No. 4, a member of the Gospel and Male Choirs, the Steward Board and the Hospitality Club. His community affiliations included membership in the NAACP. Since September 25, 1954 he abided in Holy Matrimony with the former **Hessie Armstrong** (August 21, 1932 – May 5, 2013).

Standing in this moving family photo is **Hessie Armstrong Wilson** and her ten children: **Solomon (Pee Wee), Teddy, Donnie, Jacqueline, Hestina, Willie, Sylvia, Floyd, Jimmie** and **Roosevelt**. **(Courtesy of Solomon Wilson)**

This beautiful original photo at left is **Hessie Armstrong Wilson** (August 21, 1932 – May 5, 2013), daughter of **Silas** and **Bertha Franklin Armstrong** and beloved wife of **Edward Wilson**. At right is an undated photo of elderly **Carrie Moyd Wilson** (April 6, 1904 – April 26, 1997), the daughter of **Etta Moyd**. Her obituary stated, "She was united in holy matrimony to **William Wilson** of Sampit and blessed with the birth of thirteen children." **(Courtesy of Solomon Wilson)**

The Wilson's Family of **Sampit**: **Willie,** his wife of 35 years, **Christine,** and their remarkable daughters, **IRissa, Krystal,** and **VeTarya. (Courtesy of Willie Wilson)**

This old time faded picture is **Johnny Lee Fraser** (November 17, 1934 – April 24, 1982) and **Mary Funnye Frasier** (February 12, 1938 – August 11, 1996) of Sampit. At right are **Mary**, her daughters, **Christine, Mary Alice** and grandchildren. **(Courtesy of Willie Wilson)**

Before the death of **David Smith**, his nephew **Vernon Smith** brought out the **David S. Smith Logging Company**. **Vernon** renamed the lucrative business "**The Sampit Logging Company."** One of the unique things about **Vernon** the owner is that he kept the same employees that his Uncle David hired for years. Among them were: **Edward Wilson, Franklin Grant** and **Bernie Washington**. Today, **Vernon** is self-employed "trucking" for the International Paper Company (IPC). He carries wood from IPC to the company wood yard several miles away. Vernon is an active member of St. Paul A.M.E. Church, the family church of Sampit. He also serves on the St. Paul AME Church Trustee Board, Usher Board, Male Chorus and Church Usher Board.
(Courtesy of the Lil Eff Affikan Cump'ny)

Glennie Grant (August 27, 1924 – March 2, 1970) is photographed in this picture all dressed up in his Sunday's best suit with matching tie and pocket square. Glennie' wife **Dorothy Smith Grant** (August 19, 1929 – February 26, 2006) is standing in front of St. Paul AME Church with an fashionable dress with matching hat and pocket book. Glennie and Dorothy were married in 1947. **(Courtesy of the Lil Eff Affikan Cump'ny)**

The International Paper Company (IPC), Georgetown was established in 1936. In the 1950's IPC contracted or employed many blacks from Sampit to work in pulp work or their plant in Georgetown. Some of the well-known blacks that were contracted with **IPC** were **Ross Stafford, Moody Stafford, Tom Moultrie, David Smith, Charles Smith, Henry Deas, James Deas, Milford Darby, Demphis Wragg** and **Vernord Smith**. At one time blacks were hired by IPC only as laborers; given the toughest jobs and worked very long hours with little pay. It was said by several older black employees that blacks had to use what is unofficially known as the "colored" bathroom at the mill.
(Courtesy of the Lil Eff Affikan Cump'ny)

Pictured above are logs trucks entering and lining up at **the International Paper Company,** Georgetown to be unloaded off! **(Courtesy of the Lil Eff Affikan Cump'ny)**

My father, **Eff Bryant** (July 12, 1914 - May 19, 1975 received this certificate of employment of twenty-five years from the **Quarter Century Society, Inc.** at the International Paper Company. It reads: **The Quarter Century Society, Inc.** Be it known that **Eff Bryant** is a Member of the Quarterly Century Society Having Completed 25 Years of Service. Attested by J. F. Mixon (The Quarter Century Society, Inc. Gus T. Ward President.
(Courtesy of the Lil Eff Affikan Cump'ny)

My father, **Eff Bryant** treasured this retirement certificate from The International Paper Company in Georgetown, nickname "The Paper Company" after being employed for thirty-two years.

Certificate of Retirement
International Paper Company
Presented Grateful
Appreciation to
Eff Bryant
Who has served this company Loyally, Faithfully and Well for thirty-two years and who retired on the 1st day of April one thousand nine hundred and seventy-one. **J. F. Mixon (Manager)**

(Courtesy of the Lil Eff Affikan Cump'ny)

This wooden case at left contained a King James Bible (white in color) that was presented to my mother, **Bernice Jackson Bryant** by the International Paper Company at the time of my father, Eff **Bryant's death** on May 19, 1975.
(Courtesy of the Lil Eff Affikan Cump'ny)

The BB Smith's Grocery Store was owned and operated by **Benjamin Bourne "BB" Smith** (August 13, 1927 - December 22, 2013), nicknamed "**BB**" located on St. Delight Road, Smith. He was born in Georgetown on August 13, 1927, a son of the late **John Benjamin Smith** and **Ellen Timmons Smith**. He graduated from Andrews High School and served in the US Army during World War II. BB was a Mason and Shriner and a member of Sampit United Methodist Church, where he was a former chairman of the cemetery committee.
(Courtesy of the Lil Eff Affikan Cump'ny)

The **B.B. Smith Washer** is located next to the **B.B. Smith's Grocery Store**. At one times the B.B. Smith Washer was the only laundry mat opened and used in Sampit.
(Courtesy of the Lil Eff Affikan Cump'ny)

The Reverend Wallace J. McKnight, Sr. is **Owner/Operator of McKnight-Fraser Funeral Home**s of Georgetown and Andrews, South Carolina. **The McKnight Funeral Home**, Andrews, South Carolina was started in 1956. He is also owner and operator of **Morning Glory Cemetery, Inc**. in Sampit, South Carolina.
(**Courtesy of Reverend Wallace J. McKnight, Sr.**)

Reverend Wallace J. McKnight, Sr. was born to the parenthood of the **Richard** and **Mary Cooper McKnight**; reared in Williamsburg County, South Carolina, the son of sharecroppers. He graduated from Battery Park High School, Atlanta College of Mortuary Science, Atlanta, Georgia, and received his theology training at Dickerson Theological Seminary at Allen University, Columbia, South Carolina.
(**Courtesy of Reverend Wallace J. McKnight, Jr.**)

Reverend Wallace J. McKnight, Sr. was the first black member of Andrews Town Council, and the first black member of the State Democratic Executive Committee from Georgetown County. **Gov. Richard Riley** appointed **Reverend McKnight** to the Comprehensive Employment and Training Commission of South Carolina. During his tenure as a trustee of Georgetown Memorial Hospital, **Reverend McKnight** advocated hiring more doctors and other African-American employees. In roles with the Chamber of Commerce and the Georgetown board of Directors of Wachovia Bank, he has promoted minority business development.

Reverend McKnight also served as a district highway commissioner. Other community activities include life membership in the NAACP, membership in Beech Street Masonic Lodge No. 398, the Andrews Industrial Development Committee, South Carolina Morticians Association, Inc., Board of Directors and Former Chaplain for the National Funeral Directors and Morticians Association, Wachovia Bank MEBLO Board of Directors for Minority Enterprise Business, Georgetown County Chambers of Commerce, the Georgetown County Transportation Committee and a member of the Georgetown Hospital System's Board of Trustee. **(Courtesy of the Lil Eff Affikan Cump'ny)**

Reverend McKnight has received many honors and awards: He is past President of South Carolina Morticians Association, past President of the South Carolina State Board of Funeral Services, past President of the Andrews Branch of the NAACP, the first black to be Council; the first black appointed to the State Executive Committeeman for Georgetown; he was appointed by Governor Richard Riley to serve on the Comprehensive Employment and Training Commission for the State of South Carolina; 1979, he was elected Mortician of the year by the South Carolina Morticians Association, Inc., and listed among "Who's Who" in Funeral Services. He received the Citizen of the year award in 1980 presented by The Iota Tau Chapter, Omega Psi Phi Fraternity; he also received this award again in 1984. A former District Highway Commissioner, The Georgetown Motor Vehicle Building is named in his honor. He is also a former member of the Chamber of Congress.

Reverend McKnight is married to the former **Alvina Bolton** of Reading, Pa. The have two children, **Walletta Joyce McKnight Thornton** and **Wallace J. McKnight, Jr.**; and six grandchildren: **Adrianne, James, Jr., Kristen, Wallace III, Christopher**, and **Brittany**. **(Courtesy of the Lil Eff Affikan Cump'ny)**

The McKnight Fraser Funeral Home
1423 Front Street
P.O. Box 779 Georgetown, South Carolina 29440

The McKnight Fraser Funeral Home
406 West Ashland St.
P.O. Box 499 Andrews, South Carolina

The Dedication Ceremony of the **W. J. McKnight** and **Son Memorial Chapel** at 406 West Ashland Avenue, Andrews, South Carolina was held n Saturday, April 14, 1990 at 5:00 P.M. The Chapel was dedicated to the memories of **Richard** and **Mary McKnight** (Reverend Wallace J. McKnight's parents) and **Pierce** and **Lillie Mae Bolton** (Mrs. Alvina Bolton McKnight's parents).
(Courtesy of the Lil Eff Affikan Cump'ny)

Thomas James Deas (February 8, 1940 – April 30, 2013) and **Henry Clemons** (June 16, 1937 – June 7, 2013) were two brothers from Sampit that had a lucrative logging business for over 40 years before retiring. The two brothers were the sons of **Walter** (July 31, 1900 – June 1978) and **Essie Duncan Deas** (October 29, 1903 – December 2, 1979) of Sampit. Logging was hard work and very demanding said James. During daddy's **(Eff)** vacation time from IPC he worked as a logger with **Henry** and **James**. **Deas.** This helped my father to earn extra money for his large family. The family was very appreciative to the two brothers to help the family out financially. **(Courtesy of the Lil Eff Affikan Cump'ny)**

Here is businessman **Thomas James Deas** (February 8, 1940 – April 30, 2013) standing in front of a handmade wooden chicken coop made on wheels.
(Courtesy of the Lil Eff Affikan Cump'ny)

Standing in front of **Deas' Shop** is **Weldon Deas**, owner and his two sons, **Thomas** and **Clemnite Deas**. **(Courtesy of the Lil Eff Affikan Cump'ny)**

In this 1970's family photograph is **Henry Deas Sr.** (June 16, 1937 – June 7, 2013), his wife, **Lou Pearl**, and their children, **Henry Jr.** and **Dianna**. **Henry** was in partnership with his brother, **James** in the pulp wood business for over 40 years. The two brothers, Henry and James were also known for their love of their cars. Both of them drove some of the finest cars in Sampit and kept them split clean and polished.

Henry Deas Jr. at right follows in his father's footstep for his love of cars.
(Courtesy of Henry Deas)

Joe Cooper (August 15 1903 – April 18 1963) of the New Hope section of Sampit was another "pulp wood" business manager and owner. He was a faithful member in regular and good standard of **New Hope Union Methodist Episcopal Church**. He served as a Church Trustee. Joe is pictured here directing his crew as they loaded recently cut pinewood on the pulpwood truck. **Joe Cooper** is the crew leader; **Nathaniel Cooper**, his son (standing at truck door) is the truck driver; **Robert Lee Knowlin** (October 12, 1931 – January 7, 2004) is standing on top loading logs and **Francis Bells Trappier** (May 10, 1915 – January 7, 1982) standing in his work clothes. **(Courtesy of Carrie Bell Copper)**

The much-loved children of **Thomas** and **Hattie Smith Cooper**: **John, Thomasina, Johnny, Sylvia, Rosalyn, Jeffery, Joseph,** and **Carlos Cooper**.
(Courtesy of Thomasina C. Scott)

Luechen Wragg, Sr. was born December 24, 1930 in Sampit, the son of **Samuel Wragg Sr.** and **Cardell Rhue Wragg**. He received his formal education from Georgetown County Schools. At the age of 15, **Luechen** began an apprenticeship in brick masonry under his uncle, **Samuel Rhue**. This brought about a thriving and lucrative career in brick masonry, which spanned over 47 years. **Luechen** started the **Lucheon Wragg Brick Work** in 1947. His marvelous and creative brickwork can be seen throughout the low country. He retired in 2002 after working some forty-seven (47) years as a brick mason. It is unknown how many homes or businesses he bricked in during this forty-seven years.

Luechen joined the United States Army in 1951 and fought on the front line in the Korean conflict. After serving meritoriously, he was honorably discharged.

In 1953 he met his loving and devoted wife, the former **Wilhelmina White**, daughter of **Lidia White Hanna Green**, They courted until marrying on March 17, 19555, at the Georgetown Court House. Their children: **Lue Jean, Debbra, Melissa, Luechen, Jr., Audrey, Mark, Monique, Jefferson, Leonard,** and **Verleria.** The **Wragg'** are members of Cumberland African Methodist Episcopal in good and regular standard. **Lucheon** served on the Usher Board, Senior Choir, Male Chorus, the Steward Board (Steward Pro-Tem), the Trustee Board, Class Leader, and grounds keeper. He was also instrumental in the construction and brickwork on the New Cumberland A.M.E. Church.

Wilhelmina is a member of the Cardell Wragg Missionary Society and the Willing Workers Club of Cumberland A.M.E. One of the stained glass windows inside the Cumberland A.M.E. Church is a window denoted by **Luechen** and **Wilhelmina** in the Loving Memory of **Luechen Jefferson & Monique Wragg**.

Luechen entered into eternal rest on May 19, 2016 at Georgetown Memorial Hospital. Funeral service in honor of **Luechen Wragg** was held on Monday, May 23, 2016, Cumberland A.M.E. Church, at 11:00 A.M. **Reverend Barbara Nelson** (Pastor) preached "the Word of Comfort" to a pack church with family members, friends, community leaders and ministers.

This is **Luechen** standing in front of the old homestead house.

(Courtesy of the Lil Eff Affikan Cump'ny)

Jerome Bryant, Specialty Contractor of Sampit, started the "Bryant's Electric" business in 1986. He is the son of Roland Bryant and Martha Bryant of Sampit. Other siblings: Lauretta, Rosetta and Patricia. His sister Patricia also is the owner of the "Tricia's Beauty Salon" located off the Pennyroyal Road. Patricia is married to John Grant of the Pennyroyal section of Sampit. "John-John" and Craig are their children. Jerome attended Sampit Elementary School, Sampit and Rosemary High School in Andrews, South Carolina. He graduated from Rosemary in 1968. After graduation from Rosemary, he went to Denmark Technical College, Denmark, South Carolina and graduated with a degree in Electronics 1970. He then moved back home to Sampit and was employed by the Georgetown Steel Company, Georgetown since 1970 as an Electric Technician. Jerome retired from Arcellor Mittal Steel Company in 2010. Jerome is a member of St. Paul A.M.E. Church, Sampit. He is a full member of the church in good and regular standing. He has held membership with the Senior Trustee Board, the Mass Choir, Usher and St. Paul Planning Committee. In 1975, he married Barbara Brown, the daughter of William and Marie Brown at Mt. Zion A.M.E. Church, McClellanville, South Carolina. Barbara's siblings are Jane, Dorothy, Evon, Aldeen, Verlette, and Leroy. Barbara graduated from Lincoln High School, McClellanville in 1971. After her marriage to Jerome, she moved to Sampit and became a full member of St. Paul A.M.E. Church. She held membership as Junior Trustee President, Christian Education Department, Church School Teacher, Stewardess Board President, and St. Paul Planning Committee. Barbara is now retired from the Georgetown County School Board working as a Teacher's Assistant at Sampit Elementary School, Sampit since 2009. Patrice, Jerome and Beatrice are their gifted and talented children. (Courtesy of Jerome Bryant)

Bryant Road sign!
Photograph here (standing) is Jeff Grant, Patricia Grant, Barbara Bryant, Jerome Bryant, Rosetta, Lauretta Ray, (sitting) Rollin Bryant, Martha Bryant, Annie Laura (Martha's sister) and Robert Ray. (Courtesy of Rollin and Martha Bryant)

This stunning couple, **Rollin** and **Martha Bryant** commemorated 68 years on marriage on **December 31, 1947**. **Rollin** retired in 1990 from the Georgetown Steel Company, Georgetown and **Martha** from the Georgetown County School District in 1987. They are the parents of three daughters, **Lauretta, Rosetta, Patricia**, and one son, **Jerome**. They have 7 grandchildren and 2 great grandchildren. **Rollin** is the **Patriarch** of the **Bryant's Family**.

At right is **Robert Bryant,** nicknamed **Bob** (June 10, 1932 – August 26, 1992) was the devoted brother of **Rollin, Ollin, Lucille** and **Lila Mae Bryant**. **Bob** was known as one of the most devoted and dedicated member of St. Paul AME Church, Sampit.
(Courtesy of Rollin Bryant)

The Pittman's Sisters: Martha (sitting), **Annie Laura, Almeter, Ollie** and **Dora** (standing). **(Courtesy of Martha Pittman Bryant)**

This faithful couple, **Rollin** and **Martha Pittman Bryant** commemorated five decades of marriage (**50th Wedding Anniversary**) with their children, **Lauretta, Rosetta, Jerome** and **Patricia**, Grandchildren, **Patrice, Aisha, John Jr., Patrick, Chris, Craig** and **Bianca** at the **Wallace J. McKnight Christian Education Building** in 1997. **Reverend Wallace J. McKnight,** Pastor of St. Paul A.M.E. Church renewed their wedding vows. The beautiful program included the Master of ceremony, Joseph Bryant, Musical Selection by The Knowlin Brothers, Prayer by Reverend Joe Knowlin, Grand Entrance, **Rollin** and **Martha Bryant**, Tribute and presentation by their children. The hostesses were Emma Holmes, Cleo Smith, Oden Moultie and Veronica Gasque and organist, William Whitehurst.
(Courtesy of Rollin Bryant)

This image on left is from of the wedding program **"As You Celebrate 50 Special Years -** Rollin and **Martha P. Bryant.** The stunning wedding picture on right is **Rollin** and **Martha Bryant** on their 50th Wedding Day. **(Courtesy of Rollin and Martha Bryant)**

This precious and undated picture is **Rome** and **Rosa Pittman,** parents of Martha Pittman Bryant. **(Courtesy of Jerome Bryant)**

This lovely and smiling couple is **Rollin** and **Martha Pittman Bryant** sitting in their home at Bryant Road in Sampit. **(Courtesy of the Lil Eff Affikan Cump'ny)**

Martha Pittman Bryant (July 12, 1926 - August 24, 2015) was born to the martial union of **Rome** and **Rosa (Gray) Pittman** in the Pleasant Hill Community, Georgetown County, South Carolina.

Martha received her education in the Georgetown School, where she graduated from Howard High School in Georgetown.

On December 31, 1947 she was joined in holy matrimony to **Rollin Bryant**, Sampit, S.C. This union was blessed with the birth of four children. **Martha** was a devoted wife, mother and a child of God. She joined St. Paul A.M.E. Church and accepted Jesus Christ as her personal Savior. She worked in the youth department for many years, faithful member of Stewardess, Usher Board and Steward Board. **Martha** also received many citations and recognitions for her community and church work. But most of all her dedication and personal walk with the Master left an imprint and touched the lives of many youth and elderly.

Martha was a true Proverb 31 Women! She opened her mouth with wisdom, stretched forth her hands to the needy, and did so much more. **Martha** loved her family and told everyone that came to see her that she was blessed with a loving and caring family.

Martha worked for the Georgetown Country Schools and was known as a superb cooker and baker. She was best known for her finger licking "cinnamon rolls with raisins" and other delicious treats for many years.

On Saturday, August 22, 2015, God called **Martha** home to be with Him.

Martha leaves to cherish her memory a devoted husband Rollin Bryant of 68 years; four children: Lauretta (Robert) Ray, Rosetta (Maceo) Martin, Jerome (Barbara) Bryant and Patricia (John) Grant, all of Georgetown, S.C., seven grandchildren: Aisha and Christopher Ray, Patrice, Patrick, and Bianca Bryant; John and Craig Grant; two great grand-children: Jeremiah Ray and Isaiah Grant; one sister Annie Selph of Philadelphia, Pennsylvania; two sisters-in-law: Lucille Drayton and Lila Prout of Georgetown, SC; a host of nieces, nephews, other relatives and friends.

Home Going Celebration for **Martha Magdalene Pittman Bryant** was held on Thursday, August 27, 2015 at St. Paul African Methodist Episcopal Church, Sampit at 1:00 P.M. Pastor Kelly Spann II preached the Words of Comfort "Victory of Death." Reverend Effson C. Bryant, Pastor of Youngs Chapel A.M.E. Church, Irmo, SC presided; Bishop Floyd A. Knowlin, Pastor of Light House Church, Georgetown prayed; Reverend Adams, Pastor of Adams A.M.E Church read the Old Testament Reading; Reverend Teddy Wilson, Associate Pastor of St. Paul A.M.E. Church read the New Testament Reading; Solo by Mary Brown/St. Paul AME Church Choir "Don't Call The Roll Until I Get There; Remarks by Emma Holmes (Class Leader #18); Family Tribute by Granddaughters, Patrice Bryant and Aisha Ray; Resolution and Acknowledgements by Bernida W. Trappier and Committal at St. Paul A.M.E. Church Cemetery. **(Courtesy of the Lil Eff Affikan Cump'ny)**

Cuz Rollin and **Cuz Martha** posing for this unique picture following a powerful and moving worship service at St. Paul African Methodist Episcopal Church, Sampit.
(Courtesy of the Lil Eff Affikan Cump'ny)

The Bryant's Family donated this beautiful stained glass window displaying "**CHRIST AT HEART'S DOOR KNOCKING**" at St. Paul AME Church.

The inscription reads: **BRYANTS: Rollin** and **Martha; Jerome** and **Barbara; Maceo** and **Rosetta John** & **Patricia.**

The stained glass window is based on Revelation 3:20 which reads, "Here I am! I stand at the door and knock. If anyone hears my voice and opens the door, I will come in and eat with that person, and they with me."

(Courtesy of the Lil Eff Affikan Cump'ny)

Cuz Rollin Bryant and his adorable and treasured wife, **Cuz Martha Pittman Bryant.**
(Courtesy of Rollin Bryant)

The precious children of **Rollin** and **Martha Bryant - Jerome, Lauretta, Patricia** and **Rosetta Bryant** posing for a sibling photograph.
(Courtesy of the Lil Eff Affikan Cump'ny)

Marie Brown Green (November 15, 1925 - March 26, 2015), affectionately called "Sister", was born on November 15, 1925, to the **Henrietta Brown Colleton Grant.** She was reared in the home of **Daniel** and **Emma Deas**.

Marie attended McClellanville School, McClellanville, SC. During those days, the school only went to the 8th grade. She moved to Charleston and continued her studies at Burke High School.

Sister was one of the first women of color to be employed at he cigar factory in Charleston, SC. After her children became of age, she worked for **Dr. Wallace** (Orthopedic Surgeon) for seven years.

Marie dated her schoolmate, **William Green**, the love of her life. In 1946, **Marie** and **William** were joined in holy matrimony and married for 69 years. They were indeed one in body and spirit. You would seldom see one without the other said by family members. To this marriage, seven daughters were born: **Jane, Dorothy, Evon, Delories, Barbara, Verletta** and one died at birth.

Marie began her Christian journey at an early age. She attended Old Bethel A.M.E. Church, now Bethel A.M.E. Church, McClellanville, SC. After her marriage, she transferred her membership to Mount Zion A.M.E. Church, South Santee Section of McClellanville, SC. She served under the class leadership of the late Henry Simmons and Harry Manigault. Sister was a faithful member and kept her daughters in Sunday School and worship services.

After her children entered adulthood, Sister returned to her home church, Bethel A.M.E. Church. She continued to serve the Lord faithfully and served under the class leadership of Sonny Gamble, Leader White and Lucretia Swinton.

Marie was a member of the Women Missionary Society (WMS) and the Berkeley Electric Cooperative Women Involved Rural Electrification (BEC-WIRE).

Marie was a supportive Christian. She would attend church functions even if it meant catching a ride. Her words were: "Just get me there and I will get home or stay at the church until I get a ride."

She loved the Lord, gospel songs, old hymns and reading the Bible. Her favorite scriptures were Psalms 91, 121 and the book of Deuteronomy. Her favorite songs were "I Trust In God" and "Sending Up My Timber." She that that she found the Lord while listening to the songs "Tell Me How Do You Feel When You Come Out The Wilderness."

Sister was the "**Neighborhood Mom**." There are many who called her "Mom."

Home Going Celebration was held 1:00 pm Friday, April 3, 2015 at Bethel AME Church in McClellanville, SC with Rev. Francis McPherson, officiating. Burial follows in the Church Cemetery. A Wake Service will be held Thursday, April 2, 2015 at the Church from 6:00 to 8:00 pm. **(Courtesy of Barbara Green Bryant)**

Honor Flight Network is a non-profit organization created solely to honor America's veterans for all their sacrifices. Honor Flight Network transport our heroes (Veterans) to Washington, D.C. to visit and reflect at their War memorials. Top priority is given to the senior veterans – World War II survivors, along with those other veterans who may be terminally ill. **William Green**, South Santee (WWII Veteran) was aboard the Honor Flight in November 2012. Accompanying him was his son-in-law **Jerome Bryant** from Sampit. **Patrice Bryant** (Granddaughter) said "my grandfather (**William Green**) was aboard the Honor Flight in November 2012. He and my dad had a blast. **Grandpa** wears his cap daily. Thank you SC Honor Flight!"

Two World War II (WWII) Veterans Heroes: **William Green** and **Rollin Bryant** (At Right)

At right is **William Green** – all dress up in his Sunday's best - wearing his Army World War II (WWII) cap. **(Courtesy of the Lil Eff Affikan Cump'ny)**

Jerome & Kimberly Houston Bryant's Wedding Day

The Conservatory at Waterstone
4849 North Main Street
Acworth, GA

Saturday, April 18, 2015
11:00 AM
(Courtesy of the Lil Eff Affikan Cump'ny)

The **Delta Sigma Theta Sorority, Inc.** posing on the steps of the State House, Columbia, South Carolina throwing up the Delta Sigma Theta Sorority, Inc.'s (Pyramid) hand sign. **Patrice Bryant,** from Sampit is sixth Delta standing on the front row. (L to R)
(Courtesy of the Lil Eff Affikan Cump'ny)

These two beautiful and stylist sisters are **Beatrice** and **Patrice Bryant** posting for this picture at their brother, Jerome's wedding on **Saturday, April 18, 2015.**
(Courtesy of the Lil Eff Affikan Cump'ny)

Patrice Bryant is pictured here throwing up the Delta Sigma Theta Sorority, Inc.'s (Pyramid) hand sign. **(Courtesy of the Lil Eff Affikan Cump'ny)**

Nothing like siblings - **Patrice, Beatrice** and **Jerome (Patrick) Bryant.**
(Courtesy of the Lil Eff Affikan Cump'ny)

Beatrice and **Patrice Bryant,** two fashion passion sisters posing for this exclusive picture at Bethel A.M.E. Church, Columbia, SC, their church away from home.
(Courtesy of the Lil Eff Affikan Cump'ny)

This little handsome lad is **Paul Bryant** being babysat by his Uncle **Wesley Bryant** and his wife, Aunt **Rebecca Stafford Bryant** **(Courtesy of the Lil Eff Affikan Cump'ny)**

This exclusive oil painting canvas print are **Ollin Bryant, Sr.** (January 16, 1927 – May 2, 1982) and his wife **Sadie Bryant** (April 24, 1928 – December 15, 2008). **Ollin** and **Sadie** married in June 12, 1947. **Rebecca, Everline, Frazell, Ollin Jr., Leveron** (July 29, 1949 – April 12, 2010), **Daniel** and **Kenneth** are their children. **(Courtesy of Rebecca Bryant)**

To the right is **Lila Mae Bryant Prout**, another daughter of **Wesley** and **Rebecca Stafford Bryant**, married on June 29, 1969 to **Earl Edwin Prout** (May 31, 1927 – March 5, 1999). **Lila Mae** is a devoted member and Steward at St. Paul AME Church, Sampit. **(Courtesy of the Lil Eff Affikan Cump'ny)**

The Children of **Olin** and **Sadie Bryant**: Rebecca, Everline, Frazell, Ollin Jr., Leveron (July 29, 1949 – April 12, 2010), **Daniel** and **Kenneth** are their children.
(Courtesy of Rebecca Bryant)

Here are two GQ Brother-in-laws pictured together: **Earl Prout** (May 31, 1927 – March 5, 1999) and **Ollin Bryant, Sr.** (January 16, 1927 – May 2, 1982). Here at right is **Ollin Bryant, Sr.** bedecked wearing his fashionable suit, colorful matching tie, pocket-handkerchief, and 1960' popular style hat. **(Courtesy of Lila Mae Bryant Prout)**

Samuel James Holmes (March 3, 1938 – September 23, 2011) of Sampit was known throughout the East Coast for his electrical and building working skills. **Samuel** was the son of **Cecil** and **Tisby Bryant Holmes**. As a child **Samuel** attended the New Hope Elementary School, a small two-room school in the New Hope Section of Sampit. It is said the small school was located close to the property of Joe and Hester Drayton Bryant. After graduating from New Hope Elementary School, he attended Rosemary High School, Andrews and graduated in the Class of 1957.

From Rosemary, **Samuel** joined the **United States Air Force** and stayed in the military until 1961. While in the military he worked as an Aircraft Electrician. After his four years of military duty, he moved to Philadelphia where he worked many jobs, construction, electrical, and for the City of Philadelphia. In 1965, he opened his own business in electrical and building construction. In 1973, Sam moved back to his hometown of Sampit. He was employed as an electrician at The Georgetown Steel Company, Georgetown, South Carolina. While employed at The Steel Company, he continued to work in his business - building and wiring homes. He stayed at the Steel Company for 10 years after which he went into full time business for himself.

On May 2, 1962 **Samuel Holmes** married the former **Emma Davis** of the Big Dam Community outside of Andrews, South Carolina. **Emma** was a former member of Piney Groves Baptist Church in Andrews. She earned her bachelor's degree in education from Cheyney State College in Pennsylvania and completed graduate studies in educational administration at S.C. State University and the University of South Carolina. For 36 years she has been an employee for the Georgetown County School District working as a School Counselor. She is a retired School Counselor working for the Georgetown School District. She is very active at St. Paul A.M.E. Church and serves in several capacities; Trustee, Layman, Vacation Bible School Director, Area Chairperson, Women Missionary Society for the Georgetown District of the A.M.E. Church and attended four General Conferences of the A.M.E. Church as a Delegate. Their children are **Dr. Yolanda Holmes** and **Edwin Holmes**. **(Courtesy of the Lil Eff Affikan Cump'ny)**

Here is the matriarch of the **Davis Family: Bertha Davis** at 95th young in 2015! This beloved is the mother of **Emma Davis Holmes** celebrated her birthday.
(Courtesy of Emma Davis Holmes)

Dr. Yolanda C. Holmes, the medical maker and **Edwin Holmes,** the music maker are the children of **Samuel** and **Emma Holmes. Dr. Yolanda C. Holmes** is Dermatology, the owner of **Washington DC Dermatology**, Washington, DC. **Edwin Holmes**, her brother is **Founder** and **CEO** at **RetroFuture Music**.
(Courtesy of the Lil Eff Affikan Cump'ny)

James E. Smith, Sr. (February 25, 1937 – November 27, 2009) nicknamed **Smitty** started "**Smitty's Lawnmower Repair Shop**" in 1978. **Smitty** was born in Vaughan, North Carolina on February 25, 1937, the son of **Solomon** and **Beulah Harris Smith**. He attended Warren County, North Carolina Training School, North Carolina. In 1956 he left home and joined the United States Navy. He was honorably discharged in 1960 and reached the rank of E3. As a Navy seaman he worked aboard the Warschestiz Little Cruise Ship stationed at Long Beach, California. Leaving California, his permanent change station was Guam, where he stayed until his enlistment was over. As a seaman he works with the Communication Squadron. **(Courtesy of the Lil Eff Affikan Cump'ny)**

After **Smitty** was discharged from the Navy, he moved to Philadelphia and married **Mable Bryant** (January 30, 1931 – June 10, 1974) of Sampit, the daughter of **Wesley** and **Rebecca Bryant**. To this union two beautiful children were born: **Linda and James Jr.** After the death of **Mable**, **Smitty** married **Cleo Stafford**, daughter of **Thomas** and **Bessie Bryant Stafford** of Sampit on November 8, 1975 at Charles Street A.M.E Church, Boston, Mass. at 3:00 PM. **Reverend Donald Luster**, Senior Pastor performed the wedding ceremony. **(Courtesy of James Smith)**

This Atlanta Beach souvenir picture is **Mable Bryant Smith**, a young Sampit resident enjoying a day of fun and sun at Atlanta Beach. Atlanta Beach once used to be all-black beach popular vacation stop based on the racial and segregated laws in South Carolina. At right are her son, **Jerome Rodgers** and wife, **Nina Rodges**.
(Courtesy of the Lil Eff Affikan Cump'ny)

Here are siblings **Linda** and **James E. Smith, Jr.**, the incredibly cute children of **James** and **Mable Bryant Smith**. **(Courtesy of the Linda Smith)**

Another black female business entrepreneur from Sampit was **Linnie Grant Knowlin** (November 22, 1919 – January 28, 2006), daughter of **Mannie Grant** (and **Florence White Grant**. She was married to **Luther Knowlin** in 1937 and blessed with the births of ten children: **Amos, Leroy, Hassie, Jimmy, Mannie, Juanita, Florence, Elizabeth, Magnolia,** and **Dorothy.** She was educated in the public schools of Georgetown County. She was a faithful member of St. Paul A.M.E. Church, Sampit. Linnie loved to sing and praise the Lord. She was a member of the Gospel Choir, Missionary Society, Sanders Singers, Usher Board No. 1, and served as Stewardess Board President. Her community affiliations included membership with the Order of the Eastern Star, Commander Chapter #344, and the United Order of Tents, Ruth Tent #149. **Linnie** was a very active member of the Sampit Senior Citizen where she made quilts and trashcans made out of newspapers.
(Courtesy of the Lil Eff Affikan Cump'ny)

For years **Linnie** was employed at **Tika Motel, Myrtle Beach, South Carolina**. She also provided transportation for many people of Sampit and surrounding communities, who worked in the motel and hotel industry in Myrtle Beach, South Carolina. She provided transportation using a blue 28-passenger bus and then later used smaller vans driving to and from Myrtle Beach on a daily basis. It is unknown how many people of Sampit were hired in Myrtle Beach with her assistance. The old bus can still be seen located on the left side of her house next to a "grape harbor." After the death of **Linnie**, her daughter **Elizabeth** took over the business and continues to drive to and from Myrtle Beach.
(Courtesy of the Lil Eff Affikan Cump'ny)

In this undated four generations picture standing in front of St. Paul AME Church are **Milford Louis Darby** (February 21, 1944 – April 12, 2013, **David Benjamin Darby** (June 11, 1903 – April 15, 1981), **Rosa Darby Trappier** (June 30, 1909 – April 11, 2005), **Emma Darby Cooper** (July 8, 1906 – September 1 1987), **Leslie Mae Darby Britton** (November 9, 1925 – August 9, 1987), **Darlene Darby** and **Kenneth Darby**.
(Courtesy of the Lil Eff Affikan Cump'ny)

Milford Louis Darby (February 21, 1944 – April 12, 2013) son of **John Myers and Lessie Mae Darby Britton** was owner and operator of **Darby & Son Trucking Company**. He married **Mary Montgomery Darby** and the father of two children: **Darlene** and **Kenneth Darby**. The photograph at left is taken at the Bryant and Stafford's Family Reunion Dinner, Pawley's Plantation Golf & Country Club House in 2012. **(Courtesy of the Lil Eff Affikan Cump'ny)**

This glamour shot at right portrayed **Juanita Cooper**, the daughter of **Herman Duncan** and **Annie Mae Cooper Duncan**. **(Courtesy of Juanita Cooper)**

These trusted siblings are **David Benjamin Darby** (June 11, 1903 – April 15, 1981), and **Emma Darby Cooper** (July 8, 1906 – September 1 1987).
(**Courtesy of Juanita Cooper**)

At left is **Annie Mae Cooper Duncan** (May 4, 1930 – August 30, 1963) the beloved mother of Juanita Cooper. At right are **Leroy (Baby) Duncan** (1933 – 2008) and his brother **Herman Duncan** (December 24, 1932 – September 13, 1964).
(**Courtesy of Juanita Cooper**)

In 1978, **Moody Stafford, Jr.**, founded a small monument business in Sampit. The company is located in Georgetown, South Carolina, in the Sampit community. **Moody** and his son worked the business together until such time he retired. **Moody** asked his son to keep the business going, he honored his father's wish and continued the family tradition, in the spirit of his father. With the knowledge and skills he gained by working with him for many years the business continues.

The company provides a wide variety of services including custom and specialty items. He said, "Our product line includes but is not limited too; Monuments, Bronze, Marble, Granite Signs, Benches, Grave Covers, Memorials, Etching and Sand Blasting."

"**Sampit Monument** prides itself in the personal service we provide to the individual that is looking to memorialize their lost loved ones. We also offer a variety of sales and marketing options with account online services available directly to Mortuaries."

We provide excellent professional care with customized management of both the individual customer and business needs. Please give us an opportunity to help you create a lasting memory for your loved ones. We guarantee satisfaction, because were not satisfied until you're satisfied.

Above are **Moody Stafford Sr**. (April 4, 1904 – February 16, 1986) and **Martha Hawkins Stafford** ((August 13, 1910 – March 21, 1994), the parents of **Moody Stafford, Jr**.

At right are **Moody** and his mother, **Martha. (Courtesy of the Lil Eff Affikan Cump'ny)**

Country Committee.

Moody Stafford served in the United States Air Force during World War II. He received several citations and decorations including the American Theater Service Medal, the Good Conduct Medal and the World War II Victory Medal. Three sons, **Joe Nathan, Lorenza** and **Perry** followed their dad in the military.

From the late 1940's to the early 107's he worked at the International Paper Company, Georgetown, and then as a logger with Canal Woods. He later continued in the logging business as a pulpwood company proprietor. From August 19, 1975 to December 31, 1988 he worked in the security division at Georgetown Steel Corporation. One of his most notable memorial stones is in Kingstree, South Carolina created in honor of Dr. Martin Luther King, Jr., commissioned by the Williamsburg

In 1949, **Moody** married **Marie Johnson**, the daughter of **Walter** and **Maggie Deas Johnson** of Pawleys Island, South Carolina.

Mrs. Marie, as she was so lovely called, spent the greater part of her life in Georgetown, South Carolina. In her youth, she attended the public schools of both Charleston and Georgetown Counties.

For ten years, from 1968 to 1978, **Marie** worked for the public school system of Georgetown County.

She was well loved and deeply respected. Known for her kind, easy manner and loving ways, she has truly touched the lives of those who remain.

She was exceptionally proud of her children and their accomplishments, and often shared news of them and their achievements with friends and acquaintances.

From their blessed union, eight children were born, **Joe N., Allen, Lorenzo, Milton, Perry, Josephine, Gwendolyn, Vernecia** and **Janie**. Throughout her life, she imparted honesty, integrity and the ethics of honest and hard work.

These co-partners are **Lorenza** and **Perry Stafford** standing beside their work truck with advertising on side of door of their business - Sampit Monument Co. and telephone number. **(Courtesy of the Lil Eff Affikan Cump'ny)**

When my father, **Eff** took his family to the Cumberland Section, he always made a visit to the well-kept home of **Mr. Ben** and **Mrs. Margaret Greene**. They lived in a beautiful large white wooden house. Mrs. Margaret was an excellent cook and we ate many hot buttered biscuits and cakes there. They always showed us "great hospitality" within their home. **Mr. Ben** and **Mrs. Margaret** are buried at the Cumberland A.M.E. Church cemetery. **Mrs. Green** is described as a caring mother, grandmother, aunt and friend. This word "caring" exemplified the life of **Marguerite Holmes Green**. She was the seventh of nine children of the union of **Samuel Holmes** and **Ida K. Homes**. She was well loved by all. "**Margaret**" was educated in Georgetown County schools and became a member of Cumberland A.M.E. Church at an early age. She loved God and sought to serve him daily in all her works. She was a Class Leader for Class No. 6, a member of the Stewardess Board No. 2, Steward Board, Senior Choir, Pulpit Aid Club, Cardell's Missionary Society, and the Sunday school.
(Courtesy of the Lil Eff Affikan Cump'ny)

Benjamin E. (September 27, 1913 - July 1, 1970) and **Marguerite Holmes Green** (September 7, 1914 – October 27, 1997) are from the Cumberland Section of Sampit. They were both members and officers of the Cumberland African Methodist Episcopal Church, off Pennyroyal Road. I recall as a child **Ben Greene** working for the **Barrineau Laundry** in Andrews, South Carolina. He would pick up your laundry and take it to the cleaners in Andrews and returned them a few days later well cleaned and press. He probably was the first native of Sampit who was employed by a white laundry cleaning company. **Mr. Ben** as he is called by many of his customers was a gentleman in heart. He was very friendly and well liked. He was distinguished and known by his sharp looking suits, matching ties, and well-polished shoes. **(Courtesy of the Lil Eff Affikan Cump'ny)**

This old time picture is Manny Leo Grant and Rosa Grant Duncan.

Rosa Grant Duncan (April 14, 1923 - March 12, 1981) was the owner and manager of the **"Sunset Inn"** a small community club located off Columbus Road. The "Sunset Inn" was a wooden building built in 1970 by a carpenter from Georgetown. It was a cozy little club where you came to have fun and try out your "dancing shoes" on the wooden dance floor. **Rosa** always made you welcome to the shop. **Rosa** had a great sense of humor and often told many jokes. Not only did she have a jovial personality, she often told us many stories or tales about her growing up in Sampit. She was born on April 14, 1923 in the Sampit Section of Georgetown County where she spent her entire life. She departed from this life March 12, 1981. In April of 1941, she joined in holy wedlock to the late Arthur Lee Duncan. Their children are **Arthur, Clevie, Joe, Henry, Junior Lee, Mary** and **Peggy**. **Manny Leo Grant** (September 11, 1931 – April 7, 2004) nicknamed "**Fudd**" is all dressed up with his hat on standing in the "Sunset). **(Courtesy of Junior Lee Duncan)**

After the death of **Rosa**, her youngest son, **Junior Lee**, who the family called "**Bubba**" ran the shop. Family members still call him by that nickname today. He ran the shop from 1981 – 1985. **Junior Lee** was a savvy and respected business owner. From 1985 – 1989, **Mary**, the oldest daughter took over ownership of the "Sunset Inn." **Mary** is nicknamed "**Mae**" by families and friends. In 1989, Hurricane Hugo ripped through Sampit with 135 miles per hour winds, torrential rain and damaging winds blew "The Sunset Inn" down to the ground. Since the club was severely damaged, the family decided not to rebuild it. Today, the only reminder of **The Sunset Inn** is the large oak tree that stood right beside the club. The oak tree was a fun place where relatives and friends would sit on wooden benches to "shoot the breeze to talk trash." Daughter, **Peggy** lives on the property next to the old "**Sunset Inn**. **(Courtesy of Junior Lee Duncan)**

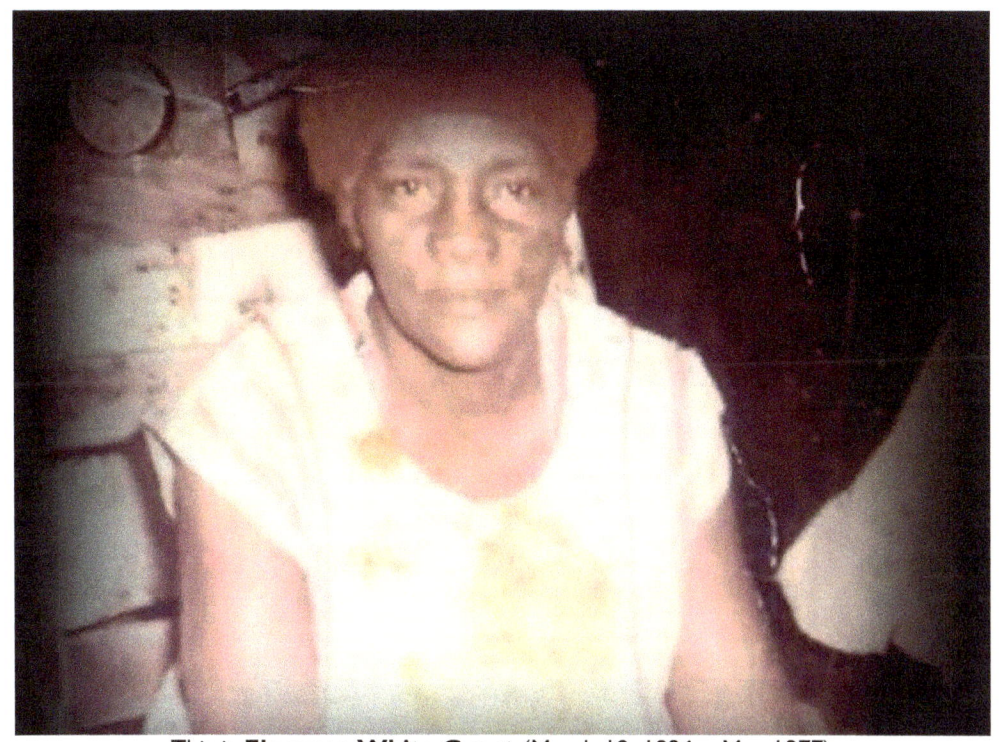

This is **Florence White Grant** (March 19, 1926 – May 1977).
(Courtesy of the Lil Eff Affikan Cump'ny)

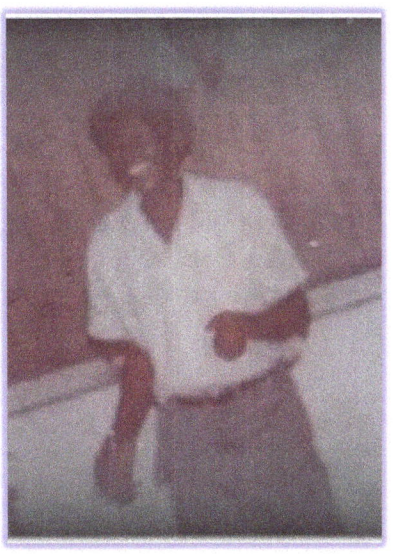 

This old school guy at left is **Willard Grant** (September 14 1917 - January 29 1980) from the big city Sampit.   At right is youthful, high-spirited and cheerful **Etta Johnson** from Sampit.
(Courtesy of the Lil Eff Affikan Cump'ny)

Ricky Joe McKnight of the Woodland Section of Sampit established the **McKnight Professional Gardening & Cleaning Services** in 1995. **Ricky** is the son of **Leon** and **Jannie Mae McKnight**. Photographed above is **Ricky**, his wife, **Clarice** and children, **Charlene**, **RJ**, and **Jon**. (**Courtesy of Ricky Joe McKnight**)

Pictured above are **Leon** (October 13, 1927 – December 23, 1984) and his wife, **Jannie Mae Berry McKnigh**t (September 5, 1934 – December 23, 1984) of the Woodland Section of Sampit. This lovely couple, **Leon a**nd **Jannie Mae** married on December 23, 1948. **Alfair, Charlie Mae, Venus, Doward** (August 26, 1949 – April 22, 1994), **Rickie, Sylvester and Bexter** are their children.
(**Courtesy of the Venus McKnight Sabb**)

Francis Arthur Bones opened the **Bone's Radiation Shop** around 1949 in a small building on Highway 521, the Andrews Highway. It is said by many blacks of Sampit that the **Francis A. Bones** and his employees at the **Bone's Radiation Shop** was the only white business that would repair black owned businesses equipment such as pulpwood trucks, tractors, cars and flat tires. **(Courtesy of the Lil Eff Affikan Cump'ny)**

In 1975 **Francis Arthur Bone's** son, **W. T. Bones**, who's nicknamed, **Penny Bones**, took over the family business and renamed it **W. L. Bone Radiator Repair Service.** He served in the United States Army from 1962-1965 during the Vietnam War. He married the former **Nancy Nichols** from Rock Hill, South Carolina. At right is **Penny** standing in his business all dressed up in his work uniform with matching work cap! **(Courtesy of W. T. Bones)– (Francis Arthur Bone's Picture - Courtesy of the Lil Eff Affikan Cump'ny)**

Holt Lindbergh and **Verna Lee Powell Smith** (August 12, 1928 - August 24, 2004) opened the "**Smith General Merchandise Store**" known as the **Holt Smith Grocery Store**" in October 1952. The store was located about 1/10 mile after you crossed the Sampit River on Saint Delights Road. It was a productive business for years and served many customers from Sampit and the surrounding communities. **Holt** and **Verna** were very friendly and displayed professional business skills to their customers. On the first floor of the shop, the shelves were packed with many can goods, dry items, and powdered products. On the second floor, they sold hardware products such as nails, hammers, locks, wires, tools, etc. The store also had a self-serving gasoline pumps on the property.
(Courtesy of the Lil Eff Affikan Cump'ny)

In 1968, **the Smith's**, **Holt** and **Verna** opened the first **Liquor Store** in Sampit. The store served the community well for many years. **The Liquor Store** stood out; a stone building painted in white with some large red polka dots on it. **The Liquor Store** was packed with consumers, especially on Fridays, for their "drink" for the weekend. In 1978, the Smith's opened the first **Gun Shop** in Sampit. The **Gun Shop** was built by **Richard Smith** and stayed open for six years; closed its door in 1986.
(Courtesy of the Lil Eff Affikan Cump'ny)

The **Beverage Depot** is located off the Saints Delight Road in the Sampit Community. **Roy** and **Edna Ward Bones** opened the original shop in the early 1950s. At first, it was a small wooden grocery store. The store was divided into two sections, groceries and hardware supplies. In the hardware department, one found chain saws, parts for small engines and fishing and tackling items. After the death of **Roy Bones** in 1985, his son **Ricky Bones** took over the family business. The store was made into a larger convenient store with an attached Food Deli Bar. In 2003, gas pumps were added to the shop. Today the **Beverage Depot** is a fast growing business and serve as a stopping place for travelers on Highway 17A.
(Courtesy of the Lil Eff Affikan Cump'ny)

At left is the **Beverage Depot** sign advertising gas prices and the time that the **Grill** is open to service breakfast, lunch, and dinner. At right are **Ricky Bones**, owner and two of his employees. **(Courtesy of the Lil Eff Affikan Cump'ny)**

Lamar's Fish and Chips, owned by **Lamar** and **Annie Cooper Iszard** is located at 205 Merriman Road, in the center of Georgetown's black historical district. His father, **Edward Iszard** opened the first black owned fish market in Georgetown in 1954. Located on 14 ½ Church Street, he ran the business until his death in 1972. **Lamar** then returned back to Georgetown (GT) and took over the family's growing business. The next year in 1973 he added a restaurant next to the fish market and named it **"Lamar's Fish and Chips."** Four years later in 1977 he moved **Lamar's Fish and Chips** to the present location at 205 Merriman Road. **(Courtesy of Lamar Iszard)**

Lamar is known throughout Georgetown as the '**Fish Man."** **The Lamar's Fish** and **Chip** cooks a finger-licking seafood breakfast (shrimp and grit), and lunch (red rice and fish).

The owners of **"Lamar's Fish and Chips."** are **Lamar and Annie Cooper Iszard.** In 2002 **Lamar** married the former **Annie Cooper** of Sampit, daughter of **Marion, (JC) Cooper** (January 30, 1926 – December 11, 1972) and **Lillie Mae Cooper. Annie** is a former member of New Hope Union Methodist Church in Sampit.
(Courtesy of Annie Cooper Iszard)

Here are **Marion (JC) Cooper** (January 30, 1926 –December 11, 1972) and wife **Lillie Mae Duncan Cooper** (1929 – 2008) of the New Hope Section of Sampit.
(Courtesy of Annie Cooper Iszard)

Vervitine, **Shirvey**, **Patricia**, **Mary**, **Annie** and **Diane Coopers** are the beautiful daughters of **Marion** and **Lillie Mae Duncan Cooper**. Their brothers **J.D**, **Jimmy**, **Marion Jr.**, **Joseph** and **Solomon** (March 19, 1968 – January 7, 2013) are not pictured.

(Courtesy of Annie Cooper Iszard)

Nurse Ethel Bolden Small (July 4, 1904 - March 15, 1995) was born in Newport News, Virginia to the union of **William** and **Mattie Bolden**.

She attended the public schools of Newport News and was a member of the family church there.

On June 25, 1918, she married **Samuel R. Small.** They moved to Washington, D.C. and lived there for thirty-seven years before moving to Sampit, South Carolina. In Washington, **Nurse Ethel** worked for a number of years as a practical nurse.

She was a member of Third Baptist Church where she was a Deaconess for thirty-six years, a member of the Usher Board, and helped to form the Nursing Unit and the Helping Hand Club. Her community affiliations included membership in the Sisterhood of the United Order of Tents.

After coming to Sampit, Nurse Ethel joined Brown Chapel Baptist Church, Oceda Community in Andrews, South Carolina. She served faithfully as a Deaconess and in various other capacities as she was needed. Her loving and warm personality brought joy to all who were fortunate to have known her. **(Courtesy of the Lil Eff Affikan Cump'ny)**

She went home to be with our Lord on Wednesday, March 15, 1995 at the Georgetown Memorial Hospital, Georgetown, South Carolina.

In Loving Memory of **Ethel Bolden Small** Service was held on Monday, March 20, 1995 at Brown Chapel Baptist Church, Oceda Community, Andrews, at 3:00 P.M. The Reverend **Thomas S. Lance** served as Liturgist and preached the "Message of Hope" to family members and friends.

Remarks were made by Deacon William Prince; Poem by Barbara Huell; Solo by Reverend Floyd Knowlin "Somebody Prayed for Me." Interment was at the Brown Chapel Cemetery.

At right is **Nurse Ethel Bolden Small** dressed in her white nurse dress uniform with nurse's cap. **(Courtesy of the Lil Eff Affikan Cump'ny)**

Maunie White, Sr. and his son, **Maunie White Jr**. are the proud owners of **Maunie J. White & Son**. The family owned business specialized in building custom made wooden cabinets. **Maunie** is the son of **Herbert Sr.** and **Rosa Bell White** born in the New Hope Section of Sampit. As a youth he attended the New Hope School, Sampit Elementary School and graduated from Rosemary, Andrews, South Carolina in 1962. After graduation he moved to Hartford, Conn., entered the United States Army for three years and moved back to Hartford where he served on the Hartford Police Force for five years. In 1972 **Maunie** returned back to his hometown of Sampit. **(Courtesy of Maunie White, Sr.)**

<u>The White Family photograph</u>: Father Herbert Sr. (November 9, 1907 – November 23, 1968) and his wife, **Rosa Bell White** (March 11, 1911 – February 21, 1982) pictured with their children: **Beulah, Herbert Jr., Albertha, Isiah Roberta, Lila, Mary C., Joe, Benjamin, James** and **Maunie**. **(Courtesy of the Maunie White, Sr.)**

Rosa Lee Stafford and **Minnie Stafford** are the daughters of **Ben** and **Mary Funnye Stafford** of Sampit. **Minnie** attended Sampit Elementary School as a youth and graduated from Rosemary High School, Andrews, SC in 1965. After graduating, she attended the Georgetown Technical College and the H & R Block classes. **Minnie** is a member in good and regular standing at St. Paul A.M.E. Church, where she is a member of the Steward Board, Usher Board, Mass Choir, Young Adult Choir, Senior Choir, the planning committee and served as ministry of music. For many years she developed and typed the weekly Sunday Worship Church Bulletins and a member of the Sampit Action Group. In 1974 **the International Paper Company, Georgetown** hired Minnie in the payroll department as clerk. In 1993 Minnie opened her own tax business. **(Courtesy of Glen Levi Stafford)**

Glen Levi Stafford is the owner of the **Glen Stafford Residential Electrician Business** - opened in 2000. **Glen** is the youngest of nine children born to **Ben & Mary Funnye Stafford**. He was born in Sampit, South in what we called the "**Backwoods**" area of Sampit. He attended Sampit Elementary School from 1st to 6th grade (1962 – 1967), Rosemary Middle School (1968 – 1970) and Andrews High School, (1971 – 1973). After graduating from Andrews High he attended Denmark Technical College, Denmark, South Carolina and graduated with a Residential Electrician Degree in 1974. After graduating from Denmark Tech, he was employed for six months by Westova monitoring the growth of trees. In 1974 he was employed by the International Paper Company and worked there over thirty-five years. Today he works as a Leader Operator at the Paper Mill. He also serves as Vice-President of the United States Steelworker's Union. **Glen** married the former **Debra Johnson**, the daughter of **Clifton** (November 10, 1920 – February 21, 2000) and **Ella Mae Davis Johnson** (January 15, 1921 – June 29, 1997) of Sampit in 1979. She is member of St. Paul A.M.E. Church where she is a member of the Stewardess Board and Usher Board. **Glen** is an active member of St. Paul A.M.E. Church, Sampit where he is a member of the Trustee Board. He is a member of the Sampit Community Organization, a community based organization. **Debra** is a Certified Nursing Assistant and works for Southern Care. They have two sons: **Damien** (Engineer) and **Josiah Stafford** (Policeman). **Josiah** is also an active member of the Omega Psi Phi Fraternity, Inc. **(Courtesy of the Lil Eff Affikan Cump'ny)**

The old weathered beat barn is a treasure of our past - located on the property of **Rufus** and **Mary Stafford**. **(Courtesy of the Lil Eff Affikan Cump'ny)**

These two super fly gentlemen are **Glen Levi Stafford** and **Effson Chester Bryant** posing together in the above photograph. **(Courtesy of the Lil Eff Affikan Cump'ny)**

"A Beacon of Integrity Since 1925" was the motto of the **Atlantic Coast Life Insurance Company of Charleston**, organized in 1925. It was one of the premier providers of life insurance and annuities to blacks in the early 1900s throughout the southeast. This policy above, underwritten by **Atlanta Coast Life Insurance Company** was written to **Williams Stafford** (September 7 1871 - September 5, 1938) of Sampit. **(Courtesy of Glen Levi Stafford)**

The policy reads: **The Atlanta Coast Insurance Company**, Charleston, South Carolina offers its Deepest Sympathy to the family and loved ones of **Williams Stafford**, who was a member of this Company and who departed this Life on September 5, 1938. "As the Eventide of Life draws nigh – Be Prepared!" **(Courtesy of Glen Levi Stafford)**

These two fellas (teenager lads) are photograph of **Ruf**us (June 22, 1909 – April 6, 2002) and his brother, **Ben Stafford (hat).** **(Courtesy of Glen Levi Stafford)**

This is the sixty (60) wedding anniversary picture of **Ben E. Stafford, Sr.** (July 16, 1906 – January 19, 1996) and **Mary Magalene Funny Stafford** (January 1, 1918 - August 18, 2002). **Ben** and **Mary** married in April 1932, sharing 63 years of marriage. Their children: **Ben Jr., Glen, Tommy, William, Sarah, Minnie, Geneva, Freddie** and **Rosa**. **(Courtesy of Glen Levi Stafford)**

Mary E. Stafford, her daughter, **Sarah**, grandchildren and great grandchildren are pictured together for this kinfolks family picture. **Courtesy of Glen Levi Stafford)**

Here are **Samuel Holmes, William Stafford, Willie Kennedy, Jr.** and **Johnny Lee Stafford** (standing) enjoying a family get-together.
(Courtesy of the Lil Eff Affikan Cump'ny)

For over fifty years **Clifton Johnson, Sr.** (November 10, **1920** – February 21, 2000) and **Ella Mae Davis Johnson** (January 15, 1921 – June 29, 1997) were married. **Rovina, Mary Nell, Ethel Mae, Vivian, Debra, Besselee, Clifton Jr. and Isreal Johnson** are their children. **(Courtesy of Debra Johnson Stafford)**

Here is **Ella Mae Johnson** sitting with fine-looking children, **Vivian, Rovina, Debra, Ethel Mae, Mary**, and **Isreal Johnson. (Courtesy of Debra Johnson Stafford)**

In 1990 **Vincent Drayton** opened **Drayton's Auto Salvage** at 9908 Powell Road in North Santee, son of **Willie Alexander Drayton, Sr.** and **Lucille Bryant Drayton**. He is known as the **"Fred Sanford"** the seller of junk cars and used car parts throughout Georgetown County. **(Courtesy of the Lil Eff Affikan Cump'ny)**

Here is **Vincent Drayton** posing in front of his business, displaying some of the used car parts for sale such as car motors, hubcaps, tires, car doors, windows, and radiators, etc.
(Courtesy of the Lil Eff Affikan Cump'ny)

Photographed above are **Willie Alexander Drayton, Sr**. (April 16, 1921 – January 2, 2001) and his wife, **Lucille Bryant Drayton.** This beautiful couple married on June 28, 1952 and four children were born, **Willie** (Billy), **Odell** (Dell), **Rebecca** (Becca) and **Vincent**. **(Courtesy of Lashawn Drayton)**

At right is Willie Edward Drayton, Jr. (November 4, 1952 – February 5, 1986) called "Billy" by family members and friends. On August 25, 1975, he married **Shirley Frasier**. **(Courtesy of Lashawn Drayton)**

In this undated Sunday picture at St. Paul African Methodist Episcopal Church are **Odell (Dell) Drayton** (September 23, 1953 – January 9, 2015), **Rebecca (Becca) Drayton**, and **Jerome Rodgers**. **(Courtesy of the Lil Eff Affikan Cump'ny)**

Pictured above are **Willie Edward Drayton, Jr.** and his wife, **Shirley Frasier Drayton**. This happy couple was married on **August 25, 1975**. (Courtesy of Lashawn Drayton)

At left are **Lucille B. Drayton** and her son, **Billy Drayton**. Willie E. Drayton, Jr., his wife, **Shirley** and their two sons, **Rodney** & **Lashawn Drayton** posing together in this picture at right. **(Courtesy of Lashawn Drayton)**

Here is **Shirley Frasier Drayton** and her two remarkable sons, **Rodney & Shawn Drayton.** (Courtesy of Lashawn Drayton)

Shirley F. Drayton is sharing an evening with her mother, **Ollie Frasier** – at left. **(Courtesy of the Lil Eff Affikan Cump'ny)**

At Right are **Willie A. Drayton, Jr**. and **Ross Stafford** all decked out in their two pieces suits. **(Courtesy of Lashawn Drayton)**

Three generations of Drayton's: Ki Asti (Granddaughter), **Odell** (Mother), **Krishona** (Granddaughter) and **Kim (Daughter)**. (Courtesy of Kim Bell)

This unforgettable family picture was taken about the **Homegoing Ceremony** of **Odell Drayton Moultrie** on Tuesday, 13 January 2015, Mt. Zion AME Church, North Santee at 1:30. Pictured is **Odell's husband, John Moultrie**, their son and daughters **Krishona Gilliard, Kim Bell, Brian Moultrie** and **Marquise Drayton**. (Courtesy of Kim Bell)

John Moultrie, Vincent Drayton, Melvin Gerald, Frances D. Gerald, Reverend Kelly Spann II, and **Odell D. Moultrie** standing on the outside ground of **St. Paul AME Church**, Sampit, SC. **(Courtesy of the Lil Eff Affikan Cump'ny)**

Straight Outta Sampit/North Santee - Lila Mae Prout, Cleo S. Smith, Jimmy Stafford, Jerome Rodges, Barbara G. Bryant, Jerome Bryant, Nina Rogers, Edison Stafford, and **Frances D. Gerald** at the funeral of **Cuz Edward Brown**, Ebenezer A.M.E. Church, Mullins, SC. **(Courtesy of the Lil Eff Affikan Cump'ny)**

Owner **Clarence Keith Jr.** opens the **Keith Builders & Home Improvement** in 2008. He operates out of Georgetown, SC and holds a Home Builders, Roofing license according to the contractors' license board. **(Courtesy of the Lil Eff Affikan Cump'ny)**

Henry R. Grant is the son of **Lucius Sr.** and **Reverend Bertie Moyd Frasier Grant**. He attended Sampit Elementary and graduated from Andrews High, Andrews in 1975. After graduation he attended Denmark Area Trade School, Denmark, South Carolina (1975 – 1977) and graduated with a degree in Plumbing. He then moved back home to **Sampit** and gained employment at the Power Plant on the Penny Royal Road on August 13, 1979 working as a heavy equipment operator. He retired on August 13, 2007 after working there for twenty-eight years. He opened the **Henry R. Grant Plumbing & Repair Services** right after graduating from Denmark Area Trade School. **Henry** is a hard working young man and assisted in doing plumbing repairs especially to the elderly of Sampit. In his spare time he enjoys riding his Gold Wing Motorcycle. **Henry** is a member of St. Paul AME Church, Sampit where he is a member of the Trustee Board.
(Courtesy of the Lil Eff Affikan Cump'ny)

This music maker is **Harrison Bryant** better known as **"DJ Lord Jazz"** one of the top most talented **DJs** in the southeast. He is the owner of **Quiet Storm Electronics** in Sumter, South Carolina. His fans and several local radio stations label him as South Carolina's No. 1 video DJ. He has been featured on BET four times, on MTV and on BET's "Rap City." He has been featured in several newspapers and magazines. In the March/April 2008 of IMARA Women's Magazine, a Lifestyle and Personal Growth Magazine, his featured article was "Mr. Entertainment-Popular DJ Does More Than Play Music." In this article he spoke of his love for music, how he became a professional **DJ**, his admiration for his parents and a message to young people wanting to get in the business of music. **(Courtesy of Harrison Bryant)**

Harrison Bryant (DJ Lord Jazz", is the oldest son of **Huey and Janet Geathers Bryant.** Photographed above is **Harrison**, his parents **Huey** and **Janet** and brother, **Marcus Bryant. (Courtesy of Huey Bryant)**

I Am Yours - Richard Gethers and Carrie Gethers – the parents of Janet G. Bryant.
(Courtesy of Huey Bryant)

The stunning and beautiful daughters of Richard and Carrie Gethers: (From left to right) Carol, Doretha, Ruth Mae, Betty and Janet Geathers. Janet, my sister-in-law is married to my oldest brother, Huey B. Bryant. **(Courtesy of Huey Bryant)**

Here are **Harrison, Diana, Justice** and **I'Yanna Bryant**. **(Courtesy of Huey Bryant)**

Two brothers tied together for life, **Marcus** and **Harrison Bryant**.
(Courtesy of Huey Bryant)

DJ Lord JAZZ
WWW.DJLORDJAZZ.COM
(Courtesy of the Lil Eff Affikan Cump'ny)

The young and talented innovator in the field of music - **DJ Lord JAZZ** - **SC's #1 Video DJ**.
The hardest working **DJ** in town! **(Courtesy of DJ Lord JAZZ)**

Marcus, Twyla, Harrison, Janet, and **Huey Bryant. (Courtesy of Huey Bryant)**

Thanksgiving Day 2015 Dinner served at the home of Huey and Janet Bryant, Sumter, South Carolina). **(Courtesy of Huey Bryant)**

George and **Loretta Swayzer** celebrated thirty years (30) of love at **CELEBRATION CASTLE** in Ludowici, Georgia, 19 July 2014.
(Courtesy of the Lil Eff Affikan Cump'ny)

Huey B. Bryant, Janet Bryant, Effson C. Bryant, Wesley M. Bryant, Zilcia E. Bryant, Gladys Bryant Scott, Iesha A. Scott, and **Pompey Scott (Scotty)**, celebrated with **George** and **Loretta Swayzer** at their thirty years celebration.
(Courtesy of the Lil Eff Affikan Cump'ny)

Family Members attending the wedding anniversary celebration of **George** and **Loretta Swayzer. (Courtesy of the Lil Eff Affikan Cump'ny).**

Numerous family members from Georgia and Louisiana attending the thirty years wedding anniversary celebration of **George** & **Loretta Swayzer.**
(Courtesy of the Lil Eff Affikan Cump'ny)

Eva Knowlin, right, poses with one of the cooks, Kim Francis, in front of her new restaurant, Eve's Southern Cafe, located at 865 N. Morgan Ave., in Andrews.

Eve's Southern Cafe

Medical coder opens restaurant on Morgan Avenue

Andrews residents now have a new place to eat. Eve's Southern Cafe opened late last month, offering a variety of food not usually found in this small town.

"This is a dream come true for me," said owner Eva Knowlin, who held the grand opening on Saturday, July 28. "I have always wanted to open a restaurant. I had looked at the property a year ago, but didn't have the funds. This year it was still available and I got it. I couldn't have done it without my partner George Britton."

The restaurant specializes in Southern cuisine, but the cooks use a lot of West Indian seasonings. The menu also includes Jamaican beef patties, as well as Saturday and Sunday specials of ox tails and curry goat and chicken.

"Restaurants in this area offer Chinese, Mexican, Italian and Greek foods, but none with the West Indian taste," Knowlin said.

Knowlin, who grew up in the Sampit community, has recently returned to the area after living in Florida and New York for the past 28 years. She is a medical coder and the mother of two grown children, with two grandchildren.

The restaurant is located at 865 North Morgan Avenue in Andrews.

Serving hours are Monday through Saturday from 6 a.m. to 5 p.m. and Sunday from noon to 4 p.m.

For more information, call 267-6833.

This advertising **Newspaper Article** from the **Georgetown Times** shows the **Grand Opening for Eve's Southern Café** on July 2, 2000 located at 865 N. Morgan Avenue, Andrews, South Carolina. Standing in front of **Eve's Southern Café** is **Eve Knowlin**, the business pro and owner with **Kim Francis**, one of the superb cooks. **(Courtesy of Eve Knowlin)**

These Kinfolks are the **Thompson Family of Columbia, South Carolina: William, Hurbert, Lila, Olive Lee, Richard, Doris, James, Daisy, Francis, Edgar, Edgar, Ricky (Richard's son), Maggie Ann, Pearl, William,** and **Sarah.** (Courtesy of James Thompson)

James & Daisy Thompson

65 Wedding Anniversary
July 9, 2006
Cecil A. Tillis Family Life Center
Columbia, South Carolina

This charming couple, **James** and **Daisy Brown Thompson** "jumped the broom" on July 15, 1941, seventy-five years ago. This picture is taken at their **66 Wedding Anniversary** on July 9, 2006 at the **Cecil A. Tillis Family Life Center, Columbia, South Carolina**. July 15, 2017 marked their **75th Wedding Anniversary**. They are the proud parents of five beautiful daughters: **Thedra, Laura, Levora, Francis** and **LaTonya.** (Courtesy of the Lil Eff Affikan Cump'ny)

In these modest old photographs is **Benjamin Brown, Sr.** (June 20, 1916 – March 20, 1994) at left and his wife, **Daisy Bryant Brown** of Sampit at right.
(Courtesy of James Thompson)

Photographed are **Patriarch William Jefferson Thompson** and **Matriarch Laura Ella Lorick Thompson** of the **Thompson's Family** of **Columbia, South Carolina**. Their children are **Maggie Ann, Olive Lee, Sarah, Edgar, James, Richard, William** and **Hurbert**. **(Courtesy of James Thompson)**

This captivating picture on left is **James** and **Daisy Brown Thompson**. James worked at Fort Jackson as a Civil Service Worker and retired in 1983 after 32 years; **Daisy** worked for the **South Carolina State Mental Institution** and retired in 1981 after 30 years. **Daisy** is also known throughout the community for her cake baking skills, probably would have won the "**Next Great Baker**" contest. This official military photograph at right is **Private First Class James Thompson** - served in the **United States Army Air Force** from 1943 – 1949 (World War II) with assignment at Kessler Field, Mississippi and Lackland Field in San Antonia, Texas. **(Courtesy of James Thompson)**

Here are **James**, his wife **Daisy**, and their beautiful daughters, **LaTonya, Thedra, Laura, Levora and Francis Thompson. (Courtesy of James Thompson)**

Nurse Susan Brown Clark, daughter of **Benjamin** and **Daisy Brown** was born February 3, 1917 in Mullins, South Carolina. Known through her community as **"Momma Susie"**, graduated from Mullins Colored School and went to Howard High School, Georgetown, SC to continue her education. Upon graduation from Howard High, she enrolled in Waverly Nursing School, Columbia, SC, where she received her nursing degree. Upon returning to her hometown, Mullins in 1937, her career of service began.

Nurse Clark was employed at Jenkins Nursing Home, Mullins Hospital, and Sunny Acres Nursing Home where she retired after 30 plus years of dedicated service. For her commitment to others, the Palmetto Alumni Association, DHEC Home Health Care Services of Marion County and State Representative Mack T. Hines honored her for being the first African American Registered Nurse in Marion Country.

State Representative Mack T. Hines said, "Nurse Clark was known as a trailblazer and the first black Registered Nurse in Marion County, South Carolina." "People like you are trailblazers, one of the first Registered Nurses in Marion County and one of the first black nurses," Hines said.

Nurse Clark response "She had to go to several different schools and colleges to be eligible for a license. "The schools weren't integrated, and we didn't go any higher than the 10th grade here," she said. She graduated from Mullins and Georgetown schools.

Mrs. Clark was a lifetime member of New Ebenezer African Methodist Episcopal Church, Mullins, South Carolina. She was a member of Class #1, Stewardess Board #2, Pastor's Pulpit Aid Club and the Women's Missionary Society (WMS), where she served faithfully until her health declined. She also was a dedicated member of the Palmetto Chapter 262 OES, and Palmetto Tent #1.

She was married to **Gus Clark** and their union brought together a beautiful, loving family: **Rita, Rosita, George** and **Catherine Sue** who both preceded her in eternal life, and one granddaughter **Keisha,** who also preceded her in eternal life.

Nurse Clark ends her marvelous life on Tuesday, February 19, 2013, with her daughter Rita at bedside. Homegoing Celebration honoring the **Life of Susan B. Clark** was held on Saturday, February 23, 2013, New Ebenezer A.M.E. Church, Mullins, South Carolina, where **Reverend Felix Jordan**, Pastor at 2:00 P.M.

The Reverend Cynthia V. Brown, Niece (Pastor, East Gate Non-Denominational Church, Marion, SC) preached the Eulogistic Message. Committal-Benediction-Interment was held at Devotions Garden, Hwy 76, Marion, South Carolina. **(Courtesy of the Lil Eff Affikan Cump'ny)**

James, Daisy Brown Thompson (left) and Susan Brown Clark (right) are posing for a photo at The Bryant – Stafford Family Reunion held at St. Paul A.M.E. Church, Sampit, SC. (Courtesy of the Lil Eff Affikan Cump'ny)

Pictured above are James, his wife Daisy, daughters, LaTonya, Thedra, Laura, Levora, Francis Thompson and son in laws, Floyd and Charles. (Courtesy of James Thompson)

Surrounding **Edward** and his wife, **Joann Brown** with love and affection are several generations of their rich family heritage. **(Courtesy of KarCelia Brown German)**

Edward Lee Brown (June 13, 1921 – January 11, 2012) affectionately called **"Snookum"** graduated from Mullins Colored School, Allen University, USC and North Carolina A and T. He served as Steward Pro Tem, President of the Laymen League, Church Treasurer and Class Leader of his home church, New Ebenezer A.M.E. Church, Mullins. **Edward** was an Educator, Teacher, Vice-Principal, Principal and Coach. He was a life member of the Omega Psi Phi Fraternity, Incorporated and served on many local and State organizations. Edward married his high school sweetheart, **Joann Cooper Brown; Robert Edward, William, Cynthia, Anne** and **KarCelia Daisyette** are their children.
(Courtesy of KarCelia Brown German)

Here are the children of **Benjamin** and **Daisy Brown**: **Benjamin "Little Ben" Brown, Daisy Brown, Edward** (Snookum) **Brown,** (June 13, 1921 – January 11, 2012), **Susan Brown** (February 3, 1917 – February 19, 2013) **and Robert "Buster' Brown. (Courtesy of Rita Clark Davis)**

This is **Edward (Snookum) Brown** (Seventh Episcopal District Lay Delegate to the African Methodist Episcopal Church 48th Quadrennial Session of the General Conference at the America's Center, St. Louis, MO) posing for a picture down town in St. Louis, Missouri on June 30, 1996. **(Courtesy of the Lil Eff Affikan Cump'ny)**

Rare picture captures these three handsome gentlemen - **Edward Brown, James Smith, Sr**. and **James Thompson** at St. Paul A.M.E. Church after The Bryant-Stafford Family Reunion Dinner held at the McKnight Education Center.
(Courtesy of the Lil Eff Affikan Cump'ny)

My mother **Bernice Jackson Bryant** and Cuz **Edward Brown** from Mullins, SC wearing their fashionable hat in this picture taken at St. Paul A.M.E. Church, Sampit, SC after the **Bryant-Stafford Family Reunion**. At right are siblings, Daisy Thompson and Edward Brown. **(Courtesy of the Lil Eff Affikan Cump'ny)**

Daisy Brown Thompson was born June 20, 1919 in Mullins, SC, the fourth of five children born to Benjamin Brown (Mullins) and Daisy Bryant Brown (Sampit). God called Daisy home on September 5, 2016 at the age of 97.

Daisy was educated in the public schools of Mullins, SC. After graduating from Mullins Colored School, she moved to Columbia to join her sister, Susan Robinson. Very shortly after her arrival, she met James "Jim" Thompson at Emmanuel AME Church, where she had introduced herself as a visitor and new resident of Columbia. It was love at first sight. That chance meeting resulted in marriage a few months later. On July 15, James and Daisy celebrated 75 years of marriage.

Daisy was a licensed cosmetologist, receiving a certificate in cosmetology from Caroline Beauty College in Atlanta, GA. Her career, however, was in food service, starting out at Columbia Hospital. She later began employment in the cafeteria of C. A. Johnson High School, where for over 20 years she helped prepare the nutritious and delicious meals enjoyed by students and staff. She was promoted to Assistant Manager of the cafeteria and from that position, was hired as Manager of the cafeteria at Florence C. Benson Elementary School for five years. She retired from food service, when she left a position with the S. C. Department of Mental Health, after thirty (30) years of dedicated work in this area.

Daisy joined Emmanuel AME Church, and was an active member for over 75 years. She was a member of the Jubilee Choir, Stewardess Board #1, and was the lead person on the Kitchen Staff for many years. She held various offices in these organizations. Her favorite scripture was the Psalm 23, which she said that she repeated to herself all the time. Daisy loved music, and although she said that she didn't have a favorite hymn, the hymn that she said came to mind most often was "Jesus Keep Me Near the Cross." She loved the Lord, and so enjoyed worshipping and fellowshipping with her church family.

Daisy was widely known for her delicious cakes, particularly her pound cakes, chocolate cakes, and carrot cakes, which she generously shared with neighbors, friends, and her church throughout the years. She loved flowers, and had a "green thumb," resulting in beautiful flowerbeds of begonias and lovely greenery that overflowed their pots. She was creative with crafts and crocheted many beautiful Afghans, and created little crocheted flowers, all sweet reminders of the beauty of her spirit.

Daisy will be remembered for her deep love for her family, her beloved Jim, of 75 years and specially five daughters, Thedra (Floyd) Bullock, Laura Thompson Hall, Frances Thompson, Levora (Laddie) Gray, and LaTonya Rish; ten grandchildren, Dalita Bullock, James (Heather) Bullock, Stephanie Solomon, Ina (Federico) Anderson, Jamal, Yusef and Turiya Gray, Alstreater, Jessica, and Brandon Rish; two great-grandsons, Brandon Rish, Jr. and Christian James Bullock; sister-in-law Joanne Brown, brother-in-law, Richard Carroll Thompson; and a host of nieces, nephews, and relatives who will miss her dearly.

In Loving Memory of Daisy Brown Thompson Funeral services was held on Saturday, September 10, 2016 at 11:00 a.m. (viewing at 10:00 a.m.) at Emmanuel A.M.E. Church where Pastor Tabitha Miller is Senior Pastor. Pastor Miller preached "The Words of Comfort.'

Visitation was held Friday evening, September 9, 2016 from 6:00 8:00 at Leevy's Funeral Home, Taylor Street Chapel, Columbia, SC. Committal, Benediction and Interment took place on Monday, September 12, at 11:00 a.m. at the Fort Jackson Cemetery.

(Courtesy of the Lil Eff Affikan Cump'ny)

The **Baker Family** of the Oak Grove Section of Sampit ran the **Baker Welding Company** of Georgetown: **Alvin, Hercules, Thomas Sr.** (April 10, 1919 – January 11, 1988), **Ruth** (December 5, 1919 – October 24, 2002), **Elbert** (1956 – June 29, 2013), **Kariconious, Wanda, Runnette, Occureda, Hercules, Clayton, Alvin, Earl, Twilar** (August 29, 1958 – September 2, 2011) **Thomas Jr., Fred, Clyde** and **Cornelius** (October 7, 1950 – July 10, 1988). **(Courtesy of Hercules Baker)**

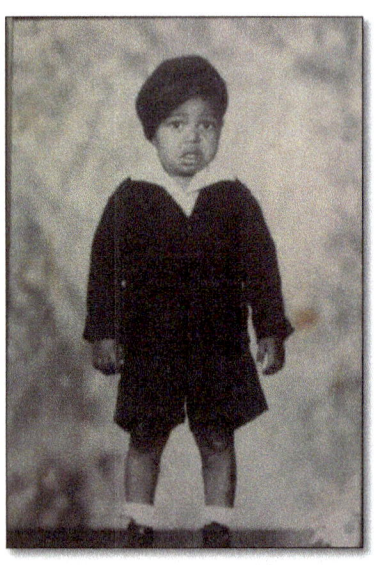 

This handsome little fella (gentleman) is **Hercules Baker** at the age of the big four! **(Courtesy of Hercules Baker)**

At right are **Alvin Baker,** his wife, **Regena** and their **children, Jason, Jade,** and **Alton Baker. (Courtesy of Alvin Baker)**

Mother Ruth Baker, sitting in chair is surrounded by her precious thirteen chillum (children). **(Courtesy of Hercules Baker)**

Here is **Alvin Baker** (knelling on far left) posing with the **Allen University Class** of **1976**. **(Courtesy of the Lil Eff Affikan Cump'ny)**

This photograph of **Francis Grant Sanders** (September 7, 1921 – June 9, 1996) and **Nurse Roxie Sanders Giles** was taken in 1982 while attending the **Georgetown Tech Nursing School** graduation. **Nurse Giles** retired on March 26, 2014 after 28 years as a **Nurse** at the **Georgetown Memorial Hospital**, Georgetown. **(Courtesy of Roxie Sanders Giles)**

Private First Class (PFC) Thomas O. Sanders (October 10, 1917 – June 21, 1965) on left is dress in his United States Army Class "A" Uniform. PFC Thomas O. Sanders served in WWII or WW2. At right is his beloved wife, **Francis Grant Sanders** (September 7, 1921 – June 9, 1996). Their children: **Annie, Shirley, Roxie, Elizabeth** and **Thomas L. Sanders** (April 24, 1951 – March 18, 1977). **(Courtesy of Roxie Sanders Giles)**

Dress in his United States Army Class "A" Uniform is **Thomas Leroy Sanders** (April 24, 1951 – March 18, 1977), son of **Thomas O. Sanders** and **Francis Grant Sanders**. At right are **Annie Sanders** and her son **Curtis Sanders**.
(Courtesy of Roxie Sanders Giles)

Nothing like cousins sharing in a special picture moment: **Annie Sanders McGainey**, **Geraldine Keith**, **Heyward Keith**, **Roxy Sanders Giles**, **Johusa Stafford**, **Shirley Sanders** and **James Sanders**. **(Courtesy of Roxie Sanders Giles)**

Evangelist Rebecca Holmes Wilson, the wife of **Grady Wilson, Sr.** opened the "**Linda's Gifts & Crafts Shop** in Sampit, SC." **Evangelist Rebecca** is very gifted in making handmade arts and crafts and sold them in her small colorful shop.
(Courtesy of Belinda Wilson Conyers)

Evangelist Rebecca Holmes Wilson is standing in her front yard, all dressed up getting ready to "praise the Lord" or "have a good ole time" at Church.
(Courtesy of Belinda Wilson Conyers)

In this undated family photograph are **Grady Sr.,** (December 12, 1928 – September 23, 2005**),** his wife, **Rebecca** and daughter, **Belinda Wilson**.
(Courtesy of Belinda Wilson Conyers)

This beautiful family photograph belongs to **Terryus Conyers**, his wife, **Belinda Wilson Conyers**, and their children, **Jaylen Conyers, Serena Conyers** and **Tianna Conyers**. **(Courtesy of Belinda Wilson Conyers)**

Mother Sara Wilson Washington is surrounded by her children, **Myra, Gregory Marcus Tara**, and grandchildren, **Jada Simone Washington** (in red dress, Greg's daughter; **Chandler Perry** (in green shirt; **Jordyn Ashley Aikens** (pink sweater, Tara's daughter, **Justin Aikens**, (in blue/white shirt, Tara's son).
(Courtesy of Tara Washington-Aikens)

Benjamin Washington (August 16, 1947 – February 7, 1989**)** the husband of **Sarah Wilson Washington** standing in door way with their baby daughter, **Myra Washington. (Courtesy of Myra Washington)**

At right are **Grady Wilson** Sr. (December 12, 1928 – September 23, 2005) and his daughter **Evelyn Wilson** (December 5, 1955 – March 15, 1955) enjoying a bike ride together.
(Courtesy of the Lil Eff Affikan Cump'ny)

The Holmes Family: Gabriel Holmes, Adrian Grate, Meshana Holmes, Brookes Larnell Knox, Savanda La'Trece, Skinny Minnie, Stace Marie Shackleford, Audrey Holmes, Takia Daniels, Daivon McCrea, Freddie Darby, Vanessa Holmes, Cassandra Holmes Manick, Daniel Holmes, Tall Bigdaddy Mac, Miranda Princess Wilson, Erica, Barry Holmes, Belinda Wilson Conyers, Donnell Scott, Stanley Smith and Nell Morris. **(Courtesy of Luke Smith)**

Posing in the picture on left is **Luke Smith** (cap on), his wife, **Rose**, son, and other family members. Luke Smith is the son of Buster and Mary Smith was born "Round the Gully" nowadays, Village Road.

At right is The Holmes' Family from Greentown. Sitting are **Reverend Levi Holmes, Sr.**, his wife, **Mary Holmes**. Standing is their beloved daughters, **Martha**, **Nell**, **Evone**, **Lizzie**, **Claudetta**, **Peggy** and **Rose**. (Courtesy of Luke Smith)

Leona Myers-Miller of Sampit, the daughter of Isiah and Leila Myers opens the Disnee Day Care, 499 Powell Road in 1994. The Day Care slogan was "We Rock, Cuddle & Talk To Your Baby!" **(Courtesy of the Lil Eff Affikan Cump'ny)**

Here are **Leona Myers-Miller, George Miller III, George C. Miller II** and **Sara Myers Keith**. (Courtesy of the Lil Eff Affikan Cump'ny)
De (The) Gullah-Geechee Legend

Artist Vermelle "Bunny" Smith Rodrigues

Vermelle "Bunny" Smith Rodrigues is known as an artist, educator, folklorist, Gullah elder, historian, advocate, sister, mother and wife. She is co-founder and curator of the **Gullah Museum**, was all of those and more to her family, friends, community and state.

A native of Georgetown, S.C., **Bunn**y was proud of her Gullah heritage and became a tireless advocate for her people, culture and traditions. She and husband **Andrew J. Rodrigues, J.D**., worked tirelessly for more than three years – conducting the research that helped gain federal approval of the Gullah Geechee Heritage Corridors, a site designed by the United States Congress to recognize and preserve the important contributions made to our nation's culture and history by the Gullah Geechee of the coastal counties of South Carolina, Georgia, North Carolina and Florida.

This Gullah maker is a nationally recognized artist in the folk tradition and a South Carolina Arts Commission fellow, **Bunny** is perhaps be known for her **Story Quilts**. Her unique work has been displayed in a number of national museums, institutions and events, including the second Inaugural Parade of President Barack Obama; the U.S State Department "Art in the Embassies" exhibit in the U.S. Embassy in Luanda, Angola; the Historical Society of Washington, D.C.; and the Children's Museum of Houston. Her best known works are the "Gullah 'Ooman' quilt and the "Michelle Obama Family History Quilt – From a Gullah Slave Cabin to the White House." In 2003, the Smithsonian Institution asked **Bunny** and **Andrew** to donate the original **Michelle Obama quilt** to the nation's museum. They agreed and are now part of the Smithsonian's permanent collection in Washington, D.C.

Bunny came into the world on April 19, 1938, in Georgetown, S.C. The fifth of 11 children born to **Anna** and **Edward** "**Hamp**" **Smith**. Raised in Dickerson African Methodist Episcopal church, she was a graduate of Howard Elementary and Howard High Schools. She

went on to earn a bachelor's degree in home economics from South Carolina State College, now South Carolina State University. After teaching in the Georgetown and Boston, Mass., school systems, she worked as a home economics consultant for Boston's Head Start Program, where she was invited to a White House conference on early childhood education.

After she and her family moved to Easton, Pa., she decided to open a series of businesses, including Vermelle's Boutique and Rodney's Restaurant. During that time, she and Andrew raised four daughters and put them all through college. **Bunny** was known for her volunteer work with groups focused on education, children, senior citizens and the A.M.E. church.

In 1997, Bunny and Andrew "retired" to Georgetown and opened the **Gullah 'Ooman Gift and Collectibles Shop** in Pawley's Island. There she really came into her own as an artist, educator, storyteller and passionate advocate for preserving her people's culture, traditions and history. She and Andrew conducted lectures daily, educating visitors about the true history and culture of the Gullah people. After she

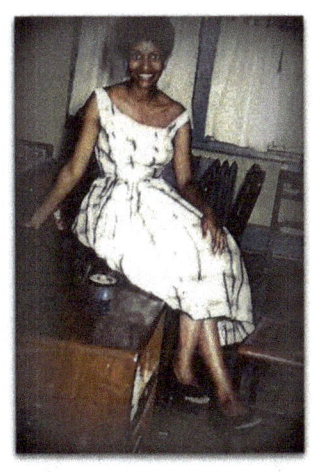

became a South Carolina Arts Commission fellow, she helped a traditional Gullah boat builder and a traditional hammock maker earn the prestigious honor.

The shop evolved into the **Gullah Museum**, now located in downtown Georgetown. Over the years, Bunny traveled the country as an artist-in-residence at schools, colleges and museums, teaching school children and adults about Gullah culture and giving demonstrations on quilting, traditional sweetgrass doll making and other crafts. She was a fixture at the Penn Center in St. Helena Island, S.C., and Gullah-related festivals in South Carolina and Georgia. She was also the founder of the Gullah Rice Festival, a local event to celebrate and promote Gullah Geechee culture.

Bunny was preceded in death by her parents, Anna Simmons-Smith and Edward "Hamp" Smith; sisters Francine Anderson and Betty Lou Sumpter; brothers Harold Smith, Rodney Smith and William Smith; and her mother-in-law, Beatrice Graham Rodrigues. The following are left to cherish her memory: husband Andrew; daughters Julia House (William) off Mitchellville, Md., Janette Rodrigues of Washington, D.C., Anna Freeman of Aiken, S.C., and Beatrice Rodrigues of Georgetown; grandchildren Autumn Freeman Moultrie (Brandon), Jakob Freeman and Jordan House; sisters Ruth Simmons (Alexander) of Louisville, K.Y.; Edna McPherson (Peter) of Litchfield, S.C.; Jeanette Anderson (Milton) of Maryville, S.C.; and Hershular Goff (Robert) of Mechanicsville, VA; fourteen nieces and nine nephews and a host of relatives, friends, adopted sons and daughters and other admirers.

Memorial service for **Vernelle "Bunny" Smith Rodrigues** was held on Friday, December 11, 2015 at Dickerson African Methodist Episcopal Church at 2:00 PM. Reverend McNeil Evans, Jr., Senior Pastor of Dickerson A.M.E. Church preached the Words of Comfort. Remarks was made by: Reverend Dr. Sandy W. Drayton, Presiding Elder of the Georgetown District; Norma Grant, Classmate; Michael Allen, Gullah Geechee Community and Reverend Dr. Richard Allen Brown, Friend and Family. Interment was held at the Bethesda Baptist Church Cemetery, Georgetown, South Carolina.

The Rodrigues' Family
(Courtesy of Andrew Rodrigues and **Bunny** (Vermelle) **Rodrigues)**

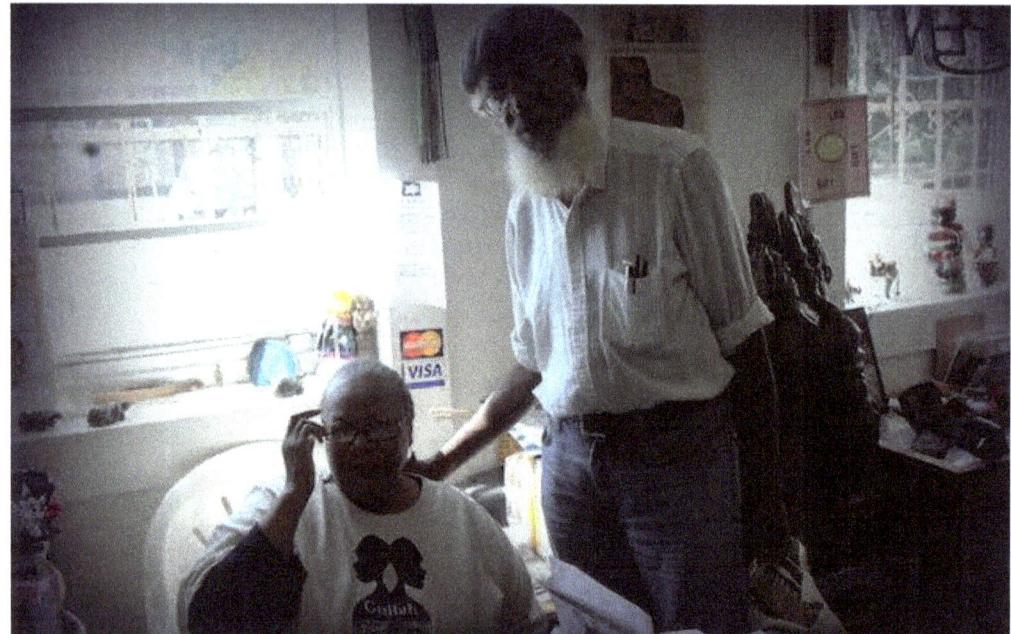

Andrew Rodrigues and **Vermelle "Bunny" Smith Rodrigues,** a Gullah Geechee woman and native of the lower Grand Strand, is the Owner and Operator located in The Gullah Museum and Gift Shop located in the Georgetown Historical District, 123-7 King St. (behind the Wells Fargo Bank building. In the Museum, the Rodrigues sells Gullah Geechee books and displayed quilts made by hand, one of which is displayed at the Angolan Embassy. **(Courtesy of Andrew Rodrigues** and **Bunny** (Vermelle) **Rodrigues)**

The Gullah Museum presents literature on historical and cultural information relating to the Gullah/Geechie people in Georgetown County, as well as those within the Gullah/Geechie Historical and Cultural Corridor from Jacksonville, NC to St. Augustine, FL. That information will demonstrate the important role that the Gullah/Geechie people played in the economic and cultural development of South Carolina and the U.S. of America from 1670 to the present time. In addition, Gullah/Geechie and/or African gifts and artifacts will be on sale. **(Courtesy of Andrew Rodrigues** and **Bunny** (Vermelle) **Rodrigues)**

Vermelle "Bunny" Smith Rodrigues,
May The Works I've Done Speak For Me."
April 19, 1938 – December 6, 2015

The Michelle Obama Family History Quilt

The Quilt Depicts: Michelle Obama's family's historical journey, "From a Gullah Slave Cabin to the White House.

The **Michelle Obama History Quilt** chronicles her family's journey – from a Gullah slave cabin on a plantation in coastal South Carolina, to the White House – in a series of "story quilt" panels. The centerpiece panel depicts the **First Lady**, whose Gullah ancestor's valued education, graduating from Princeton University and Harvard Law School. It also depicts the results of the impression that he great grandfather, **Frasier Robinson, Sr.**, a former illiterate had developed regarding the importance of not just a good education but also an excellent one.

The ten panels surrounding the centerpiece tell how the family found their version of the American dream. **(Courtesy of Andrew Rodrigues)**

De Gullah History–Culture Room at the Gullah Museum – Andrew Rodrigues (Curator) (Courtesy of Lil Eff Affikan Cump'ny)

De (The) Culture Room at the **Gullah Museum** contains old hand tools used during and after slavery. **(Courtesy of Andrew Rodrigues)**

De (The) Gullah Museum (Curator Andrew Rodrigues standing in doorway)
(Courtesy of Lil Eff Affikan Cump'ny)

Ms. Babe Grayson – AKA "Makeba" story telling at The Gullah Museum"
(Courtesy of the Lil Eff Affikan Cump'ny)

De Georgetown Outreach Ministries, Inc., GOMInc.   168 - 173

De (The) Reverend Rosalyn Grant Coleman, Presiding Elder of the Columbia District
De (The) Reverend Joseph J. Grant - Family
De (The) Kristen Michelle Coleman - Noluthando Ntsangani
De (The) Reverend Melvin Coleman
DE (THE) MEETING PLACE: MINISTRY BEYOND THE WALLS
De (The) Columbia District Office

Reverend Rosalyn Grant Coleman is a native of Georgetown, South Carolina. She is the eight of nine children born to **Reverend Joseph J. Grant** (February 10, 1917 – November 16, 2009), and **Lillie Mae Ward Grant** (June 5, 1920 – November 14, 2009). Other siblings are **Joseph H.** (October 8, 1941 - January 11, 2010), **Frank, Dell Omega, Patricia Ann**, **Jacquelyn** and **Deborah Grant**. There were four other ministers in her immediate family; her father, **Reverend Joseph J. Grant**, who retired after 37 years as a pastor and 42 years in the ministry, two sisters, **Dr. Jacquelyn Grant,** Director of **Black Women** in Church and Society and Womanist Scholars Program, Callaway Professor of Systematic Theology, Area II, Interdenominational Theological Center, Atlanta, Georgia and **Dr. Deborah Grant**, Pastor of St. John AME Church, Columbus, GA and one brother, **Reverend Joseph H. Grant.**

Presiding Elder Coleman earned her B.A. Degree in Psychology from Morris Brown College and a Master of Divinity Degree in Pastoral Care and Counseling from the Interdenominational Theological Center – Turner Theological Seminary in Atlanta, Georgia. She has had five years of clinical training in Clinical Pastoral Education (CPE) with the Academy for Pastoral Education, South Carolina Department of Mental Health.

She has served as Chaplain in the United States Air Force Chaplaincy Corps for a total of four (4) years on extended and reserve duty. Reverend Coleman pastored Bethel A.M.E. Church, Laurens, South Carolina for one (1) years, and Bishop's Memorial A.M.E. Church, Columbia for sixteen 16) years. In November 1996, **Bishop John Hurst Adams,** Presiding Prelate of the Seventh Episcopal District, appointed her to the office of Presiding Elder of the Newberry-Spartanburg District, the first woman to hold this office in the State of South Carolina. In November 2006, **Bishop Preston Warren Williams II**, Presiding Bishop of the Seventh Episcopal District appointed her to serve in her home Conference (Palmetto) as Presiding Elder of the Georgetown District. In November 2014, **Bishop Franklin Norris**, Presiding Bishop of the Seventh Episcopal District appointed her to the Columbia Conference as Presiding Elder of the Columbia District. Presiding Elder Coleman serves 26 churches and 5,368 members in her District.

Presiding Elder Coleman is a retired Chaplain at William S. Psychiatric Institute, South Carolina Department of Mental Health (SCDMH). She served as a Supervisor in Training at the Academy for Pastoral Education (DMH) while pursing certification as a Clinical Pastoral Educator and served as an Instructor in the Religion Department of Allen University, Columbia, South Carolina.

Presiding Elder Coleman has chaired and served on several boards, committees, civic, community and religious organizations, most recently among them; she is Chair of the Board for the Georgetown Outreach Ministries, Inc. She is a member of Sigma Gamma Rho Society, Inc. She is married to **Reverend Melvin Coleman**, Pastor of Bethel A.M.E. Church (Central Annual Conference – Wateree District) in the St. Matthews of Calhoun County and together they have one daughter, **Kristen Michelle Coleman**.

Reverend Joseph J. Grant (February 10, 1917 – November 16, 2009), **Lillie Mae Ward Grant** (June 5, 1920 – November 14, 2009) celebrated their 65th Wedding Anniversary, **Joseph H.** (October 8, 1941 – January 11, 2010, with their children, Frank, Dell, Patricia, Rosalyn, Jacquelyn, Deborah. **(Courtesy of Presiding Elder Rosalyn G. Coleman)**

At left are **Reverend Joseph J. Grant** and his lovely wife, **Lillie Mae Ward Grant**. At right are **Reverend Rosalyn G. Coleman** (Presiding Elder of the Columbia District) and her husband, **Reverend Melvin Coleman** (Pastor of Bethel A.M.E. Church, St. Matthews). **(Courtesy of Presiding Elder Rosalyn G. Coleman)**

Kristen Michelle Coleman, Reverend Melvin Coleman, Marline Robinson, Presiding Elder Rosalyn G. Coleman, and **Noluthando Ntsangani**
posing for this beautiful Christmas picture in 2016.
(Courtesy of the Lil Eff Affikan Cump'ny)

Reverend Rosalyn Grant Coleman,
Presiding Elder of the Captivating
Columbia District.

Reverend Melvin Coleman
Senior Pastor of Bethel AME Church
St. Matthew, SC

(Courtesy of the Lil Eff Affikan Cump'ny)

Marline Robinson, Noluthando Ntsangani, Kristen Michelle Coleman, Presiding Elder Rosalyn G. Coleman, and Reverend Wanda Rapley at the Allen University's Richard Allen Awards/UNCF Gala Masquerade Scholarship Luncheon, Marriott Hotel, Columbia, SC on February 13, 2016. (Courtesy of the Lil Eff Affikan Cump'ny)

Presiding Elder Rosalyn Grant Coleman and Reverend Melvin Coleman posing for this picture at The Retirement Dinner Celebration in honor of Bishop Richard Franklin Norris and Mother Mary Ann Norris.
(Courtesy of the Lil Eff Affikan Cump'ny)

THE MEETING PLACE: MINISTRY BEYOND THE WALLS, the **Georgetown Outreach Ministries, Inc., GOMInc** was born out of assessed community needs and concerns. Presiding Elder Coleman was assigned to the Georgetown District in November 2007. She came with a vision for ministry that went far beyond the walls of the sanctuary – ministry that involves more than church attendance and worship – ministry that meets the needs of our times. In order to accomplish these goals, Presiding Elder Coleman identified, trained and utilized the Local Preachers, Evangelists, some lay and the Ministers of Music of the District. After Clinical Pastoral Education (CPE) training was provided, these individuals then set out in various communities of Georgetown and portions of Williamsburg Counties to assess individual and community needs and concerns. From the overwhelming responses, specific ministries were developed to help to meet those needs identified through community surveys. **GOMInc** identified ministry needs in the areas of Youth Services, Parenting Services, Addiction Services, Senior Services, Educational Services, Veteran Services, Entrepreneurial Young Adult Services, and Artistic Expressions.
(Courtesy of the Lil Eff Affikan Cump'ny)

In seeking to "make a difference - one community at a time", **GOMInc's** goal is to impact, engage, enhance and empower the community through leadership and personal development workshops, wellness clinics, skills assessments, training and educational alternatives. In order to provide all of the ministries established by GOMInc, the Georgetown District was successful in purchasing a building, which serves as and is appropriately named "The Meeting Place". District leadership meetings, some CPE classes, GOMInc outreach services, the Music and Arts Program and the newly established Low Country Veteran's Group Ministry are housed at this prime location within the City of Georgetown. It is the shared vision of Presiding Elder Coleman, the Pastors, clergy and the lay of the Georgetown District to transform the site of "The Meeting Place" to a state of the art green building that will house the ministries of GOMInc, a Christian Book Store, a Health Food Restaurant, a Banquet facility and much more.
(Courtesy of Presiding Elder Rosalyn G. Coleman)

The Captivating Columbia District Office at 1529 Hampton Street, Suite 100, Columbia, South Carolina. **(Courtesy of the Lil Eff Affikan Cump'ny)**

This is the **Columbia District Office Conference Room, Columbia, South Carolina**. On the District Conference room walls are pictures of Former Presiding Elders of the Columbia District (Columbia Annual Conference). These Former Elders are **Presiding Elder J. Arthur Holmes, Jr.**, **Presiding Elder B. C. Cunningham** (1952 – 1976), **Presiding Elder Lee M. Seward** (1976 – 1980), **Presiding Elder Clarke R. Hawthorne, Sr.** (1980 – 1998), **Presiding Elder Willie J. Nelson** (1998 – 2004), and **Presiding Elder William Smith, Jr.** (2004 – 2006). **(Courtesy of the Lil Eff Affikan Cump'ny)**

De (The) Sampit Masonic Lodge #429   175 -176
Sam Pitt (Sampit)

De (The) Rising Sons and Daughters Lodge Hall
Woodland

This 1990s photograph of the **Sampit Masonic Lodge #429**, located off **Powell Road,** Sampit, SC shows the front view of this two-story stone structure. **(Courtesy of the Lil Eff Affikan Cump'ny)**

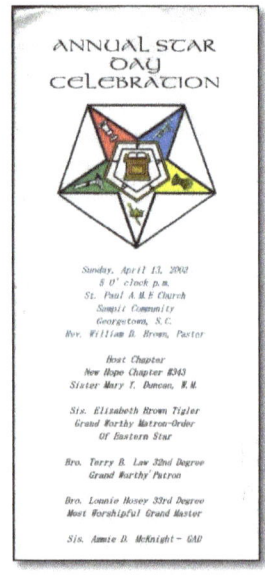

Chapter #343 held its Annual Star Day Celebration on Sunday, April 13, 2003 at St. Paul A.M.E. Church, Sampit Community – **Reverend William B. Brown**, Pastor. Host Chapter was New Hope Chapter #343 – **Sister Mary T. Duncan** - WM, **Sister Elizabeth Brown Tigler** – Grand Worthy Matron of the Order of Eastern Star, **Brother Terry B. Law** - 32nd Degree Grand Worthy Patron, Bro. Lonnie Hosey – 33rd Degree Most Worshipful Grand Master and **Sister Annie D. McKnight** – GAD.
(Courtesy of the Lil Eff Affikan Cump'ny)

The old wooden historical building with roof tin top is the **Rising Sons** and **Daughters Lodge Hall** located in the Woodland Section of Sampit.
(Courtesy of the Lil Eff Affikan Cump'ny)

These pictorial sketches or drawings are **Charlie Berry, Jr. and Laura Trappier Berry from the Woodland Section of Sampit. Charlie Berry, Jr.**, the son of **Deacon Charles Berry, Sr**. and the **Lucille Ward Berry**, was born February 17, 1936, in the Woodland Section of Sampit, South Carolina. He joined Gethsemane Baptist Church where he was baptized under the leadership of the **Reverend Lewis Felder**, the sixth Pastor of the Gethsemane Baptist Church. There he was a dutiful member and taught Sunday School for many years.

His early education was received in the public schools of Georgetown County and in 1957 he graduated from Rosemary High School, Andrews, South Carolina. In 1958, he was united in Holy Matrimony with the former **Laura Trappier** of the Sampit Community, the daughter of **Isaac** and **Lillie Trappier**.

Well known and respected throughout Sampit, Georgetown and surrounding counties for his exemplary athletic ability, he was an outstanding coach of baseball and softball; working closely with area youth and adults, coaching baseballs teams for over 36 years. He organized the Sampit Hawks, a men's softball team and the Sampit Eagles, a men's baseball team that later changed its name to the Georgetown Steel Eagles. The Sampit Shamrocks and the TKO's are two women's softball teams also organized by **Charlie Berry**. His teams traveled throughout the southeast playing in championships and winning trophies.

On Tuesday, May 17, 1998 at the Georgetown County Memorial Hospital, he transcended this life to another of eternal joy and rest. His passing is deeply felt by his family, many friends, colleagues, and all who were fortunate to have known him.

Left to cherish fond memories of him are: a loving wife, Laura Trappier Berry, four daughters, Prestena Trappier, Julia Armstrong, Ella Thompson, Sincera Berry, all of Georgetown, S.C., five sons, Ronson Trappier, Eric Berry, Clyde Berry, Stacy Berry and Darrell Berry. His father, Deacon Charlie Berry, Sr., and stepmother, Addie Berry; one sister, Jannie Mae McKnight, one adopted sister, Berry; one adopted brother, Thomas Berry.
(Courtesy of Laura Trappier Berry)

De (The) Sam Pitt (Sampit) Gospel Singers 178 - 185

De (The) Four Gospel Jubilee Singers
De (The) Chosen Sisters
De (The) Knowlin's Singers
De (The) Sensational Brown Brothers
De (The) Southern Six
De (The) John Duncan and the Singing Stars
De (The) Knowlin's Brothers
De (The) Original Truetone Singers

The Four Gospel Jubilee of Sampit, South Carolina was one of the well-known and most beloved Gospel Groups throughout Georgetown County. The Four Gospel got it beginning in the 1960s with four dedicated singers. **The Four-Gospel Jubilee's** members since the 1970s were **Grady Wilson** (Mr. Grady), **Francis Trapper** (Trap), **Leroy Gasque, Sr**. (Roy), **Thomas Cooper** (Sunny), **Joe Louis Bryant** (Big Joe), **J. W. Gasque** (Tillie), **John Funnye** (Funnye), **Jacob Smith**, and **Thomas Frazier**. **Tec** and **John White** served as their guitarists for many years. The Four Gospel often would sing on the Sunday Morning Gospel Radio Program, Georgetown at 9:00 a.m. I recalled my parents huddled around the radio every Sunday morning just to hear them sing their moving songs. One of the most requested songs was "**Let Jesus Fix It for You**". **Oh, He Knows Just What To Do. Whenever You Pray Let Him Have It Way, Let Jesus Will Fix It For You."**

The Four Gospel Jubilee, Leroy Gasque, Sr., Thomas Cooper, Grady Wilson, Frances Trappier and Jacob Smith recorded this CD "Some Sweet Day." (Courtesy of the Lil Eff Affikan Cump'ny)

The Chosen Sisters (Rosa Mae, Albertha and **Martha Tucker)** from Plantersville, SC singing at the Knowlin's Brothers Anniversary at Saint Paul African Methodist Episcopal Church, Sampit. Their most requested song was **"I Want To Be Ready To Walk Into Jerusalem Just Like John."** **(Courtesy of the Lil Eff Affikan Cump'ny)**

Another nationally acclaimed Gospel group with **Sampit root** is the **Knowlin's Singers** from Jamaica Long Island, New York. **The Knowlin's Singers** was founded in 1968 in Jamaica Long Island with six members: **Wilma, Jake, Dorothy, Ruth, Luther**, **Margaret, Dorothy, Ruth,** and **Luther** were born and raised in Sampit before they journeyed North to New York. **(Courtesy of Dorothy Knowlin)**

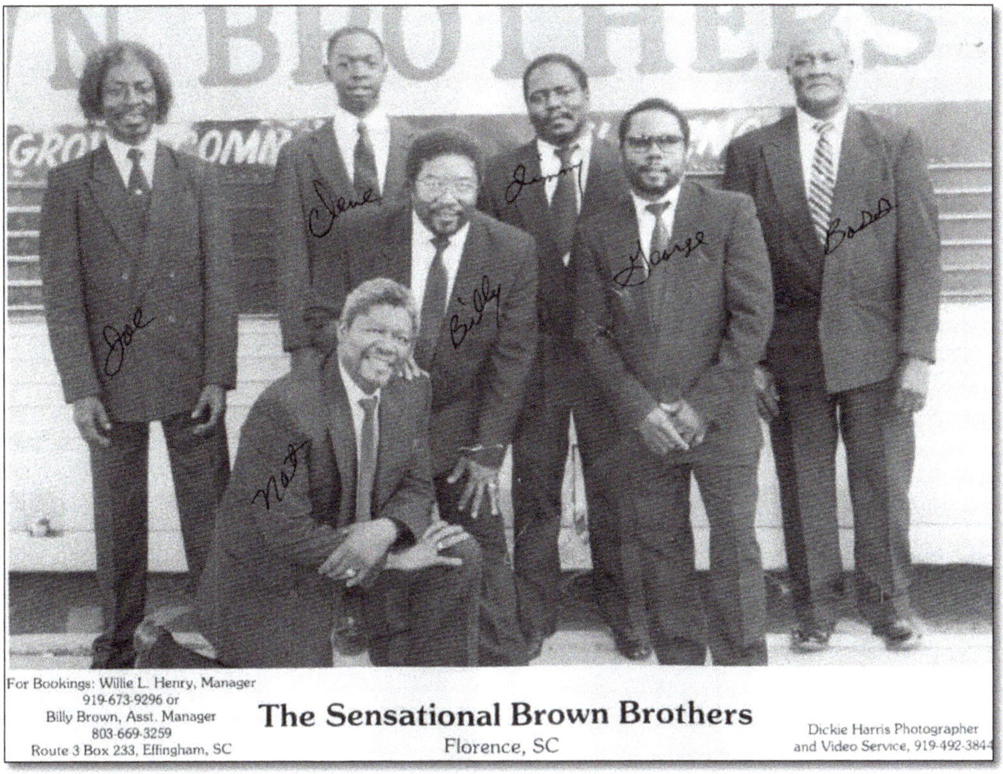
For Bookings: Willie L. Henry, Manager
919-673-9296 or
Billy Brown, Asst. Manager
803-669-3259
Route 3 Box 233, Effingham, SC
The Sensational Brown Brothers
Florence, SC
Dickie Harris Photographer
and Video Service, 919-492-3844

This autographed black and white photo above is the one and only Sensational Brown Brothers from Florence, SC. The brothers signed this copy after singing at St. Paul African Methodist Episcopal Church, Sampit, South Carolina, my home Church. Joe, Nate, Billy, George, Boss, Jimmy and Cleve are the signed names on the pictures.

The brother often time told the story in one of their songs that they were raised on a small farm in the Savannah Grove area in Florence, SC- start singing together on Easter Sunday, Washington, DC in 1960. They also said that their parents had nine (9) sons and nine (9) mules to help plowed the large fields around their small farm.

The Sensational Brown Brothers
"At The Cross"

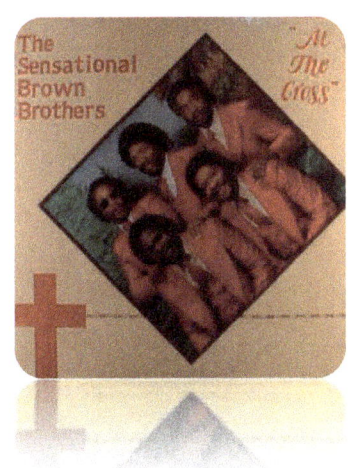

My most favorite-recorded Album by the Sensational Brown Brother was "At the Cross." My three most remarkable songs were "Kneel At The Cross, Lord You Spared Me Over and What A Friend."

(Courtesy of the Lil Eff Affikan Cump'ny)

The Southern Six Singers - (Left to right) **Arthur Hemingway, Henry Holmes, Jr., Clarence Lewis, William Grant, Joseph Ward, James Green, Sr.,** (guitar) and **Reverend Willie Hemingway** (at microphone). **(Courtesy of Joseph Ward)**

John Duncan and the **Singing Stars**
Here are **Vincent Drayton, Eric Clark, Mark Duncan, Robert Cooper, John Duncan Lynn Stafford,** and **Adrea Cooper. (Courtesy of the Lil Eff Affikan Cump'ny)**

The Knowlin Brothers, Floyd and **Charles Knowlin** began singing together in the 1970s at the St. Paul African Methodist Episcopal Church, Sampit. **Emma B. Stafford** gave them the name "**Knowlin Brothers**" at a Gospel singing program held at St. Paul A.M.E. Church

The story was told that in the 1970s as the sun was brightly shining in the woods behind the house of where **Charles** and **Floyd** lives, they were having church together and singing the songs of praise. Upon hearing what sounded like angels from heaven, their **Mother**, **Lizzie** walked onto the back porch and said, "The next time that there's a singing program at the church, you guys will sing."

When the next program was held, their mother requested them to sing. The two brothers did not have a name. Then **Emma Stafford**, who served as Mistress of Ceremony said, "Let's call them the **Knowlin Brothers**." From that day until this, they are known as the Knowlin Brothers. The first song they ever sang was "**God's Grace and Mercy**." The gifted singing brothers electrified the congregation with their magnetic and melodious voices. For twenty-two years the **Knowlin Brothers** sang at church singing programs, church musicals, anniversaries, funerals and revivals from South Carolina to New York. The brothers were known as "the greatest gospel singers of all time."

The Knowlin Brothers held their anniversary once a year at St. Paul AME Church with standing room only. One of my favorite songs sung by the Knowlin Brothers was "**Jesus, The Best Thing That Ever Happened To Me.**" In the song, **Floyd** would share his upbringing being born in a large and loving family. He would talk about the death of his parents, but stated "**Jesus - Is the Best Thing That Ever Happened to Me!**"

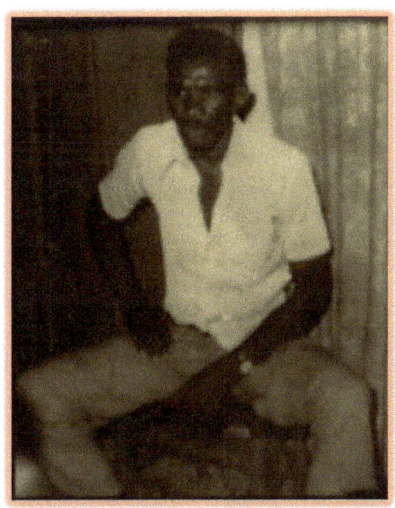 

These two flashback old photos are **John R. Knowlin** (February 12, 1916 – June 24, 1977) and **Lizzie Bell Duncan Knowlin** (March 21, 1919 – December 13, 1973).
(Courtesy of Bishop Floyd Knowlin)

In this classic black and white family photograph are the twelve (12) children of **John** and **Lizzie Knowlin** posing for a family photo. In the picture from left to right are **Gertrude, Ida, Charles, Floyd, Gale, Robell Duncan, John, Willie J., Gale, Sarah, Myrtle, Blondell, Patricia,** and **Denise Knowlin.** **(Courtesy of Bishop Floyd Knowlin)**

Charles was known as the Sampit singing bird. He loved to sing, could sing, and people loved to hear him sing.

After having sung together for twenty-two years, separate paths were chosen by God. **Floyd** was called in the ministry. **Charles** began singing alone, only singing with **Floyd** on occasions such as funerals, wedding and banquets. **Charles** went on to start his own choir, the Metro-Denominational Mass Choir, which is still going strong, entering into its eighth year.

Some of Charles' favorite songs were 'When I've Done All I Can Do," "Jesus Is Everywhere," "I Won't Complain," "Walk Around Heaven," "My Lord Is Getting Us Ready," "I'll Fly Away," "Lord, Do It," "Pass Me Not O Gentle Saviour," "Jesus Got His Arms Wrapped All Around Me," "Keep In Touch With Jesus," "When I Call On God," and "God Bless Our Love," which was his favorite wedding song.

The last time the brothers sang together was January 3, 1998. The last song they sang as the Knowlin Brothers was "When the Roll Is Called Up Yonder." Then on Saturday, January 21, 1998 at a family gathering, Charles began to sing. His last song was "Pass Me Not O Gentle Savior." God called the roll for Charles on February 22, 1998 at 10:10 A.M. and now he is living up and singing "Up Yonder with the Lord!" Family members, gospel singers, and friends mourns the death of Charles, a former member of the legendary brother's group, the Knowlin Brothers at a standing room only home going services.

I recalled while pastoring at Fairview A.M.E. Church, Clinton, South Carolina in 1984 that the Knowlin Brothers came and did a musical concert for the church. What a great celebration we had in the Lord! They spiritual electrified the waiting congregation.

I (**Effson**) was deployed to Prince Sultan Air Base, Kingdom of Saudi Arabia at the time of Charles' untimely death. I called Reverend Floyd Knowlin and gave him some words of hope and healing.

Reverend Floyd mailed me a copy of **Charles' obituary** and he wrote these moving words: "**Hi Man! I love you and thank GOD for you. I did my best for Charles and this is a copy of his obituary! Love you. Your Pal!**" Reverend Floyd Knowlin.

The Home Going Services for Charles Louis Knowlin was held on Saturday, February 28, 1998 at St. Paul A.M.E. Church, Sampit. **Pastor Wallace J. McKnight** delivered Word of Comfort and Hope. Interment at St. Paul A.M.E. Church Cemetery.
(Courtesy of Bishop Floyd Knowlin)

Deacon William Rutledge, Raymond Alston, Deacon Lee Jay Cooper, Leon Cooper and Jonathan Cooper started the Original Truetone Singers of Andrews, South Carolina in 1973. In this photograph is The Original Truetone Singers of Andrews, South Carolina. Sitting on top of the travelling van is Lee Jay Cooper (Husband of Louedith Cooper) and Raymond Alston, Leader Singer. Standing and kneeing are Singers Jonathan Cooper, Leon Cooper, Jr., Derrick Moyd, Albert Chandler, Darryl Moyd and Curtis Moyd. (Courtesy of Louedith Cooper)

A young Cooper's Family from Oceda: Lee Jay, Louedith, Lai, Michelle, Katrina Leeann, Jermaine and Elizabeth Cooper. (Courtesy of Louedith Cooper)

Here are Louedith Cooper and her two beautiful daughters, Michelle and Katrina Leeann Cooper – at right. (Courtesy of Louedith Cooper)

De Sam Pitt (Sampit) Eddycashum (Education) 181-266

De Sam Pitt (Sampit) School

De (The) Allen University – Columbia, South Carolina	181-182
De (The) Campus View of Allen University	183-185
De (The) Reverend (Dr.) Charles E. Young	186
De (The) James Square Shopping Center	187
De (The) Right Reverend Frederick Calhoun James, Retired	188-189
De (The) Mother Theressa Gregg James - Episcopal Supervisor (Retired)	189
De (The) Right Reverend Benjamin W. Arnett	190
De (The) Reverend William Conyers Ervin, Jr.	191-193
De (The) Doris Green	193
De (The) Jerome Lavern Knowlin (Hunk)	194
De (The) Black Church Are Still Burning - We Are Not Satisfied" Monument	195
De (The) Preston Warren Williams II Student Residence Hall	196
De (The) Wilma Deloris Webb Residence Hall	197
De (The) Omega Psi Phi Fraternity	198
De (The) Allen University Remembers Gerry Lee Gilliam	198-201
De (The) Allen University's United Negro College Fund (UNCF) Gala	202-205
De (The) Male Leadership Empowerment Symposium	206
De (The) Allen University Homecoming – 2015	207-211
De (The) Allen University vs. USC Baseball Game	212-215
De (The) 146th Founder's Day – 2016	216
De (The) Bishop Richard Allen Stamp Unveiled	217-221
De (The) Oak Grove School	222
De (The) Cumberland A.M.E. Church School	223
De (The) Oak Grove Colored School	224
De (The) Saint Paul A.ME. Church ABC School	225-226
De (The) Sam Pitt (Sampit) Senior Citizen's Center	227-229
De (The) Bernice Frasier	230-231
De (The) Sam Pitt (Sampit) Head Start	232
De (The) Rosemary High School	233-237
De (The) Joseph Abraham (Abe) Bryant	238-239
De (The) Ellis Calvin Mean, Sr. – Arnetha Smith Means	240
De (The) Jessie & Rosa Lee Robinson	241
De (The) Teacher Emma Brewington Stafford	241
De (The) Teacher Essie Graham Britton	242-243
De (The) Rosemary Class of 1964	244-245
De (The) Rosemary Class of 1970	246
De (The) Mother Ada Edith Brown Cokley	247
De (The) Teacher Vera Cokley	247
De (The) Reverend (Dr.) James H. Cokley	248-249
De (The) Mt. Zion African Methodist Episcopal Church School	250
De (The) (Sam Pitt) Sampit Elementary School	251-261
De (The) Staff Sergeant Leroy McDonald	262
De (The) Reverend Alphonso N. Scott	263
De (The) Claudia Sherald Wright	264
De (The) Interdenominational Theological Center (ITC) – Atlanta, Georgia	265-266

Allen University was founded in Cokesbury, South Carolina in 1870 as Payne Institute. Its initial mission was to provide education to freed African American slaves. In 1880, it was moved to Columbia and renamed Allen University in honor of **Bishop Richard Allen**, founder of the African Methodist Episcopal Church. The university remains connected to the denomination, which is in the Methodist family of churches. As one of two black colleges located in Columbia, Allen has a very strong presence in the African American community. **Allen University** initially focused on training ministers and teachers, and over the years has enlarged its scope to produce graduates in other academic areas. **(Courtesy of the Lil Eff Affikan Cump'ny)**

Payne Institute Marker

Erected by
The Allen University Alumni Club of Greenville County
November 1970
In Honor of **Payne Institute**
Established in 1870 by
The African Methodist Episcopal Church
Moved to Columbia, South Carolina in 1860
And Renamed Allen University
Payne Institute Marker
Marker is in Hodges, South Carolina, in Greenwood County
N Marker is on Allen University Road
(Courtesy of the Lil Eff Affikan Cump'ny)

Allen University has one of the most beautiful campus views in Columbia, SC
(Courtesy of the Lil Eff Affikan Cump'ny)

Completed in 1870, **Allen University is on the National Register of Historical** Places.
(Courtesy of the Lil Eff Affikan Cump'ny)

Bird's eye view of selected buildings at Allen University - **J. S. Flipper Library**

Allen University Student Center

John Hurst Adams Gym
Allen University
(Courtesy of the Lil Eff Affikan Cump'ny)

The Allen University historic **Levi J. Coppin Hal,** a four-story dormitory located on the corner of Harden and Hampton Street in the Waverly Community was constructed in 1906; renovated in 1956and 2006. **(Courtesy of the Lil Eff Affikan Cump'ny)**

This view from **Allen University Allen University** shows **Coppin Hall Historic Restoration 2002 Cornerstone.** **(Courtesy of the Lil Eff Affikan Cump'ny)**

Reverend (Dr.) Charles E. Young, a native Georgetonians served as **President of Allen University,** Columbia, South Carolina **from** 2001-2010.
(Courtesy of the Lil Eff Affikan Cump'ny)

Reverend (Dr.) Charles E. Young is the Senior Pastor of Pine Grove African Methodist Episcopal Church, 120 Steward Road, Columbia, South Carolina. **Dr. Young** was assigned to Pine Grove AME Church in March of 2015. He is married to the former **Sandra Archer** and together they have two children **Charlotte** (Shola) and **Christopher** and one granddaughter **Tolu.** A native of Georgetown County, South Carolina and educated in Georgetown County public schools he set his goals on service to humankind early in his career.

After serving two years in the United States Army, his desire to improve himself led him to Virginia Union University in Richmond, Virginia where he earned a Bachelor of Science degree in Biology. However, after his conversion and receiving the call to preach he set aside his pursuit of medical science and enrolled at Columbia International University, Columbia, South Carolina where he earned his Master of Divinity. He later earned a Doctoral degree in Urban Anthropology from Westminster Theological Seminary in Philadelphia, Pennsylvania.

Dr. Young taught Church Ministry and Urban Anthropology at Columbia International University for fifteen years. During this time he participated in several overseas study tours as well as led seminary students in urban study research in major US cities. His professional career also includes President of Allen University, Prison Chaplain for the South Carolina Department of Corrections, and Probation and Parole Agent for the state of South Carolina.

Dr. Young served several congregations in South Carolina focusing his ministry on church growth, discipleship training and developing ministries to the elderly and youth. He has worked extensively with persons with chemical dependency and other life crises. During his pastoral ministry he led his congregations in capital improvements, community development, housing initiatives and economic development.

Dr. Young is the Presiding Elder of the Orangeburg District in the Central Annual Conference and overseas 18 Churches. **(Courtesy of the Lil Eff Affikan Cump'ny)**

The governance of policy and general administration of **Allen University** is a function of the University's Board of Trustees. **Joseph Thompson,** Principal of Rosemary High School, Andrews, SC served as a member of the Board members.
(Courtesy of the Lil Eff Affikan Cump'ny)

The James Square Shopping Center located at 2300 Taylor Street, Columbia, South Carolina is named in honor of **Bishop Frederick Calhoun James,** Ecumenical theologian. In this photograph taken on June 19, 1996 is **Bishop James** and **Mother Theresa James** dressed up in their African Attire. **(Courtesy of the Lil Eff Affikan Cump'ny)**

Ecumenical theologian, advocate for fair and decent housing, proponent of civil rights, political leader and public servant are only a few of the characteristics of **Bishop Frederick Calhoun James**. He was born on April 7, 1922, in Prosperity, S.C., the son of Rosa Lee Gray James and Edward James. He graduated from Drayton Street High School, Newberry, South Carolina, and earned his B.A. degree in History/English from Allen University (1943), and his Master's of Divinity degree from Howard University School of Religion (1947). He also studied at Union Theological Seminary in New York.

James returned to South Carolina in 1947 to become pastor of Wayman African Methodist Episcopal Church, Winnsboro; Chappelle Memorial African Methodist Episcopal Church, Columbia; and Mt. Pisgah African Methodist Episcopal Church in Sumter, a position that he held for 19 years. He was also a professor at Allen University in Columbia, and, later, Dean of Allen's Dickerson School of Theology. As a champion for civil rights, he also became a community and state social and political action leader. In 1960, he was elected Consultant/Director of Social Action of the African Methodist Episcopal Church. In this position, he formed a close relationship with Dr. Martin Luther King, Jr. In 1963, he became President of the Effective Sumter Movement of Sumter, South Carolina, a historic chapter in civil rights.

In 1967, as pastor of Mt. Pisgah A.M.E. Church, Rev. James led the sponsorship of the first 221(d) Rent Supplement Housing Project in South Carolina. In 1969, he initiated the first 221-(h) Home Ownership Project in the state. He was South Carolina's first African American Congressional District member of the Department of Alcohol and Drug Abuse and the Department of Social Services. From 1987 to 1992 he was a member of the Columbia Housing Authority and served as vice chair. He also served as Vice President of the S. C. Christian Action Council.

In 1972, this eminent theologian and champion of civil rights was elected to the AME Bishopric and was assigned Presiding Bishop of the AME Church in South Africa, Lesotho, Botswana, Swaziland, Namibia, and Mozambique. Headquartered in Cape Town, South Africa, he established schools, a publishing house, churches, and other institutions. Bishop James later was assigned bishop in Arkansas and Oklahoma (1976). He formed a lifelong friendship with then Attorney Bill Clinton. In 1984, he was assigned to the 7th Episcopal District,

Dr. George Flowers, Bishop Z.L. Grady, Bishop Frederick Calhoun James, and Presiding Elder Novel Goff, Sr.

State of South Carolina. In each of these positions, he built housing projects, strengthened schools and led two colleges to full accreditation; Shorter College, N. Little Rock, Arkansas in 1981 and Allen University, Columbia, South Carolina in 1992.

In 1992, Bishop James was assigned Ecumenical Bishop and Chaplaincy Endorsement Officer of the African Methodist Episcopal Church International. In 1993, he was given major fiscal and reconciliation duties as Bishop of the Second Episcopal District (Maryland, Washington, D.C., Virginia, and North Carolina) of the African Methodist Episcopal Church and he stabilized the District.

In 1994, he was selected by **President William Clinton** as an official member of the delegation to attend the inauguration of **South African President Nelson Mandela**, and in 1998 he was again chosen to accompany President and Mrs. Clinton on an official visit to South Africa. He and his wife, Theressa, had retired from active duty in 1996 and returned to live at home in Columbia, South Carolina.

Bishop James is a former member of the White House Advisory Board on Historical Black Colleges and Universities, the U.S. State Department's Advisory Board on Religious Freedom, and National Vice President of the Interfaith Alliance. A life member of the NAACP, Alpha Phi Alpha Fraternity, and a 33-degree Mason, he was inducted into the South Carolina Black Hall of Fame (1991) and the Columbia Housing Authority Wall of Fame (1994).

In January of 2003, Bishop James was awarded the state's highest honor, The Order of the Palmetto, for his significant contributions to South Carolina.

Episcopal Supervisor (Retired) Theressa Gregg James was born in Marion, South Carolina. Her educational experience included Kittrell College, Allen University, Bachelor of Arts Degree in History, Cum Laude Graduate, Masters Degree Teachers College- Columbia University, major Childhood Education-Older Children and Doctorate of Humanities Degree – Monrovia College, Liberia West Africa.

Professionally, she worked as a public school educator and administrator. Civically, she is a member of the Alpha Kappa Alpha Sorority, and a Life Member and Legacy Life Member of the National Council of Negro Women.

She is the spouse of Bishop F. C. James (Retired) the 93rd elected and consecrated Bishop of the African Methodist Episcopal Church. Her church work included the Women's Missionary Society, Church Women United, World Federation of Methodist Women, the Bishop's Spouses Council, Governing Board of The National Council of Churches of America, Church World Service Committee and the National Council of Churches.

She and her husband served the 15th (South Africa and South West Africa), 18th (Lesotho, Swaziland, Botswana and Mozambique), 12th (Oklahoma and Arkansas), 7th Episcopal District (South Carolina), the Ecumenical and Urban Affairs Office of the African Methodist Episcopal Church and the 2nd (Washington, D.C., North Carolina, Virginia and Maryland, respectively. Mrs. James is an author, "An Historical Review of Missions In South Africa." **(Courtesy of the Lil Eff Affikan Cump'ny)**

The Right Reverend Benjamin W. Arnett served as **CHAIRMAN OF BOARD OF TRUSTEES** of Allen University from 1888 – 1892. The historical **Arnett Hall** is named in his honor! **(Courtesy of the Lil Eff Affikan Cump'ny)**

Bishop B. W. Arnett (1838-1906) was an African-American educator, minister, and elected official. He was born a free man in 1838 in Brownsville, Pennsylvania, where he taught school from1859 to 1867. In his youth, Arnett lost a leg to cancer. As an African Methodist Episcopal pastor, Arnett served parishes in Toledo, Cincinnati and Columbus. In 1888, he was elected bishop, a position he held until his death in 1906. In 1872 Arnett became the first black man serve as foreman of an all-white jury, and in 1885 he was elected to the Ohio State Legislature from a district with a white majority. He was the author of the bill, which repealed the Black Laws of Ohio. A forceful and compelling speaker, he was influential in Republican politics, thanks, in part, to his friendship with fellow legislator (and later president), William McKinley.

This photograph has been identified as that of the Combined Normal and Industrial Board, Wilberforce University, Wilberforce, Ohio, 1893. **Bishop Benjamin W. Arnett,** though, appears to be standing second from left in the front row.
(Courtesy of the Lil Eff Affikan Cump'ny)

Reverend William Conyers Ervin, Jr. received his "Bachelor of Arts Degree" from Allen Univeristy, Columbia, SC on May 25, 1950. Samuel R. Higgins, President, Frank M. Reid, Sr., Chairman of the Board/Bishop, T. O. Greene, Dean, J.E. Thomas, Secretary, Gwendolyn O. Hadden, Secretary.
(Courtesy of Luisa Ervin Hughie)

Allen University, Columbia, S.C

William Conyers Ervin
The Degree of
Bachelor of Arts
May 25, 1950.

(Courtesy of Luisa Ervin Hughie)

Allen University, Columbia, South Carolina – Graduation Class of 1950. **Reverend William C. Ervin, Jr.** is standing on front row (left) with graduation cap and gown on.

(Courtesy of Luisa Ervin Hughie)

The Seventh Episcopal District Messenger (Newsletter) was published monthly in the Seventh Episcopal District of South Carolina.

At left is Bishop Samuel R. Higgins, Presiding Prelate of the Seventh Episcopal District.

Bishop Higgins was born July 6, 1896 in Laurens, South Carolina.

He died December 31, 1961 in Charleston, South Carolina.

He was married to Eugenia DeCosta Higgins (November 22, 1898 – April 12, 1993). Robert Samuel DeCosta Higgins (1932 – 1964) was their son.

Bishop Higgins and his wife Eugenia are buried at United and Friendship Society Cemetery, Charleston, South Carolina.

(Courtesy of the Lil Eff Affikan Cump'ny)

This group picture shows **Reverend William Conyers Ervin Jr.**, (4th from right) posing with Allen University Alumnus at Allen University.
(Courtesy of the Lil Eff Affikan Cump'ny)

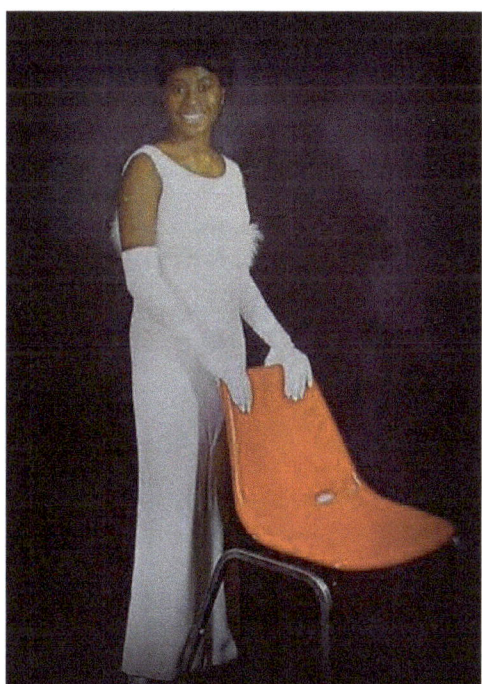

This portrait depicts **Doris Greene** from the Cumberland Section of Sampit while as student at Allen University, Columbia, SC).
(Courtesy of the Lil Eff Affikan Cump'ny)

This **Sampitonian** is **Jerome Lavern Knowlin** was the youngest son of **Gideon** and **Sarah Singleton Knowlin** was born February 12, 1957 in Georgetown, South Carolina. Both of his parents predeceased him.

Subsequent to having attended Sampit Elementary School, he graduated from Andrews High School, Andrews South Carolina. He later received the Bachelor of Arts Degree in Education with honors from Allen University, Columbia, South Carolina. He then moved to New York City and furthered his studies in the field of education at New York City College. There he graduated with honors and earned the Master of Arts Degree.

Jerome taught for thirteen years in the public schools of New York. As a resident of Yonkers, New York, he was a faithful member of Bethel A.M.E. Church there. Many characterize him, as has been a "people oriented" person. Better known as **"Hunk"** or **"Ronnie"** to those who knew him well, he was a very loving, kindhearted individual. He was one committed to the well being of those around him. Their concerns were his concerns.
(Courtesy of the Lil Eff Affikan Cump'ny)

Jerome loved to travel. God had blessed him to visit many places and to meet people only dreamed of by others. Above all, he was a child of God who always gave the Lord praise for all that he was able to achieved, and for all that he had.

He went Home to be with his Savior on Monday, May 8, 1995 at the Conway Hospital, Conway, South Carolina.

Homegoing Celebration for **Jerome** was held on Thursday, May 11, 1995, St. Paul A.M.E. Church, Sampit at 3:30 P.M. Pastor Wallace J. McKnight, Sr., preached the "Words of Comfort" to the family and friends. Rev. Floyd Knowlin, gave the invocation; Solo, Mildred Flippen; Remarks, Andrew Gasque, Sr. and Rev. William C. Ervin, Sr.

Committal, Benediction, and Interment were at the St. Paul A.M.E. Cemetery. Family, Friends and Classmates were all there to say farewell to a dear friend.
(Courtesy of the Lil Eff Affikan Cump'ny)

Allen University was founded in 1870, one hundred forty-six (146) years ago. The campus is home to several historical buildings. **(Courtesy of the Lil Eff Affikan Cump'ny)**

This white marble memorial on **Allen University campus** listed more than 200 black and multiracial churches that have burned since 1990 carries a simple message: **"Black Church Are Still Burning - We Are Not Satisfied."** The memorial was dedicated in memory of Reverend Mac Charles Jones on April 11, 1997.
(Courtesy of the Lil Eff Affikan Cump'ny)

The Preston Warren Williams II Student Residence Hall is named in honor of The Right Reverend Preston Warren Williams II – Presiding Bishop of The Seventh Episcopal District. **(Courtesy of the Lil Eff Affikan Cump'ny)**

This Plaque Reads:
BISHOP PRESTON WARREN WILLIAMS II, DMin, L.H.D
This building was erected in November 2009 under the leadership of **Bishop Preston Warren Williams II**, elected the 119th **Bishop of the African Methodist Episcopal Church**, Presiding Bishop of the Seventh Episcopal District (South Carolina) and named in honor of him for his outstanding contributions to Allen University as Chairman of the Board of Trustees from 2000 – 2012. March 26, 2012.
(Courtesy of the Lil Eff Affikan Cump'ny)

The Wilma Delores Webb Williams Student Residence Hall is named in honor of **Mother Wilma Delores Webb Williams** – Supervisor of the Women's Missionary Society of The Seventh Episcopal District **(Courtesy of the Lil Eff Affikan Cump'ny)**

This Plaque Reads:
MOTHER WILMA DELORES WEBB WILLIAMS, EdS, MA, L.H.D.
This building was erected in November 2009 under the leadership of Mother Wilma Delores Webb Williams, the wife of Bishop Preston Warren Williams II, Supervisor of the Women's Missionary Society of the Seventh Episcopal District (South Carolina) and named in honor of her outstanding contributions to Allen University from 2004 – 2012.   March 26, 2012.
(Courtesy of the Lil Eff Affikan Cump'ny)

The Omega Phi Fraternity was founded on November 17, 1911, at **Howard University in Washington, D.C.** The founders were three Howard University undergraduates, -- **Edgar Amos Love, Oscar James Cooper and Frank Coleman.** Joining them was their faculty adviser, **Dr. Ernest Everett Just.** From the initials of the Greek phrase meaning, **"friendship is essential to the soul,"** the name Omega Psi Phi was derived. That phrase was selected as the Motto.

Two line brothers **Effson Chester Bryant** (Dog #1) **and Gerry Lee Gilliam (**Dog #2**)** pledging Omega Psi Phi Fraternity **at Allen University (Mu Sigma Chapter)** getting ready for the Death March (crossing the burning sands). **Big Brother Joe Brown** is standing over his pledgees. **Dog #1** and **Dog #2** went over on **December 1977.**
(Courtesy of the Lil Eff Affikan Cump'ny)

 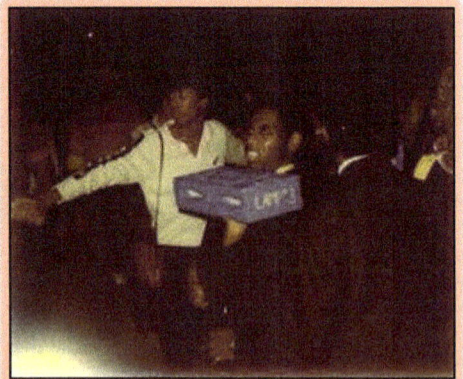

Omega Pearls, **Emma Muldrow, Glendale, Emma Gipson** posting with **Big Brother Joe Bryant** and **Dog I** (Effson) and **Dog II** (Gerry) at left. At right is **Wesley Bryant**, Omega Psi Phi pledgee carrying the stone during the death march at Benedict College.
(Courtesy of the Lil Eff Affikan Cump'ny)

This Omega Psi Phi Fraternity (Mu Sigma Chapter) plot is display on the campus of Allen University. **(Courtesy of the Lil Eff Affikan Cump'ny)**

In 1925 the **Chapelle Hall Auditorium** at Allen University was completed. It was once the largest gathering places for African Americans in the city of Columbia at one time. On Friday, 24 June 2016 at 1:00 pm this old 94 years old historical auditorium reopened after sitting empty for eight (8) years for restoration.
(Courtesy of the Lil Eff Affikan Cump'ny)

December 5, 1957 – August 18, 2014

Allen University Remembers
Melenthia Roberts, Chantay Long, Gerry Lee Gilliam
"Heavy Low"

Willie H. Johnson Center for Educational Excellence
Friday, 7 November 2014   7:00 PM

Loving Father, Esteemed Businessman, Dedicated Man of God are just a few words that describe **Gerry Gilliam** who went from his earthly labor to his heavenly reward on Monday, August 18th in Dallas, Texas. He was 56 years old. Gilliam was born in Joanna, South Carolina and lived in Texas for over thirty years. He received his Bachelor of Arts Degree from Allen University in Columbia, South Carolina where he pledged Omega Psi Phi Fraternity Inc. with his line brother, Effson C. Bryant. Gilliam owned G&G Protection, a well-known security company that provides protection for private and public entities throughout the Dallas/Fort Worth area. In the last few years, G&G Protection provided security at the XLV Super Bowl, the Dallas Cowboys Stadium, "Taste of Dallas," Omni Hotel, and several businesses around the DFW Metroplex. In February 2014, WFAA Channel 8 and the Black Chamber of Commerce as a "Quest for Success Award" Recipient honored Gilliam. The Quest for Success Award has represented the highest form of recognition for African American entrepreneurship and community service. Gilliam loved the Lord and was a hard worker not only for his business but also for his church. He was a long

time member of Christian Chapel Temple of Faith C.M.E. Church, and also fellowshipped with Greater Allen A.M.E and Carter Temple C.M.E. churches. He supported and contributed time, talent and treasure to both church and community organizations. He was revered as a big brother and father figure in the church as well as the community. Gilliam believed in helping people and employed church members and others in the community to work in his company. He had a heart of compassion and was committed to serving and supporting others. Gilliam was a lifetime member of Omega Psi Phi fraternity where his fraternity brothers affectionately called him "Heavy Low." He was affiliated with Theta Alpha Chapter where he has served as assistant keeper of records, Seals, Achievement Week and Retention Chair. Gilliam was also a lifetime member of the Irving-Carrollton Branch NAACP and served as Membership chair and First Vice-President of the chapter. He also served as a voting delegate in his neighborhood precinct for the Presidential election. Gilliam received several awards for community service and business achievements. These awards include the Black Contractors Small Business award, 2014 Dallas Black Chamber Of Commerce Quest for Success Award, 2010 NAACP Presidential Award, Theta Alpha Omega Psi Phi 2009 Founders Award, 2012 Omega Man of the Year and Minority Enterprise Development Week 2009.
(Courtesy of the Lil Eff Affikan Cump'ny)

Allenites (Allen University, Columbia, SC) at the memorial service of **Gerry Lee Gilliam, aka Heavy Low** (December 5 1057, August 18, 2014) at Mt. Zion African Methodist Episcopal Church, Joanna, South Carolina. I, Effson, Heavy Low's line brother brought the words of comfort to family members and friends. **(Courtesy of the Lil Eff Affikan Cump'ny)**

(Left to right) **Sandra Fulmore, Effson C. Bryant, Venus Sabb, Ralph Fulmore, Leroy James, Emma Muldrow, Leroy Sabb, Rose James, Willie Newman, Melody Bille-Jone**s and **Marion Smalls**. **(Courtesy of the Lil Eff Affikan Cump'ny)**

Reverend Phillip Washington, Monroe Miller, Presiding Elder Joseph Postell, Reverend Phillip Anderson and **Reverend Rufus Gaymon**, (Allen University's UNCF Gala) March 27, 2015 – Columbia Convention Center.
(Courtesy of the Lil Eff Affikan Cump'ny)

Reverend Clementa & Jennifer Pinckney   Darci Strickland & Annie G. Simmons
(Allen University's UNCF Gala) March 27, 2015 – Columbia Convention Center.
(Courtesy of the Lil Eff Affikan Cump'ny)

These two elegance couples attending the Allen University's UNCF Gala, March 27, 2015 – Columbia Convention Center are **Reverend Phillip C. Anderson**, **Sandra A. Anderson**, **Constance Washington,** and **Reverend Phillip Washington.** (Left to right)
(Courtesy of the Lil Eff Affikan Cump'ny)

Wilhelmenia Elizabeth Miller at the Allen University's UNCF Gala, March 27, 2015 – Columbia Convention Center. **(Courtesy of the Lil Eff Affikan Cump'ny)**

These glamor girls are **Ella Gadsden Richburg, Darci Strickland** (WLTX 19 News Anchor) and **Tiffany Richburg** at Allen University's UNCF Gala, March 27, 2015 – Columbia Convention Center. **(Courtesy of the Lil Eff Affikan Cump'ny)**

Reverend Rodella Burns & Edward Burns   **Reverend & Mrs. Robert Thomas**
(Allen University's UNCF Gala) March 27, 2015 – Columbia Convention Center.
(Courtesy of the Lil Eff Affikan Cump'ny)

Three notables' preachers from the Low County are **Reverend Dr. Sandy W. Drayton** (Presiding of the Georgetown District**), Reverend Robert Kennedy** (Pastor of St. Peters AME Church in North Charleston, SC) and **Reverend Dr. Allen W. Parrott** (Presiding Elder of the Kingstree District). **(Courtesy of the Lil Eff Affikan Cump'ny)**

At left are **Reverend Judy Richardson** (Presiding Elder of the Greenville District) and **Reverend (Dr.) M. Charmaine Ragin** (Presiding Elder of the Newberry-Spartanburg District). These Presiding Elders are posing for a photograph at The 10th Annual Allen University Richard Allen Awards Gala, Friday, March 27, 2015, Columbia Metropolitan Convention Center, Ballroom, Columbia, South Carolina. At right are Reverend **Phillip Washington**, Senior Pastor of Ebenezer AME Church, Mayesville and his Fraternity Brother (Alpha Phi Alpha Fraternity) **Reverend Clementa Pinckney,** Senor Pastor of Mother Emmanuel AME Church, Charleston, SC. **(Courtesy of the Lil Eff Affikan Cump'ny)**

The Male Leadership Empowerment Symposium was held on Thursday, 3 September 2015 at the Allen University – Student Center at 6:30. One of the panelists was **Effson Chester Bryant** of Sampit, South Carolina.
(Courtesy of the Lil Eff Affikan Cump'ny)

Allen University Homecoming 2015. (Courtesy of the Lil Eff Affikan Cump'ny)

Allen University Welcome Alumni at Homecoming 2015.
(Courtesy of the Lil Eff Affikan Cump'ny)

This **2016** image was taken at Allen University homecoming where the brotherhood of **Mu Sigma Fraternity - Omega Psi Phi** standing tall flashing their fraternity signs. The **Q Dogs** are in the **HOUSE!** **(Courtesy of the Lil Eff Affikan Cump'ny)**

This **Allenites** is wearing the Omega Psi Phi hoody in **Memory of Heavy Low (Gerry Gilliam).** At right is **Joseph "Abe" Bryant (Allenites) – Straight Outta Sampit** visiting his alma mater for a school homecoming in 2016.
(Courtesy of the Lil Eff Affikan Cump'ny)

Allenites sharing in a group hug picture - Allen University Homecoming 2015.
(Courtesy of the Lil Eff Affikan Cump'ny)

Kappa Alpha Psi   Phi Beta Sigma

Fun Day at Allen University Homecoming!

This Frat Bruh is **Willie T. Newman** and his beautiful wife, **Benita Baker Newman**.

Reverend Silas Spann - Willie T. NewmanWillie T. Newman/Venus M. Sabb

Nimai GarrettBernard Cook

This premier chef is **Leroy Sabb** and his wife, **Venus McKnight Sabb.** (Straight Outta Sampit). **(Courtesy of the Lil Eff Affikan Cump'ny)**

The World's Greatest Chefs (Leroy Sabb)

Allenites

Allen University Yellow Jackets VS **South Carolina Gamecocks Basketball** exhibition contest marks the first-every meeting between the two Columbia-based schools. The Yellow Jackson are led by head coach **Nelson Jones** in his first season, while Carolina is led by fourth-year head coach **Frank Martin. (Courtesy of the Lil Eff Affikan Cump'ny)**

The **Allen University Concert Choir** sang the "National Anthem" at the Basketball exhibition. **(Courtesy of the Lil Eff Affikan Cump'ny)**

Allen University Yellow Jackets VS **South Carolina Gamecocks Basketball**

This talented basketball player is **A'ja Wilson** from the University of South Carolina Gamecocks Women's Basketball Team

Allenites

Jackie Whitmore and **Family (Courtesy of the Lil Eff Affikan Cump'ny)**

At halftime during the exhibition game, a solemn moment was held to remember the nine victims of the **Emanuel AME Church** shooting with their family members in attendance.

Anne Simmons attended the Basketball exhibition.

Jenifer Pinckney and daughters, Malana and Eliana Pinckney in attendance at the Basketball exhibition.

(Courtesy of the Lil Eff Affikan Cump'ny)

The 146th Founder's Day Celebration. On February 9, 2016, Allen University hosts its 146th Founder's Day Celebration at the John Hurst Gymnatorium from 10:00 AM to 11:00 AM. Dr. Lady June Cole (President of Allen) making remarks.
(Courtesy of the Lil Eff Affikan Cump'ny)

The **Reverend E. Robert Thomas**, Allen University Chaplain and Instructor in the Division of Religion at Allen University in Columbia was the keynote speaker. Reverend Thomas is the Immediate Past Associate Commissioner for the Columbia Conference AME Church Debutante and Masters Commission and an Instructor within the Columbia Annual Conference Board of Examiners.

Reverend Thomas is the proud Pastor of Spring Hill AME Church, Gilbert, SC. He received his calling into the ministry at the age of eighteen and became ordained an Itinerant Elder at the 108th session of the Northeast South Carolina Annual Conference on September 16, 2000. Before being appointed to Spring Hill, Rev. Thomas served as Pastor of St. Luke AME Church, Sumter SC, Mt. Calvary AME Church, Hartsville, SC, Quinn Chapel AME Church, Sumter, SC and Lever Chapel AME Church in Prosperity, SC.
(Courtesy of the Lil Eff Affikan Cump'ny)

Allen University unveiled the **Richard Allen Stamp,** which coincides with the 200th anniversary of Richard Allen's founding of the African Methodist Episcopal (AME) Church. The print is from the collection of the Library Company of Philadelphia. First-Day-of-Issue ceremony will take place at the Mother Bethel A.M.E. Church in Philadelphia.

Dr. Lady June Cole (President of Allen University). (Courtesy of the Lil Eff Affikan Cump'ny)

Dr. Lady June Cole (President of Allen University) and her husband, **Dr. Bruce Cole** posing together beside the Bishop Richard Allen's Black Heritage Stamp.
(Courtesy of the Lil Eff Affikan Cump'ny)

Standing by the **Bishop Richard Allen's Black Heritage Stamp** is **Reverend (Dr.) Sandy W. Drayton**, Presiding Elder of the Georgetown District.
(Courtesy of the Lil Eff Affikan Cump'ny)

Jeremiah Hemingway (President of the General Alumni Association of Allen University) and **Nimai Garrett. (Courtesy of the Lil Eff Affikan Cump'ny)**

(Courtesy of the Lil Eff Affikan Cump'ny)

(Courtesy of the Lil Eff Affikan Cump'ny)

Reverend & Mrs. E. Robert Thomas standing beside the Black Heritage postage stamp of Bishop Richard Allen. **(Courtesy of the Lil Eff Affikan Cump'ny)**

This image above shows **Dr. Peter Felder II** - ALLEN UNIVERSITY CLASS OF '59 and Director of the Allen University Concert Choir in the far left posing with the Allen University Concert Choir. **(Courtesy of the Lil Eff Affikan Cump'ny)**

Kedric Funnie (Straight Outta Sampit) - President of Allen University Student Body. President Kedric is the son of John and Veronica Funnie.
(Courtesy of the Lil Eff Affikan Cump'ny)

The Oak Grove School was probably the first graded school in Sampit. One historian stated that the school was built between 1926-1927. Other schools were the **Britt School, Britt Branch School, Cumberland School, New Hope School, Oak Grove School,** and **Saint Paul School.** Most of the schools were located inside or near the churches in the community. Oak Grove School was only for teaching white students, and blacks were not allowed to attend. Some of the teachers that taught there was **Mrs. Laura Boatwrights**, the wife of **Ezekiel Boatwrights** who owned the No. 2 Store, **Mrs. Joe Deal Smith** from Sampit and **Mrs. A. J. Tilton** from Andrews. **The Oakgrove School** was a large wooden school with ten rooms to accommodate the white students who lived in the surrounding areas. The school had an auditorium that was centrally located with classrooms in the two wings on the sides of the auditorium. There was a cafeteria off the back, where light lunches were served. Some of the lunches consisted of soups, crackers, fruit, and peanut butter sandwiches. One of the school principals was **Mrs. Kate D. McConnell**. After the closing of the Oakgrove School, students attended school at Andrews High School, Andrews, and Winyah High School, Georgetown. **(Courtesy of the Lil Eff Affikan Cump'ny)**

It is believed that **Mr. Francis Bone** and his brother **Weldon Bone** helped to build the school around 1926 – 1927. The Bone's brothers were known as some of the greatest carpenters and blacksmiths in and around Sampit. They used handsaws to cut the lumbers for the school. As the carpenters worked on the school, it is said that many white families brought hot meals and dinners for them. Today, the old Oakgrove School is used as an apartment complex for construction workers working in Georgetown County. **(Courtesy of the Lil Eff Affikan Cump'ny)**

Historical records stated that **Cumberland African Methodist Episcopal Church** was organized in the Cumberland section (Penny Royal Road) of Sampit on April 21, 1874 under the pastoral leadership of **Reverend March Singleton** in the old church building. **Reverend Bruce Williams** served as the Presiding Elder and the **Right Reverend Jabez Pitt Campbell** was Presiding Bishop. Cumberland AME Church had an ABC school on the church property to serve the educational needs of the colored (Black) students of the Cumberland Community. The original Church **Stewards** were **Joseph Furerson, Elex Trappia, Stussant A. Green, Samuel Bryant**, and **Cornellus Clements**. The **Trustees** were **Mack Wilson, Robbin Simmon,** and **John Herbert**. The original church property was bought for $ 5.00. In 1954, Cumberland ended its service as a community based school where it had provided early childhood education to many of the present-day members.

In this c. 1900s photograph, stewards and trustees of the Cumberland AME Church gathered for a formal portrait. Worship service continued in the old building until 1893, when the church was rebuilt. The church was remodeled in 1928, under the leadership of the **Reverend C. Lewis** and the **Right Reverend John Adams**, Presiding Bishop. The Trustees were: **S. P. McCants, A. Z. Green, J. Wragg, S. Rhue, G. Green, H. Keith** and **S. D. Blandon**. **(Courtesy of the Cumberland AME Church)**

This is a picture of the old **Oakgrove Colored School** in the **Oakgrove** Section of Sampit. Most of the public school to educate black students was organized shortly after the Civil War. This school was built to educate the colored (blacks) students that lived in the community was racially separated from the white schools. Blacks were not allowed to attend the Oakgrove School (white school), which was less than 1/10 of a mile away from the Oakgrove Colored School. The **Oakgrove Colored School** was located on the property where the New Life Deliverance Church (John H. Burroughs, Senior Pastor) stands today. **David Wragg**, a resident of the **Oakgrove** community attended the school at a youth. The schoolhouse had one or two small rooms used to educate the students. The school term lasted 1 month to 10 months in the early 1900s. **(Courtesy of the Lil Eff Affikan Cump'ny)**

This is a replica of the old wooden school chair used in the Colored (Blacks) Schools in Sampit. **(Courtesy of the Lil Eff Affikan Cump'ny)**

This is a picture of the old Saint Paul African Methodist Episcopal Church ABC School

The Saint Paul African Methodist Episcopal Church School, known as the ABC School, was the first school established for **'Colored'** or **'Negro'** children in the St. Paul Section of Sampit. It is said that the Saint Paul's community raised money and built the school next to the Saint Paul African Methodist Episcopal Church.

The ABC school had three large partitioned rooms with a small kitchen. The kitchen had a large wood-burning stove with a pipe sticking out through the wall to the outside. The students were responsible for chopping wood for the large wood heaters. They normally went into the woody area that surrounded the school to cut the wood. Small kerosene lamps attached to the walls lighted the schoolroom.

The school also had large eight pane windows in each classroom. Male and female outdoor toilets were built between the church and the school. Most of the students brought their own lunch from home. When a child could not bring a lunch from home, the school gave small lunches prepared by church members for those students without a lunch. The lunches consisted of a slice of bread and a small piece of meat. Some parents who didn't have money to buy lunch for their family member would send wagonloads of cut wood for the wooden heaters or eggs from their own chickens to the school to help.

Outside the kitchen, a hand pump was located. The hand pump was used for pumping water for the kitchen and drinking. In order to get water from the pump one had to prime it with water from a small bucket. Then the water would flow. In the back of the school were two outdoor toilets, for males and female students.
(Courtesy of the Lil Eff Affikan Cump'ny)

The photograph documented **The St. Paul ABC School** three (3) days school trip to **Paradise Park, Silver Spring, Florida**. Florida's invitation to tourism in the 1950's was, unfortunately, not extended to persons of all races on the same terms. As part of the Jim Crow South prior to the passage of Civil Rights legislation in the 1960's, Florida's major attractions and beaches were, by and large, for whites only, by practice or by law, with black tourists and locals segregated to separate places like Dade County's Virginia Beach, Amelia Island's American Beach, or other areas that offered alternative facilities in 1949 Florida's Silver Springs established Paradise Park, a, as the brochure pictured here puts it, section for "colored people only" at a separate bank of the river southeast of the main dock area. Here was a bathing area and dock for glass bottom boats where black visitors could enjoy the springs without interracial mingling.

Two well-known teachers at the St. Paul AME Church School were **Charlena Greene** from Georgetown and **Emma Brewington Stafford**, (Aunt Emma), formerly of Bloomingvale gave school instruction to the sixth grade level. They taught reading, writing, and arithmetic. Upon completion of this school, some of the families were able to send their children in secondary schools in Andrews and Georgetown. They were required to receive the same state educational standard and training as white teachers.

Those that went on the three days school trip to Paradise Park, Silver Spring, Florida were Charlena Greene, Emma B. Stafford, Norine Duncan, Pearline Smith, Pressley Gasque, Samuel James Holmes, Randolph Stafford, Annie Sanders, Suziah Stafford, Hazel Greene, Willie Mae Grant, Vernell Stafford, Lila Mae Bryant Prout, Raymond Alford, George Washington, Lucille Drayton, Cleo Stafford, Leroy Duncan, Christopher Gilyard, Bus Driver, and Mrs. George Washington. One of the highlights of the trip for the teachers and students were riding in a glass bottom boat - where you were able to see abundant of wildlife and fishes underwater. It is said that each parent had to paid for his or her student's trip to Florida. The student enjoyed the trip, had a fun time, pillar fight, and oldest children had to stay with the youngest ones. It is said that Saul Smith, one of the contributors from Sampit asked the students "tells us if there were any pine trees in Florida?" Said that the student bust out and laughed! **(Courtesy of the Lila Mae Bryant Prout)**

The first **Senior Citizen Center of Sampit** was established in the 1970 in the old St. Paul ABC School house next to the St. Paul A.M.E. Church. The old school turned center was given a face-lift to meet the needs of an aged population in Sampit. Handicapped railings, wheelchair accessories and many niceties were added to the center. A wooden sign "**The Senior Citizen**" hangs on a wooden post outside the center. The center was established under the pastoral tenure of **Reverend William C. Ervin, Jr.** The Center served as a community haven where Senior Citizen gathered to participate in many social activities and functions. **(Courtesy of the Lil Eff Affikan Cump'ny)**

Almenar Mercer Elliott (March 8, 1908 - August 20, 1988) was instrumental in organizing The Senior Citizen Center in Sampit. She was the daughter of **Jessie** and **Jack Hazel**. She attended schools in Georgetown County and moved to Boston, Massachusetts. In Boston, she was self-employed as a beautician for over thirty years and rose to the highest honors in the Order of the Eastern Stars and the Elks. Almenar was an active member of the New Hope Baptist Church in Boston and was respected as a community leader. She returned to the Sampit Section of Georgetown in 1972 and became a member of St. Paul A.M.E. Church. She worked for many years in the Headstart Program and was a member of the New Hope Chapter No. 343 Order of the Eastern Stars. **Aunt Hester D. Bryant**, after her retirement from the Department of Social Services, worked with the Sampit Senior Center until her health began to fail. She worked along with **Almeta** for many years at the Sampit Senior Citizen Center. **Aunt Hester** helped with driving and picking up Senior Citizens that attended the Center with her own car for many years before a van was given for transportation. She also was instrumental in making curtains for the center. **(Courtesy of the Lil Eff Affikan Cump'ny)**

The **Sampit Senior Center** was later moved into a stone building at 92 Singleton Avenue in Sampit. This sign at left located off of Powell Road directs one to the Center.
(Courtesy of the Lil Eff Affikan Cump'ny)

It took the County Council about twenty- five years to allocate matching funds for the building of the new Sampit Senior Center. It was built with a kitchen, 2 restrooms, storage space, and a large community room. **David Smith**, community activist and church leader, donated the land for the Senior Center.
(Courtesy of the Lil Eff Affikan Cump'ny)

A Ribbon Cutting Ceremony for the **Senior Citizen Center** was held at the Center on June 26, 1999. Many family members, community leaders, church activists, local and state political leaders, and community members attended the ceremony. Among them: Sam Wragg, Hattie Mae Cooper, James Porter "JP" Jayroe, David Wragg and John Yancey McGill, SC Senate District 32: Florence, Georgetown, Horry and Williamsburg. Bernice Frazier and the members had the center very decorative and had a welcoming sign on the wall that stated, "Welcome to Sampit Senior Citizen's Dedication." Following a short program led by the Senior Citizen members. Senator J. Yancey McGill (District 32/Florence, Georgetown, Horry and Williamsburg Counties) made remarks. Then a soul food meal was served. Afterward, the cutting ribbon took place on the outside. The following persons took part in the **Ribbon-cutting ceremony**: Samuel Wragg, Hattie Mae Cooper, James Porter Jayroe, Senator J. Yancey McGill, David Wragg and other political and civil leaders.
(Courtesy of the Lil Eff Affikan Cump'ny)

This picture shows the Senior Citizens posing for this group picture at the **Ribbon Cutting Ceremony** at the Sampit Senior Center on June 26, 1999.
(Courtesy of the Lil Eff Affikan Cump'ny)

The Georgetown Council on Aging proved transportation for Senior Citizens to and from the Sampit Senior Citizens Center daily. Some of the drivers were **Grady Wilson, Junior Heywood,** and **J. W. Gasque, Jr. (Courtesy of the Lil Eff Affikan Cump'ny)**

One of the most active members of the Sampit Senior Center and Andrews Senior Citizens Center was **Bernice Louise Frasier** affectionately called **"Bez"** by family members and friends. She was born on June 20, 1940 in the Oak Grove Community of Sampit, daughter of **Arthur** and **Marie Rhue Frasier**.

At an early age, **Bernice** joined Cumberland African Methodist Episcopal Church and served faithfully in the following capacities: Stewardess Board, Women's Missionary Society (WMS), Kitchen, Usher Board and Pastor's Aide Boards.

Bernice started her formal education in the one room schoolhouse – Brick Branch School located in the Oak Grove Community across from the family home. She graduated from Rosemary High School, Andrews, South Carolina. Upon graduation, she moved to Buffalo, New York for a short period and then returned home.

Bernice was known for her culinary cooking skills that she learned from her mother, **Marie R. Frasier**. She was hired by the Georgetown County School District as a Cafeteria Worker and later promoted to Head Cook. After years as a Head Cook at Rosemary Middle School, Andrews, South Carolina she retired and was known as a Master Chef.

After retirement from the Georgetown County School District, **Bernice** started her own catering business that made very sumptuous meals and cakes. Bernice was very instrumental in coordinating the Free Lunch Program at Cumberland African Methodist Episcopal Church sponsored by Georgetown School District for many years.

On January 27, 2016 at 1:22 A.M., Bernice answered God's melodious voice and said, "Here I am." **The Celebration of Life Service** for **Bernice Louise Frasier** was held on Monday, February 1, 2016, Cumberland A.M.E. Church in the Sampit Community at 11:00 A.M. where Reverend Bernard Brown, Pastor. Reverend Francena Frasier Orr, Sister of Bernice Frasier preached the Words of Comfort. Interment was held at Cumberland A.M.E. Church Cemetery.

(Courtesy of the Lil Eff Affikan Cump'ny)

The **Sampit Senior Citizen Members** posing together for a group photograph at the Senior Citizen Center; standing, **Rosa Bell Smith, Hattie Mae Cooper, Knowlin, Linnie Knowlin, Bernice Frasier (Director), Grady Wilson (Van Driver), Bernice Bryant, Rosa Darby,** (sitting) **Ida H. Green, Pearline Smith, Stafford, Rosa Darby, Amelia Trappier, Mary Stafford** and **Lillie Bell Grant.**
(Courtesy of the Lil Eff Affikan Cump'ny)

This official school picture is the **Sampit Head Start Class** with **Teachers, Teacher's Aides** and **Students.** **(Courtesy of the Lil Eff Affikan Cump'ny)**

Sampit Head Start Class posing with their beloved teacher, **Sarah Bell Bryant** and Teacher's Aides, **Almeta Elliot** and **Mary Lou Duncan** on February 3, 1977.
(Courtesy of the Lil Eff Affikan Cump'ny)

This is the **Sampit Head Start Graduation Class** wearing their hats and holding their graduation certificate after their upcoming commencement ceremony. Their teacher was **Sarah Bell Bryant; Teacher's Aids** were **Almeta Elliot** and **Mary Lou Duncan**.
(Courtesy of the Lil Eff Affikan Cump'ny)

The **Rosemary School** on Jones Avenue, Andrews has a long and interesting history. The school term was not always as long as it is now, and neither was the building as beautiful and well equipped. There were many citizens before our time that worked hard for many years to secure adequate facilities for some of the children of the community. Among them was the late **Reverend George G. Jones** (Jones Avenue) who we might refer to as the "**Father of Rosemary School.**" The first school was a one-room building, was located in the settlement once called "**Coontown**" in 1907. Its only teacher was the late **Sulie Becton Brockington**. Later school was conducted in a building on what is now Main Street, on or near the site of Hammond's store. The school was moved to a building on North Beech Avenue. **James Woodbury** of Georgetown was principal.
(Courtesy of the Lil Eff Affikan Cump'ny)

After the school building on North Beech Avenue burned in 1930, a school was built on the corner of Main Street and Cedar Avenue. This building contained five classrooms and an auditorium that was used for classrooms and sometimes as a place to play basketball called the "matchbox." The students were proud of the fact that their school had the only indoor basketball court in the area. There was also a small stage, which doubled as a classroom and a library. Later a small office and another small room to be used as a library were added. **Jesse Edward Smith** served as principal. In the early 1930's the school grew at a moderate pace. The teachers and students enrollment showed little increase. Graduating classes continued to be small. In the spring of 1936 only four people were in the graduating class, all boys. Among them was **Joseph G. Thompson** who became principle after Jesse E. Smith left the school, then known as Andrews Training School. **Mr. Smith** loved by many for his gentleness, his generous spirit and his noble character accepted the position as supervisor of Howard High School in Georgetown. Additional buildings were added in 1947; a high school building of six classrooms, a lunchroom and an agricultural shop were added.
(Courtesy of the Lil Eff Affikan Cump'ny)

Joseph Garvin Thompson became the new principal of Rosemary High School and served as principal until his death on February 16, 1976. Under his administration a new features were added to the school. Among them was hot lunch -a bowl of soup for two cents and it was time that city water was first used.

The history of Andrews stated, "**The Negro School** also new and modern in every particular, built at a cost of about $730,000.00, and accommodates 501 elementary pupils and 403 high school pupils with a faculty of 33 teachers.

Basketball became a major sport. Football was the second major sport, it was first introduced in the School in 1955. In the fall of 1956 the school moved from Main Street to a beautiful new plant on Jones Avenue in West Andrews with grades 1 thru 12. In 1956 there were 29 teachers and 823 students in the school.

Geneva Bryant, Joe Louis Cooper, Arthur Frasier, Rutha Mae Gasque, Jefferson Grant, Dorothy L. Ladson, Gwendolyn McCants, Ethel L. Sanders, Thomasena Sanders, Carl Smith, Freddie Smith, Queen Smith, Franklin Stafford, and Rosa Lee Stafford were from Sampit and graduated in the Class of 1963.

Suziah Stafford, daughter of **Thomas** and **Bessie Bryant Stafford** being crowned Miss Queen of the football team by **Rosemary High School Cobra's Football Team Captain** with **Principal Joseph G. Thompson** looking on.
(Courtesy of the Lil Eff Affikan Cump'ny)

Demphis Wragg (29 June 1914-24 December 1961) from the Cumberland Section of Sampit provided bus services and transportation for students that attended Rosemary School in Andrews, SC. Before Demphis' bus services students from Sampit provided their own transportation "by any mean necessary" using personal cars, trucks or just "catching a ride from a stranger."

Demphis' bus services also provided transportation that took bus excursion to Atlanta Beach, North of Myrtle Beach once designated "for colored only" based on the racial and segregated laws in South Carolina.

For years Demphis was the owner of the **Demphis Wragg Logging Company**, a very lucrative business for many years.

He married **Sarah Holmes**, the daughter of *Samuel* and **Janie Holmes**. He was also a very active member of Cumberland African Methodist Episcopal Church, Sampit.

(Courtesy of Demphis Wragg)

Sarah Holmes Wragg (April 5, 1916 – November 6, 2007) was the daughter of **Samuel Holmes** and **Ida Knowlin Holmes**. She was married to **Demphis Wragg**. Their children were: **Alfrenita, Geraldine, Valerie, Samuel, John Demphis Jr., Javaughn Wragg**, and **Curtis Wragg**.

Sarah was active and devout member of the Cumberland African Methodist Episcopal Church and a homemaker.

(Courtesy of Demphis Wragg)

Bernida Washington Trappier of Sampit was employed with the Georgetown School District since December 1974 working in the old Rosemary and is now working as Senior Secretary at Rosemary Middle School. She is a graduated in the class of Rosemary High School. She is a member of St. Paul African Methodist Episcopal Church, Sampit. Bernida serves on the Steward Board, Stewardess Board, Senior Choir, and Planning Committee (planning committee is responsible for the church calendar). She was a former member of the Usher Board where my Mom served as Director. She also is a very active member of the Sampit Community Crime Watch Group Church.
(Courtesy of the Lil Eff Affikan Cump'ny)

This distinguished educational scholar and top Principal is Sampson Hughes from Andrews, South Carolina. He served as Principal of Rosemary Elementary School, Andrews, SC.
(Courtesy of the Lil Eff Affikan Cump'ny)

Huey Bryant and **Gwendolyn Stafford** from Sampit are standing with **The National Honor Society** at Rosemary High School. **(Courtesy of Huey B. Bryant)**

The **Georgetown Times** printed this news article "Rosemary High Names Valedictorian" in their edition on Thursday, May 29, 1969, Section C.

The news article stated that **Rachel Snipes**, daughter of **Mr.** and **Mrs. Acy William Snipes** of Andrews, has achieved the honor of valediction of the Class of 1969 at Rosemary School. **Oliver L. Reown**, eldest son of **Mr. & Mrs. Luther N. Reown** of the Sampit Section is salutatorian of the class. **(Courtesy of Huey B. Bryant)**

At right are **Huey Bryant** (Vice President) and other members of The National Honor Society. **(Courtesy of the Lil Eff Affikan Cump'ny)**

On Saturday, 1 July 2006, the Rosemary "Cobra" Alumni held it first banquet in the old Rosemary Gymnasium. The old school now is the property of the Jerusalem Center. The theme: "Rosemary Alumni Loyal Forever". The keynote speaker was **Alumni Joseph Abraham (Abe) Bryant**, son of the Joe and **Hester Drayton Bryant**, Sampit who graduated from Rosemary High School in 1962. **Mary Bryant Tucker**, his sister introduced her brother. Joseph, nicknamed Abe electrified the audience about of 275 with his great wits and sense of humor. In his speech, he recalled many humorous stories of **Principal Joe Thompson**, the teachers, students and school activities. The **Reverend Thomas "Earl" Drayton**, Uncle of Joseph and a member of Georgetown Country Councilman served as **Toast Master**. Other Alumni that participated on the program were: **Elaine Thompson** and **Emma "Monk" Ravennel Drayton** (President). Abe is a member of St. Paul A.M.E. Church, Sampit where he served on the Trustee Board. After graduating from Rosemary High School, he attended Allen University, Columbia, South Carolina and received a BA in Math in 1966. In 1972 he received his Masters Degree from the Citadel in Charleston, SC.

Following graduating from **Allen University**, he was employed with the Georgetown School District working at Howard High School, Georgetown (1966-1970), Winyah High School (1970-1977), Georgetown District Math Coordinator (1977-1980), Brown Ferry Middle School Principal (1980- 1990), Rosemary Middle School Principal (1990-1995) and retired in 1995. He retired on Tuesday, 30 May 1995 after 30 years of dedicated service to Georgetown County Education School system. After retirement, he moved to Brunswick, Georgia and was employed as a Math Teacher with the Glen County (1996). In 1996-1999 he served as Principal at Risley Middle School in Brunswick. In 1999 he became the Director of Transportation for the School District in McIntosh and held that position until 2006, where he retired the second time. He held membership in the Omega Psi Phi Fraternity, 14 Black Men Association, NAACP, Association of Middle School Principals, and Trustee of St. Paul A.M.E. Church, Sampit.

"We've all learned some many lessons from "Mr. Bryant that'll stay with all of us for a lifetime." **(Courtesy of the Lil Eff Affikan Cump'ny)**

This lovely and gracious couple is **Joe Luther Bryant, Sr.** (September 28, 1921 – July 6, 1982) and Hester Drayton Bryant (July 14, 1925 – June 6, 2004). Joe is the son of **Robert** and **Lula Smith Bryant** of Sampit. Joe was a **Private First Class** in the United States Army and served in World War II. He was employed at the **International Paper Company,** Georgetown for thirty-nine years. **Hester Drayton Bryant**, his wife was the daughter of **Reverend Henry Samuel** and **Sarah Williams Drayton** of North Santee, S.C. **Mrs. Hester**, as she was fondly called, graduated from Mt. Zion School, North Santee. For years **Mrs. Hester** drove school bus for the Sampit Elementary School and later retired from the Department of Social as a homemaker after 19 years. After her retirement, **Hester** worked with the Sampit Senior Citizen Center in Sampit. **Joseph (Abe), Sara Bell, Joe Jr., Betty, Mary, Pattie, Esther (Ricky), Robert** (Bobby) and **Samuel (Sammy)** are their children. **(Courtesy of the Lil Eff Affikan Cump'ny)**

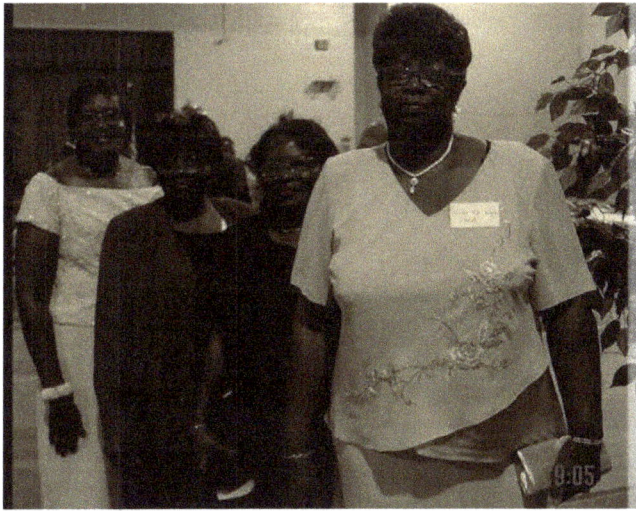

Here is **Mary Gasque, Magdelene Knowlin, Elizabeth Knowlin** and **Sarah Wilson** all dressed up at the first **Rosemary Alumni Banquet** at old **Rosemary Gymnasium**, Andrews, S.C. on July 1, 2006. **(Courtesy of the Lil Eff Affikan Cump'ny)**

Here is **Ellis Calvin Means Jr**. (April 16, 1927 – June 15, 2007) and wife **Arnetha Smith Means** holding hands singing the **Rosemary Alma Mater** at the first Alumni banquet held in the old Rosemary Gymnasium on Saturday, 1 July 2006. Student **Dorothy Burgess Thompson Mack** wrote the Alma Mater for the Rosemary High School. The old school now is the property of the **Jerusalem Missionary Baptist Association**.
(Courtesy of the Lil Eff Affikan Cump'ny)

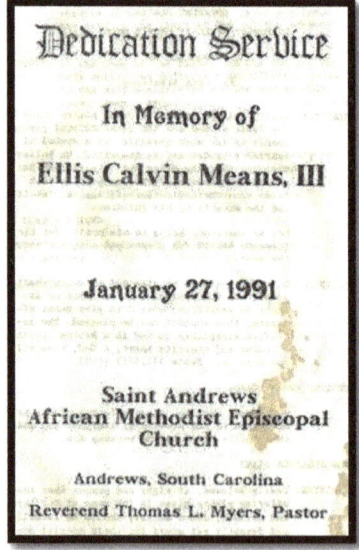

On May 5, 1995, **Jessie Robinson and his wife, Rosa L. Robinson** attended the retirement service of **Joseph A. Bryant** held at the Rosemary Middle School, Andrews, S.C. (At L) **(Courtesy of the Lil Eff Affikan Cump'ny)**

On Sunday, January 27, 1991, a **Dedication Service** (at right) was held In Memory of **Ellis Calvin Means III** at Saint Andrews African Methodist Episcopal Church, Andrews, S.C. where **Reverend Thomas L. Myers** served as Senior Pastor.
(Courtesy of the Lil Eff Affikan Cump'ny)

Teacher Rosa Lee Pressley Robinson was born February 22, 1925 in Nesmith, South Carolina to the parenthood of the **Samuel Pressley** and **Cloria McKnight Pressley**. Other siblings were **Mary, Natine, Alberta, Louise** and **Onetha Pressley**.

She was educated in the public schools of Williamsburg County, graduated from Brown Junior High School, Nesmith, South Carolina and Morris Senior High School, Sumter, South Carolina. She graduated from South Carolina State College (now South Carolina State University), Orangeburg, South Carolina with a Bachelor of Science degree in Education.

On September 21, 1946 in Andrews, South Carolina she was united in Holy Matrimony to **Jessie Robinson, Jr**. called **"Cuz' Junior."** The **Reverend Chappelle McClary**, Senior Pastor at St. Andrews African Methodist Episcopal Church, Andrews, SC performed the marriage at the church parsonage. **(Courtesy of the Lil Eff Affikan Cump'ny)**

A view of the Fourth Grade Class of **Teacher Emma Brewington Stafford** from Sampit. It is said by all students that the teachers at **Rosemary** were considered to have the best minds that the nation offered to any school. They were talented, well-educated, well dressed, professional, tough and came from the best colleges throughout the United States to teach at Rosemary. Not only did they teach us, they served as role models, community leaders, political leaders, church ministers, church officers, and entrepreneurs.
(Courtesy of the Lil Eff Affikan Cump'ny)

Mrs. Essie G. Britton
A.B. - Claflin College
M.A. - S. C. State
College - English

Essie Mae Graham Britton (January 22, 1921 - October 24, 2001) was a success who lived well, laughed often and loved much…who gained the love of children and the respect others; who left the world better that she found it whether by an improved bloom, or a rescued soul; who never lacked the appreciation of earth's beauty or failed express it; who looked for the best in others and gave her best. Essie was such a person. She was the daughter of **James** and **Martha Graham.** The thirty-seven-year marriage to **Torrence Eugene Britton, Sr**. was blessed with two children, **Karen** and **Torrence, Jr. (Tony)**. As a graduate of the Andrews area schools, she received her Bachelor of Arts degree from Claflin University and her Master of Education degree from South Carolina State University, Orangeburg, SC.

Her family and St. Andrews A.M.E. Church in Andrews, SC, nurtured her spiritual life. She served faithfully as a member of the Senior Choir, Missionary Society, Willing Workers Club, a Class Leader, and Young's Peoples Department (YPD) Director. She also held membership in numerous professional and civil organizations including Georgetown Alumnae Chapter of Delta Sigma Theta Sorority Inc., Leggette-Whittaker Order of the Eastern Star, and the Home Charity Lodge.

Some of the principals and teachers I recalled as a student: Joseph G. Thompson, Sr., Principal, Sampson D. Cooper, Assistant Principal, A.B. Dozier, Essie Britton, Margaret Hughes, Sampson A. Hughes, Etta Thompson, Acy Wm. Snipes, Carl B. Hughes, Ellis C. Means, Gilmore McManus, Naomi M. Dozier, David L. Odom, Emma B. Stafford (Sampit), Alvina B. McKnight, Arneitha S. Means, Ethel G. Smalls (Sampit), David E. Sessions, Rosa L. Robinson, Diana E. Adamson, Louise H. Kinloch, Mamie A. Tindal, Mary Hughes, Geraldine M. Bessellieu, Trudie Britton and Doris Greene (Sampit). **(Courtesy of Karen Britton)**

This cute, charming, and smiling little schoolgirl is **Karen Britton,** the beautiful daughter of **Torrence Eugene Britton, Sr.** and **Essie Mae Graham Britton.**
(Courtesy of Karen Britton)

At right is Karen with that tenuous smile standing on the outside of Allen Temple AME Church, Greenville, SC. **(Courtesy of Karen Britton)**

At left is **Torrence Eugene Britton, Jr.**, the son of **Torrence Eugene Britton, Sr.** and **Essie Mae Graham Britton** and brother of **Karen Britton.**
(Courtesy of Karen Britton)

Randolph Stafford, the son of **Thomas and Bessie Bryant Stafford** received this certificate of promotion after satisfactorily completed the Course of Study prescribed for the Rosemary Elementary School and is therefor entitled to this testimonial and to admission to the Rosemary High School given at Rosemary school on 2nd day of June 1954. Teacher was **L. H. Kinloch** and **Joseph G. Thompson** was Principal.
(Courtesy of the Lil Eff Affikan Cump'ny)

The **Rosemary High School Graduation Class of 1964** – at center is Principal Joe Thompson. **(Courtesy of the Lil Eff Affikan Cump'ny)**

Ida Evans Frasier, 8th grade mathematic teacher at Rosemary Middle School, has been teaching for thirty-three years! She was nominated for the Golden Apple Award by a niece who said lots of nice things about her aunt. Tracy Amick for Live Five News was there to present the award and to capture the surprised teacher's reaction as **Michael Caviris**; Principal of RMS presented Mrs. Frasier with a bouquet of red roses. Ida Evans Frasier is the daughter of **Reverend & Mrs. Joe Evans,** Pennyroyal Road. She is a member of St. Michael African Methodist Episcopal Church. **(Courtesy of the Georgetown Times)**

These seniors - **Gertrude Davis (left)** and **Leroy Bryant (right)** are from the Rosemary High School's graduation class of 1968. **(Courtesy of the Lil Eff Affikan Cump'ny)**

The Rosemary High School Class of 1970 were photgraphed in this "unforgettable moment" at their **40th Year Class Reunion** at **Quality Inn Motel, Georgetown SC.** Among those attended were Shirley Cumbee, Alvin Nelson, Rebecca Washington, Johnny Cokley, Brenda Prince, Margeret Green Wineglass, Tryphena Rhue, Martha Scott, Suzanna Pushia, Gwen Stafford, Sheryal Hayes, Mary Smith, Anne Grant, Shirley Frasier, Theresa Humes, Danny Nixon, Wannetta Wragg, Betty Ervin, William Ervin, Martha Graham, and Huey Bryant. **(Courtesy of Huey Bryant)**

The **Rosemary Alumni Annual Holiday Banquet** was held on December 20, 2014 at the Old Rosemary Gymnasium, Andrews SC. **(Courtesy of Huey Bryant)**

Long life is in her right hand; in her left hand are riches and honor. Her was the ways of pleasantness, and all her paths are peace. She is a tress of life to those who lay hold of her; those who hold her fast are called blessed. Proverbs 3: 16 – 18)

Long life is the ensuring epitaph of our dearly beloved, mother, grandmother, sister, and matriach, **Ada Edith Brown Cokley**. Mother Cokley was born to the John Brown and Mary Flowers Heward on December 12, 1903. In the same peaceful and pleasant way in which she lived, "Ping" (as she was known to her family), departed this life on Tuesday, June 14, 2005 at 2:50 PM in the Georgetown County Memorial Hospital, Georgetown at the wonderful age of one hundred and one (101) and a half years old.

Grew up in the Rhems Section of Williamsburg Country, she was only able to complete the seventh grade but was indeed the source of wisdom, intellect, and dignity, which proved to be a tremendous gift and blessing as she was still in her right mind at her passing. Just one year ago, she was still reciting her favorite poem that she learned in the second grade.

Mother Cokley accepted Christ as an early age and united with Weldon Hill Baptist Church where she remained active until her health failed. At that time, she was serving at the Mother of the Church. In spirite of going blind in her fifies, she remained independent, not wanting to be a burden on anyone she trusted in the Lord and continued to live in His presence daily.

She met and married **Henry Cokely Sr**. in March 1925 and to their union six children were born. **Henry Sr., Frank, Richard, Ann, Janie** and **Vera**.

Celebrating the Life and the Homegoing of the late **Mother Ada Edith Brown Cokley** was held at Weldon Hill Missionary Baptist Church, Reverend Thomas S. Lance, Pastor on Friday, June 17, 2005 at 1:00 PM. The **Reverend (Dr.) James H. Cokely,** grandson and Pastor of Cherry Hill Missionary Baptist Church, Conway, SC preached the eulogy.
(Courtesy of Vera Rowell)

Vera Cokley grew up in Andrews, South Carolina and lived with her grandmother, **Ada Edith Brown Cokley**. She attended Rosemary High School and later moved to New York.

She received her undergraduate degree in Business Administration from Lehman College in New York City and Master Degree in Teaching Students with Disabilities - Educable Mentally Disable (classified as Intellectual Disabled) from Francis Marion University, Marion, South Carolina.

Vera has worked at Marion High School, Marion, SC for the past seventeen years as a special education teacher and Math Teacher since 1998. She hold membership at the Pleasant Grove Missionary Baptist Church, Marion, SC.
(Courtesy of Vera Cokley)

The Reverend (Dr.) James H. Cokley, native of Andrews, South Carolina, graduated Valedictorian of his high school, and received scholarships from the James F. Byrnes Foundation, Alpha Phi Alpha, Fraternity, Inc., and the Vocational Rehabilitation.

While a student in high school, he accepted Christ and was baptized at the Piney Grove Missionary Baptist Church, Andrews, South Carolina and became the first black Eagle Scout of Georgetown County and the first black member of the Order of the Arrow, a program for honor scouts.

After high school, **Dr. Cokley** was a student matriculating at the University of South Carolina majoring in Biology-Pre-Medicine when he accepted the call to the ministry and became a Preacher in Learning at the Zion Baptist Church in Columbia, SC. While a student at the University of South Carolina as a Stay-in-School employee gaining expertise in rural housing, rural rental housing and business and industry with the Farmer's Home Administration.

In August 1982, he received the Bachelor of Science degree in Natural Science from the University of South Carolina just four months after receiving the call to serve as Pastor of the Pleasant Hill Baptist Church of Saluda. He served the Pleasant Hill Baptist Church faithfully for three and a half years while teaching Earth and Physical Science, Biology, and Chemistry in the middle and high schools of Lexington County School District II.

In December 1985, he accepted the call to the Mount Zion Missionary Baptist Church of Laurens where he pastored for the twelve years and three months leading the church in Christian Education, discipleship, and community development. While at Mount Zion, Reverend Cokley attended Erskine Theological Seminary, Due West and received the Master of Divinity Degree in Theology and a Doctor of Ministry in Parish Revitalization from McCormick Theological Seminary in Chicago, Illinois. He has done further studies at Preaching Symposiums at Princeton Theological Seminary and Regent's Park College of Oxford University, Oxford, England.

On April 1, 1998, **Pastor Cokley** took the reins of the **Cherry Hill Missionary Baptist Church,** Conway, SC where he has led them to do transforming work for the Lord where the church has grown spiritually, physically, fiscally, numerically, and emotionally. The church's net worth has risen from just short of one million to over four million dollars and are in the midst of a three-phase building program, which will cost $6 million.

In addition to his work as a Pastor, Dr. Cokley was appointed in September 2014 to serve as the Vice-President at Large of the National Baptist Church Congress of Christian Education and now the President of the National Baptist Congress of Christian Education for the National Baptist Convention, USA, Inc. He served as President of the South Carolina Baptist Congress of Christian Education, Assistant Dean of the National Baptist Congress of Christian Education, Assistant Dean of the National Baptist Congress of Christian Education, National Baptist, USA, Inc. and now the President of the National Baptist Congress of Christian Education for the National Baptist Convention USA, Inc., which is the largest African-American religious organization in the world; life member of the NAACP, a member of Phi Beta Sigma Fraternity, Inc., Board of Counselors, Erskine Theological Seminary, and Board of Trustees, Morris College. He also serves as adjunct professor for Erskine Theological Seminary.

He has received numerous awards including the Key to the City of Conway, SC, Who's Who Among Christian Leaders in America, and Outstanding Young Preachers Award, American Academy of Ministry.

The Reverend James H. Cokley is married to the former **Cindy Graham** of Conway and they are the proud parents of three children, two daughters, **Jami Davina, Bakir Allyne** and one son, **D'Oscar Haynes**; and one foster daughter **Adrienne LaTres Sullivan**.

Reverend (Dr.) James H. Cokley, Guest Preacher at Zion Baptist Church, 801 Washington Street, Columbia, South Carolina Sons of Zion Sesquicentennial Revival, August 25, 2015. **(Courtesy of the Lil Eff Affikan Cump'ny)**

Reverend Cokley, his wife, **Cind**y, their son, **D'Oscar Hayes** and daughter in law, **Christie. (Courtesy of the Lil Eff Affikan Cump'ny)**

This building was first used as the **Mt. Zion African Methodist Episcopal Church School, North Santee,** opened in 1946, with grades 1 to 6. Nowadays it is used as the **North Santee Senior Citizen Center**, opened in 1989, closed for sixteen years and reopened in 2005. **(Courtesy of the Lil Eff Affikan Cump'ny)**

These smiling and amused **Senior Citizens** at the **North Santee Senior Citizen Center** are posting for a group photo on **November 12, 1999.** These **Senior Citizens** are **Barbara Brown, Lucille Bryant Drayton, Caroline V. Singleton, Florie White Reather** and **Gilliard (Sug/Sugg). (Courtesy of the Lil Eff Affikan Cump'ny)**

In 1954 the **Sampit Elementary School** was built on land ceded by **Ross Stafford** and **Troy Gasque** to be used for a public elementary school for predominately African American students. The School served students in grades one through six from Sampit and North Santee areas. It is said that at a Sampit townhouse meeting the community came together to discuss the name of the newly developed school. Long debates and heated discussions took place during the meeting, several school names were suggested, but the community voted to call it "**Sampit Elementary School.**" **(Courtesy of the Lil Eff Affikan Cump'ny)**

The first principal of Sampit Elementary School was **Thaddeus L. Thompson** (September 24, 1919 – July 28, 2009) from Andrews, South Carolina. He was one of the four sons born to the late **Torrence** and **Addie Thompson**. He served as principal of Sampit Elementary from 1954 -1957 and served as Principal of Beech Swamp School, Morrisvillle Section of Williamsburg County and Mt. Zion School, North Santee. In 1957 he became the supervisor of the rural schools of Georgetown County and in 1970 he was appointed as Assistant Superintendent for Administration and Personnel for Georgetown until his retirement. He was married **Leah Shepherd Thompson** in 1957.

The second principal of Sampit Elementary School was the **Reverend James Edmund Prioleau**. He was the son of the **Reverend Edmund Prioleau** and **Maria W. Prioleau**, was born November 27, 1906, in Georgetown County, and a second-generation preacher. He served as principal of Sampit Elementary from 1957 – 1966. He was a graduate of Howard High School, Georgetown, South Carolina State College, Orangeburg, South Carolina, Union Theological Seminary, and Allen University in Columbia.
(Courtesy of the Lil Eff Affikan Cump'ny)

Rebecca Vernette Williams Prioleau was born on July 27, 1933 on Weehaw Plantation in Georgetown, SC to the marital union of **Henry Zachariah Williams** and **Rosetta Dennison Williams**. Her loving parents, husband, infant grandchild Kamone, siblings Isaac (her twin), Ella, Thelma, Seaman, and an infant brother all preceded her in death.

Rebecca received her formal education from Georgetown County Public Schools, and later moved to Virginia where she graduated from James Solomon Russell High School.

"Beck, Becky, Sister, or **Titta"** as she was lovingly called, joined Bethel AME Church at an early age and was active in a number of organizations. She was a member of the Women's Missionary Society, the Excelsior and Chancel Choirs, and Stewardess Board #2. She was also the director of Bethel's Day Care. Rebecca was a member of Mt. Olive Chapter #81 Order of the Eastern Stars, where she served as Past Worthy Matron.

The span of her career included various capacities of housekeeping. Her last place of employment was Primary Medical Associates. Known there as **Miss Becky**, her kind, calming spirit and radiant smile allowed her to form loving relationships not only with her coworkers, but their families and the patients as well. She also formed loving relationships with members of her church and community, especially when she transported workers to Myrtle Beach. She lovingly spoke about how she let "other people's children pull at my heartstrings."

She was married to **Nathaniel Young**. This union was blessed with two children. She later married **Reverend James Edmund Prioleau**. Their union was blessed with three children.

Rebecca departed this life on Tuesday, October 20th at Tidelands Community Hospice House. Those left to remember her with undying love are her children: Jamee Johnson (Milton), Austell, GA, Sharon Young, Orange, NJ, Joseph Young (Valerie), Bronx, NY, Angela Prioleau, Della Prioleau, both of Georgetown, SC, and James Prioleau, II, Norfolk, VA; two sisters, Mary Brooks, Bloomfield, NJ and Irene Hollis Newark, NJ; three brothers, Henry Williams, Jr., Lexington, SC, Robert Williams, Irvington, NJ, and Herman Williams, Lexington, SC; two sisters-in-law, Virginia Williams, Newark, NJ and Mary Williams, Georgetown, SC; 11 grandchildren and their spouses, 13 great-grandchildren, many nieces (including her goddaughter, Sherlyn Ragin), nephews, cousins, her caregivers Mae Gasque and LaTrease Graham, adopted children, longtime neighbors/extended family (including The Scott family, Bobby Ruffin, Ishmael and Juanita Knowlin, The Brave family, Idella Bradford) and family friends. **(Courtesy of Della Prioleau)**

The third **Principal of Sampit Elementary School** was **Thomas J. Robinson,** born May 21, 1928, Georgetown, son of **Frasier Robinson** and **Rosella Cohen**. He served as principal of Sampit Elementary School from 1966 - 1990. He was a graduate of Howard High School and earned the Bachelor of Science and Masters of Arts Degrees at South Carolina State College, Orangeburg, South Carolina, and studied further at Auburn University, Auburn, Alabama. He subsequently served as principal of Sampit Elementary School for twenty-five years.

Maudest Rhue-Scott is the fourth principal at Sampit Elementary School. Under her principalship, a new Sampit Elementary School was built in the Woodland Section of Sampit. **Maudest Rhue-Scott,** currently the principal with the longest tenure in the district, has decided to retire effective June 30. Rhue-Scott is completing her 40th year as an educator and said that was the reason she chose now as the time for retirement. "Forty is a divine number," Rhue-Scott said, adding she knew two years ago this would be when she retired.

Sampit Elementary School

The new Sampit Elementary School was built in the Woodland Section of Sampit in 2000. The first principal was **Dr. Maudest Rhue-Scott**. It was dedicated on **April 9, 2000**. The Georgetown District Superintendent was **Dr. Charles "Chuck" Gadsen**. School Board Members: **George R. Geer, Board Chair, Barbra G. Allen, Charlesann H. Buttone, Benny K. Elliott, Darren L. Holmes, Jody Tamsberg, Harold Jean Brown, Jim Dumm, Ben Grate, John H. Spears** and **Wayne P. Tayo**r.
(Courtesy of the Lil Eff Affikan Cump'ny)

An "Unveiling Ceremony" of Sampit Elementary past Principals took place on Sunday, May 18, 1997, 5:00 P.M. at Sampit Elementary School. At this unique ceremony, community leaders, political leaders, ministers, and former students came together to honor the past three principals.

Thaddeus Thompson 1954 – 1957
James Prioleau 1957 – 1966
Thomas Robinson 1966 – 1990

The theme: De Yesterday's Leaders-Today's Inspiration-Tomorrow's Legacy.
Mistress of Ceremonies/Mrs. Barbara Huell
Welcome/Occasion/Mrs. Erica Rembert
Recognition of Honored Guest/Mrs. Eunice Brown
Greetings/Mr. David Britton/Mrs. Theresa Humes/Attorney Johnny Morant/Mrs. Charlesann Buttone **Introduction of Speaker**/Rev. Wallace J. McKnight
Selection/Young Adult Choir (Sampit)
Speaker/Rev. Thomas Myers/Pastor of St. Andrews A.M.E. Church
The Sampit Elementary School was located at 2482 Powell Road.

The **Prioleau** from Georgetown: **Della, James II, Angela, Crystal, Kevin Greene, James Green**, and **Rebecca Prioleau**. (Courtesy of Della Prioleau)

The fifth Principle of Sampit Elementary School is **Dr. Sabrina Goff-Mack**. She was an assistant principal at Andrews Elementary School, has been named as new principal of the school to take over the position held by **Maudest Rhue-Scott** since 1990. The four finalists for the job were: Latanya Goodson, assistant principal, Georgetown Middle School, Lee Glover, assistant principal, Carvers Bay Middle School, Paula Anderson, curriculum coach, Sampit Elementary and Sabrina Goff-Mack, assistant principal, Andrews Elementary School. **Dr. Goff-Mack** takes over the school principalship on July 1 2012.
(Courtesy of the Lil Eff Affikan Cump'ny)

The **Sampit Elementary School 4th Grade Class -** standing with their Teacher, **Tajuanda Singletary**. Some of the students were Michelle White, LaKisha Joy, Wayne Grant, Tatt Sajak, Tonney Sanders, Jasper McCray, Vashawn, Chillwill Robinson, Lisa Pugh, Samantha W. Point, Maxine Livingston, Jen Grant, Ra' Grant, Gerald White, Corey R., Jefferson Grant, Jr., and Anitra Washington.
(Courtesy of Jefferson Grant, Jr.)

The **Sampit Elementary School 5 Year Old Kindergarten Class** of 1987 – 1988 stood with their Teacher, **Mrs. Scott** and Teacher's Aide, **Barbara Bryant** for their formal class picture. **(Courtesy of the Lil Eff Affikan Cump'ny)**

This formal class picture of 1991 – 1992 is the **Sampit Elementary School Grade K – Mrs. Gibson, Teacher. (Courtesy of the Lil Eff Affikan Cump'ny)**

This blurry image shows the annual **May Day** Spring festival at **Sampit Elementary School.** Dancing around and wrapping the may pole by the girls was the most celebrated and illustrious events at the festival which took place in early May. **(Courtesy of the Lil Eff Affikan Cump'ny)**

Family members enjoying **The Fun Day** celebration with their children at **Sampit Elementary School. (Courtesy of the Lil Eff Affikan Cump'ny)**

This historical room is **"The Waiting Area at Sampit Elementary School"**
(Courtesy of the Lil Eff Affikan Cump'ny)

Here is **Felitcha Cumbee Pinckney,** the Office Secretary at Sampit Elementary School. She charms visitors to the school with her big smile, great sense humor, nature beauty and professional demeanor. **Courtesy of the Lil Eff Affikan Cump'ny)**

The "Welcome to Sampit Elementary School – Together we make our
Welcome to **SAMPIT ELEMENTARY SCHOOL** – Together we make our school a success is the motto or saying that Sampit Elementary teachers and students lives by! **(Courtesy of the Lil Eff Affikan Cump'ny)**

In this featured picture are Sampit Elementary School Library Medical Center Staff, Mary Brown, Elizabeth Moss, Debra Harrison and Principal Dr. Sabrina Goff-Mack.
(Courtesy of the Lil Eff Affikan Cump'ny)

Teddy Wilson is the fourth of ten children born to **Edward** and **Hessie Armstrong Wilson.** He was born and reared in the Sampit Community of Georgetown, SC.

Teddy graduated from Andrews High School, 1978. He attended Voorhees College, graduating with a BS in Elementary Education, 1982. He earned a Master Degree from Columbia College, Columbia SC.

He has been an employee of The Georgetown County School District at Sampit Elementary School since 1984. He currently teaches Fifth grade and has been teaching this grade level for the majority of his career. His colleagues chose him as Sampit Elementary School's Teacher of the Year for the 1995-1996 and 2016-2017 school years.

In 2010, Teddy accepted his divine calling to preach the gospel and was ordained as an Itinerant Deacon in the African Methodist (AME) Church by Bishop Richard F. Norris, Bishop of the Seventh Episcopal District on August 17, 2013.

Reverend Wilson is a member of St. Paul AME Church under the current leadership of Rev. Kelly Spann II. He is married to the former **Althea Conelly** Wilson of Denmark SC. They are blessed with a son, **Kareem**, who is currently a rising junior at Winthrop University, Rock Hill, SC.

Reverend Teddy Wilson is a lifetime member of the Alpha Phi Alpha Fraternity, Inc., a member of the Sampit Watch Group, Southern Georgetown Leadership, and St. Paul Men Fellowship Organizer.

Reverend Teddy's favorite scripture: "Trust in the Lord with all your heart and do not lean on your own understanding. In all your ways acknowledge Him and He will make straight your paths." Proverbs 3:5-6.

In this school picture is **Dr. Sabrina Goff-Mack** (Principal at Sampit Elementary School) and **Teddy Wilson -** (Fifth Grade Teacher) – Taught over 31 years at Sampit Elementary School
Teddy Wilson – Teacher of the Year 2016 – 2017, 5th Grade Teacher.
(Courtesy of the Lil Eff Affikan Cump'ny)

The Ladies of **Sampit Elementary School Place** are **Kathleen Elmore, Janet Herman, Sydney Rice, Jestine Coffield** and **Dr. Sabrina Golf-Mack, Principal.**

Sampit Elementary School received these prestigious awards – **The Palmetto Gold & Sliver Awards Program – Silver School** (2001-2002). The **Palmetto Gold and Silver Awards Program** (2002 – 2003).

(Courtesy of the Lil Eff Affikan Cump'ny)

This professionally done oil painting portrait is **Staff Sergeant Leroy McDonald** taken while deployed to Camp Navistar, Iraq in support of Operation Iraqi Freedom. At right all dressed up for a loving evening out are **Leroy McDonald** and his beautiful wife, **Veronica Scott McDonald** preparing for evening of elegance. **(Courtesy of Leroy McDonald)**

The Scott Family of Georgetown: Mrs. Evelyn, Veronica, Laurietta, Benjamin, and Leroy Scott. Mrs. Scott taught at Sampit Elementary for many years.
(Courtesy of the Leroy McDonald)

Reverend Alphonso N. Scott, the 14th Pastor of Bethesda Missionary Baptist Church is the son of **Evelyn G. Scott** and **Benjamin Scott** of Georgetown, SC. After graduating from Elementary School (St. Cyprians - St. Mary) he attended and graduated from Winyah High School. He earned a Bachelor of Science Degree from Benedict College (Columbia, SC), majoring in Marketing and Economics.

While a student at Benedict College, he served as a member of Gordon - Jenkins Pre-Theological Association, President of the Benedict College Concert Choir and recipient of the Leadership Award. During the presidency of Dr. Henry Ponder, he was selected to serve as "President for a Day" and invited to dine with the late **Dr. Benjamin E. Mays**.

Pastor Scott also earned a Master of Divinity Degree from Morehouse School of Religion, the Interdenominational Theological Center in Atlanta, GA. He is listed in the 1986 edition of Outstanding Young Men of America and Who's Who Among America's Professionals. He is also a lifetime member of Alpha Phi Omega Fraternity, Inc.

Pastor Scott accepted the call to preach at a very early age. He was licensed to preach from

his home church, Bethesda on May 21, 1978 (Trial Sermon: "What's So Special about Jesus?") The Jerusalem Baptist Association later ordained him on February 10, 1985. Before accepting the call to pastor Bethesda, Reverend Scott served as Religious Program Director for the Butler Street YMCA, Atlanta, Georgia and Assistant to the Pastor of Zion Grove Baptist Church, Atlanta, GA. where The Reverend H. D. Freeman is Pastor.

Pastor Scott is a Gospel preacher, teacher and revivalist, having preached throughout South Carolina. Pastor Scott has also preached in the States of Texas, New Jersey, Kentucky, Tennessee, and Georgia. He has also preached on the national level in settings of the National Baptist Convention of America.

Pastor Scott has served in positions on both the national and local levels. He previously served as a member of the Publishing Board of the National Baptist Convention of America, Inc. and writer for the Brotherhood Manual and Young Adult/ Sunday School literature. He has served as an Associate Dean for the National Baptist Convention of America, Inc., Congress of Christian Education, Dean of the Georgetown Baptist Educational Union #1 and State Congress Regional Director for the South Carolina Baptist Educational and Missionary Convention. As a member of the Ministerial Alliance, Pastor Scott served as a Volunteer Chaplain at the Georgetown Memorial Hospital. Currently, **Pastor Scott** serves as Chairman of the Executive Board of the Jerusalem Missionary Baptist and Educational Association and continues to write Sunday School literature. **(Courtesy of the Lil Eff Affikan Cump'ny)**

Former educator, **Claudia Sherald Wright**, 87, of Georgetown, died on August 24, 2016 at her residence. Funeral services were held on August 30, 2016 at Bethel A.M.E. Church conducted by Worship Leader, Rev. Dr. Betty Deas Clarke.

Mrs. Wright was born on September 3, 1928 in Georgetown, SC, the first of three children of brother, John L. "Sonny" Sherald, Jr., all preceded her in death. She graduated from Howard High School in 1946 and attended South Carolina State College, Orangeburg, SC, where, in 1950, she earned a Bachelor of Science Degree in elementary education. During her time in college, she was initiated into the Beta Sigma Chapter of Alpha Kappa Alpha in 1949. In the 1960's she was a charter member of the Eta Pi Omega Chapter in El Paso, Texas. In 1979 she also became a charter member of the Georgetown County graduate chapter, Mu Phi Omega. A golden soror, and a life member of the sorority, she served as first Philacter, first Historian, and Anti Grammaticus.

Mrs. Wright abided in holy matrimony with George Wright, from June 20, 1950 until his death on April 7, 2012. Together they shared life, love, and the rearing of three beloved children. A granddaughter, Nicole, is deceased.

She began her teaching career at Pee Dee Elementary School in 1950 as a joint first and second grade teacher. She also taught at Dunbar Elementary and Parkersville Elementary Schools for four years. In 1956 she left the School District of Georgetown County to travel with her husband, a military officer, to Europe and on other national and international tours of duty. Having returned, in 1962 she continued her teaching career at Sampit Elementary School. In 1979 she was honored as Teacher of the Year and was among the core of teachers who brought Head Start to Georgetown. After retiring in 1988, she worked in tutorial programs in the community, and was a member and volunteer of several associations including: the National Education Association, Georgetown County Education Association, the National Association for Advancement of Colored People, the Aids Task Force of The American Legion Auxiliary, Friends of the Library, and voter registration.

Mrs. Wright joined Bethel African Methodist Episcopal Church at the age of twelve and has served in numerous areas: Junior Steward Board Secretary, the Senior Missionary Society, the Layman's Organization, Orilla Rice Missionary Society Treasurer, Vacation bible school teacher, Senior Missionary Society historian, and Usher Board No. 7.

Survivors include her children, Linda Wright Lindsey, Georgetown, SC, LCDR George Ronald Wright, Columbia, SC, and David P. Wright, Charleston, SC; one great-grandson, Nicholas George Titus Wright, Columbia, SC; her sisters, Joan Ford and Willie Lou Humes, an uncle who was reared as a brother, Leroy S. Buttone, and sister-in-law, Vera Sherald, all of Georgetown, SC. Funeral services entrusted to Wilds Funeral Home, LLC.

(Courtesy of George Wright)

These graduating seminarians of the class of 1983 are standing in front of the Interdenominational Theological Center (ITC) Atlanta, Georgia on graduation day - **Reverend Effson Chester Bryant, Reverend Dietra C. Bell, Rev. Alphonso N. Scott and Elder Jeff Mitchell.** (Left to right) **(Courtesy of the Lil Eff Affikan Cump'ny)**

From left to right are **Reverend Effson Chester Bryant, Reverend Dietra C. Bell, Reverend Alphonso N. Scott** and **Elder Jeffery Mitchell** photographed together standing in the front of the sign at **The Interdenominational Theological Center** after graduation. Morris Brown College Chapel's (AME Church College) steeple is in the far background.

(Courtesy of the Lil Eff Affikan Cump'ny)

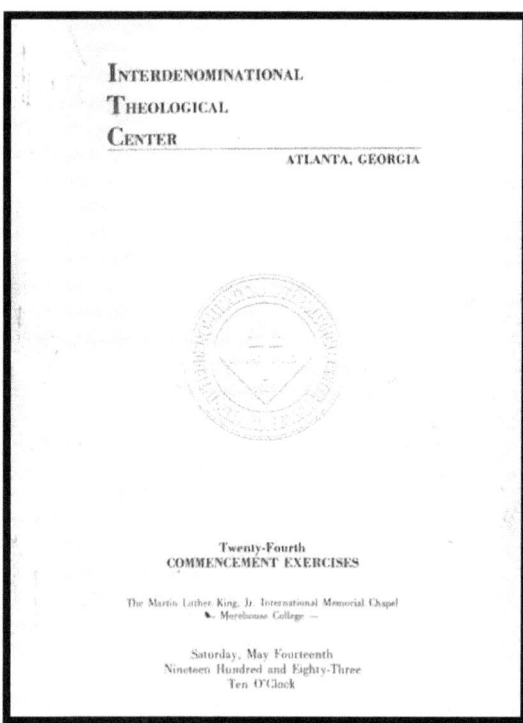

The Interdenominational Theological Center
Twenty-Fourth
Commencement Exercises

The Martin Luther King, Jr. International Memorial Chapel
Morehouse College

Saturday, May Fourteenth
Nineteen Hundred and Eight-Three
Ten O'clock
(Courtesy of the Lil Eff Affikan Cump'ny)

De (The) Doctor's Office   **274 - 283**

De (The) St. James – Santee Family Health Center
De (The) Opening of the North Santee – Sampit Health Center
De (The) Pediatric Waiting Room - In Memory of Mr. Thomas J. Robinson
De (The) First Lady Michelle Obama
De (The) Senator Barack Obama
De (The) 44th President of the United States of America - President Barack Obama –
De (The) Congressman James E. Clyburn

The St. James-Santee Family Health Center - North Santee-Sampit Health Center was built on March 4 1991 at 4145 Powell Road, Sampit. The Center was part of the St. James-Santee Family Health Center, 1189 Tibwin, McClellanville, South Carolina. The first building that housed the Health Center was a large doubled wide trailer. The sign reads: St. James-Santee Family Health Center-North Santee-Sampit Site; 401 Powell Road, Georgetown, South Carolina. This is a federally supported Community Health Center/School-Based Health Center, providing physicals, health education, counseling, and laboratory services. They treat adults and children including EPSDT (Early and Periodic Screening, Diagnoses and Treatment Program) for Medicaid eligible children, and immunizations. All Community Health Centers accept Medicaid, Medi-care and most private insurances and offer a sliding fee discount program for eligible low-income families. Health centers provide health care regardless of your ability to pay and even if you have not health insurance and people who need information about those services should phone the health center for more information or to make an appointment.

On March 4, 1991, the **North Santee-Sampit Health Center** hired it first two employees, **Dr. Henry Bowen,** North Santee and Register Nurse, (RN) **Mildred Hardee,** Lambertown.

(Courtesy of the Lil Eff Affikan Cump'ny)

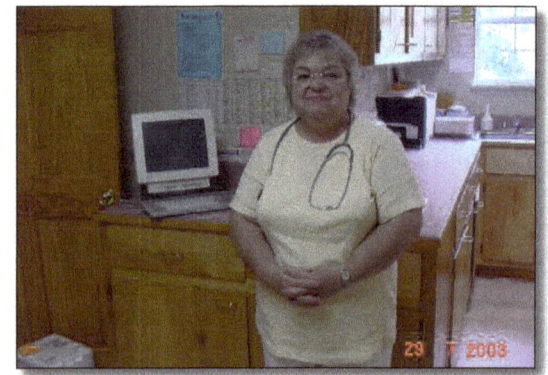

Here standing in file room is **Nurse Betty Collins** from North Santee. Medical records shows that **Marva Tompkins Elmore**, the daughter **Samuel** and **Ester Mae Tompkins** was the first recorded patient to be treated at the Medical Center. **Dianna Deas-Footman**, at right takes on the distinction of being the employee with the longest employee work history at the Center. She became an employee in 1998, seven years after the center opened. **Mary Gasque Trappier** has provided transportation for patients to and from the Center since 2000. Healthcare is now more accessible for residents of southern Georgetown County. **(Courtesy of the Lil Eff Affikan Cump'ny)**

The second doctor that worked at **The St. James-Santee Family Health Center** - North Santee-Sampit Health Center was **Dr. Wile Denwordy**. Other employees of the Center were **Mary Gasque, Smith, Nurse Betty Collins, North Santee, Cherily/ Medical Assistant, Dianna Deas Footman-Officer Manager, Dr. Joan Taylor, North Kingston, North Carolina,** and **Dr. Peterson** from Charleston, South Carolina. Photographed above is Mary Gasque aka "Mae Mae" in her work attire standing beside the Center transportation van where she is the proficient driver.
(Courtesy of the Lil Eff Affikan Cump'ny)

The Grand Opening and Ribbon Cutting Event of the branch of the **St. James-Santee Family Health Center, Inc., North Santee-Sampit Site** (Former Old Sampit Elementary School) took place at a ceremony on Friday, June 10, 2011. The guest speaker for the grand opening was **Congressman James E. Clyburn** who encouraged residents to use the facility "so we can keep people healthy." **Clyburn** also said he wanted to address concerns expressed by some that the facility was too expensive. "I don't know what dollar value you put on life. I don't want a dollar value placed on mine," he said. For the past two decades, the facility has operated out of a much smaller building on Powell Road.
(Courtesy of the Lil Eff Affikan Cump'ny)

A portion of the former **Sampit Elementary School** was renovated with a $436,000 grant from the American Recovery and Reinvestment Act (ARRA) Capital Improvement Funds. The 9,000-square foot facility includes 10 exam rooms, a large lab, comfortable waiting rooms, a conference room/patient education classroom, office space, and space for a future pharmacy. In the picture above is Congressman James Clyburn and others "cutting the ribbon" to the medical center. **(Courtesy of South Carolina Historical Society)**

The Grand Opening & Ribbon Cutting Event

St. James-Santee Family Health Center, Inc.

North Santee-Sampit Site
(Former Old Sampit Elementary School)

2482 Powell Road
Georgetown, SC 29440

Friday, June 10, 2011

Merging the Past into the Present and Beyond
Old Sampit School property donated to Georgetown Country School District by local resident, the late Ross Stafford and Troy Gasque.

The Old Sampit Elementary School opened in 1954, then closed and moved to a brand new facility in 2000.

Past Principals of the Old Sampit Elementary School
Mr. Thaddeus Thompson (1954-1957)
Mr. James Prioleau (1957-1966)
Mr. Thomas Robinson (1966-1990)
Dr. Maudest Rhue- Scott (1990-2000)

Dr. Scott continues to serve as the principal of the new Sampit Elementary School and is beginning her 22nd year. Under her leadership, the school received the National Blue Ribbon award of distinction.

Present: St. James-Sampit Family Health Center, Inc. North Santee-Sampit Site

Roberta H. Pinckney, CEO   Sandra D. Gilliard, CEO-elect

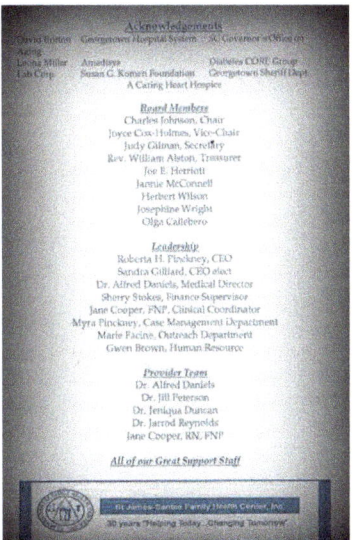

Acknowledgements
David Britton   Georgetown Hospital System
Leona Miller   SC Governor's Office on Aging
Amedisys   Diabetes CORE Group
Lab Corp   Georgetown Sheriff Department
                             Susan K. Komen Foundation
                             A Caring Heart Hospice

Board Members
Charles Johnson, Chair   Joyce Cox-Holmes, Vice-Chair
Judy Gilman, Secretary   Rev. William Alston, Treasurer
Joe E. Herriott   Jannie McConnell
Herbert Wilson   Joseph Wright
Olga Callebero

Leadership
Roberta H. Pinckney, CEO
Sandra Gilliard, CEO-elect
Dr. Alfred Daniels, Medical Director
Sherry Stokes, Finance Supervisor
Jane Cooper, FNP, Clinical Coordinator
Myra Pinckney, Case Management Department
Marie Facine, Outreach Department
Gwen Brown, Human Resource

Provider Team
Dr. Alfred Daniel   Dr. Jill Peterson   Dr. Jeniqua Duncan
Dr. Jerrod Reynolds   Jane Cooper, RN, FNP

All of our Great Staff Support
St. James-Santee Family Health Center, Inc. - 30 Years "Helping Today…Changing Tomorrow"

(Courtesy of the Lil Eff Affikan Cump'ny)

The **Pediatric Waiting Room** at the **North Santee-Sampit Family Health Center** is in memory of the **Thomas Robinson**, the longest serving principal of Sampit Elementary - 1966 - 1990. Thomas Robinson was the uncle of **Michelle Robinson Obama,** First Lady of the United States of America and wife of **President Barack Obama. Michelle** roots runs deep in Georgetown, SC – Friendfield Plantation. **First Lady Obama** sent a letter marking the occasion, which was read during the ceremony. The **First Lady** wrote she remembers "the passion" her uncle had for education. Said that she is especially proud since one of her big missions is to help improve health care for children.

"Organizations like this that are working to solve health challenges will improve lives and strengthen the community," she wrote in the letter read by **Connie Robinson Jones**, the daughter of **Thomas Robinson**.

Principal Thomas J. Robinson takes on the distinction, as being the longest served principal at Sampit Elementary from 1966-1990. Principal Robinson is remembered as a legend and master in education in is own right. (Courtesy of the **North Santee - Sampit Branch** of the **St. James-Santee Family Health Center)**

(Courtesy of the Lil Eff Affikan Cump'ny)

Mrs. Michelle Robinson Obama reunited with her kinfolks while travelling through Georgetown on a campaign trip when her husband **Senator Barrack Obama** won the Democratic nomination for the President of the United States. Michelle's Family tree has deep roots in Georgetown on the Friendfield Plantation. Their family tree begins with Jim Robinson, Michelle Obama's great-great-grandfather, who was born around 1850 and lived as a slave, at least until the Civil War, on the sprawling rice plantation. Records show he remained on the estate after the war, working as a sharecropper and living in the old slave quarters with his wife, Louiser, and their children. He could neither read nor write, according to the 1880 census. **Mary Robinson** from Sampit is standing on the last row by the window.

Mrs. Michelle Robinson Obama speaking at Bethel African Methodist Episcopal Church in Georgetown Historic District, where her grandfather, **Frasier Robinson** and **Uncle Thomas Robinson** were active members. **Bethel African Methodist Episcopal Church** was the first separate black church in Georgetown County. **The Reverend A. T. Carr** established it shortly after the 1863 Emancipation Proclamation, which freed the slaves. The church purchased this property January 15, 1866, and remodeled the present building in 1908 when **Reverend. R. W. Mance** was minister. The educational building was built in 1949 under the pastorate of **Reverend H. B. Butler, Jr. Mrs. Obama** spoke at a packed church house of South Carolina Obama's supporters that included over thirty-one of her own family members from the area. **(Courtesy of Mary Robinson)**

Behind this gate is the road that lead you to where **Mrs. Michelle Robinson Obama's great-great-grandfather**, **Jim Robinson**, worked as a slave on the **Friendfield Plantation** in Georgetown, S.C. Many of the slave quarters on the plantation still stand untouched and alone on the property. It is said that many skilled and gifted slaves built this beautiful deep-rooted plantation. **(Courtesy of the Lil Eff Affikan Cump'ny)**

This radiant and lovely **First Lady** of the **United States of America** is **Michelle Lavaughn Robinson Obama** - keynote speaker at the **African Methodist Episcopal Church 49th Quadrennial Session** of the **General Conference** of the held on July, 2012 – Nashville, Tennessee. **(Courtesy of the Lil Eff Affikan Cump'ny)**

Congressman James E. Clyburn of South Carolina was honored to receive the **Civil Rights Award** at the **African Methodist Episcopal Church** 49th Quadrennial Session of the General Conference of the held on   July, 2012 – Nashville, Tennessee. Bishop Preston W. William II, Prelate of the 7th Episcopal nominated Congressman for this prestigious award. **Congressman Clyburn,** on November 16, 2006, the House Democratic Caucus unanimously elected **Congressman James E. Clyburn** of **South Carolina Majority Whip** for the 110th Congress. This was a historic day for House Democrats, having just won back the majority for the first time in twelve years. It was also historic for **Jim Clyburn**, who became the first South Carolinian and the second African American to ascend to the third ranking position in the U.S. House of Representatives. **(Courtesy of the Lil Eff Affikan Cump'ny)**

Senator Barack Obama, of Illinois (Democratic nominee for the President of the United States of American) addressed the African Methodist Episcopal Church 48th Quadrennial Session of the General Conference at the America's Center, St. Louis, MO on Saturday, June 6, 2008. In November 2008, Senator Obama became the 44th President of the United States, and the first African American to hold the office. **(Courtesy of the Lil Eff Affikan Cump'ny)**

This history-making moment took place in November 4, 2008, **Senator Barack Hussein Obama** of Illinois defeats **Senator John McCain** of Arizona to become the 44th U.S. president, and the **first African American** elected to the **White House**. The 47-year-old Democrat garnered 365 electoral votes and nearly 53 percent of the popular vote, while his 72-year-old Republican challenger; **John McClain** captured 173 electoral votes and more than 45 percent of the popular vote. **Obama's vice-presidential running mate** was **Senator Joe Biden** of Delaware, while **McCain's** running mate was **Governor Sarah Palin** of Alaska, the first female Republican ever nominated for the vice presidency. **(Courtesy of the Lil Eff Affikan Cump'ny)**

Remarkable Moment in Black History 2009: The first inauguration of **Barack Hussein Obama** as the **44th President of the United States** took place on Tuesday, January 20, 2009 where he takes the presidential oath of office at the U.S. Capitol as his wife, Michelle, holds a bible. On the day of the Inaugural ceremony in 2012, President Obama took the oath of office using two-historic Bibles-one that belonged to Abe Lincoln and the other to Dr. Martin Luther King, Jr. The inauguration, which set a record attendance for any event held in Washington, D.C., marked the commencement of the first four-year term of **Barack Hussein Obama** as **President** and **Joe Biden** as **Vice President**. Based on the combined attendance numbers, television viewership, and Internet traffic, it was among the most-observed events ever by the global audience. **(Courtesy of the Lil Eff Affikan Cump'ny)**

This decorated Airman is **Chaplain, Major Effson Chester Bryant** (author) standing in front of the White House before the inauguration ceremony of **Barack Hussein Obama - the 44th President of the United States of America** - Tuesday, January 20, 2009. **(Courtesy of the Lil Eff Affikan Cump'ny)**

This poignant and moving scene shows thousand of people at the U.S. Capital waiting for the **President Barack Hussein Obama** to be sworn in as the 44th President of the United States of America. **(Courtesy of the Lil Eff Affikan Cump'ny)**

De (The) Nine-Miles Curve Fire Station   285 - 288

De (The) Sampit – North Santee Cucumber Market

Ground Breaking for **Fire Station (No. 5)** and **EMS Station** was held in front of New Hope Union Methodist Church. **Sam Wragg, Thomas Earl Drayton, Johnny Morant,** and **David Britton** are among those participated.
(Courtesy of The Georgetown Times)

The Nine Mile Curve Fire Station that served Sampit was located in a small tin building on the Georgetown Highway 521. This station served the Sampit community for many years. On January 10 2002 a new fire station was built about two-tenth of mile from the old location on Highway 521. The Fire Station was called "No. 5 Fire and EMS Station.
(Courtesy of the Lil Eff Affikan Cump'ny)

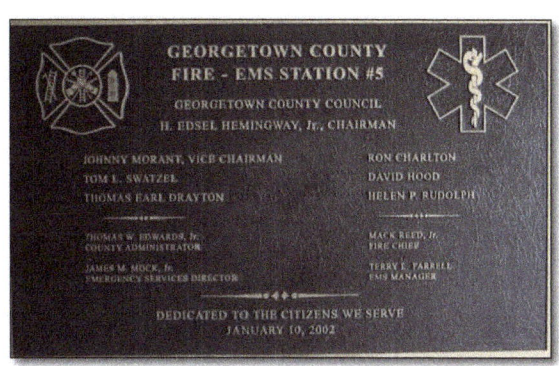

(Courtesy of the Lil Eff Affikan Cump'ny)

**Georgetown County
Fire – EMS Station #5**
Georgetown County Council
H. Edsel Hemingway, Jr. Chairman

Johnny Morant, Vice Chairman
Tom L. Swatzel
Thomas Earl Drayton
Ron Charlton
David Hood
Helen P. Rudolph

Thomas W. Edwards, Jr. County Administrator
Mack Reed, Jr. Fire Chief
James M. Mock, Jr. Emergency Services Director
Terry L. Farrell EMS Manager
Dedicated To The Citizens We Serve
January 10, 2002

The Fire Chief Georgetown County Fire – EMS Station #5 was **Mac Reed**. **Jessie Cooper,** a native of Sampit served as the **Assistant Chief**. Jessie is the son of **Nathaniel** and **Carrie Lee Myers Cooper** of Sampit. He is married to **Cathy Knowlin Cooper**. Today **Jessie** is the **Fire Marshall** for Georgetown County.
(Courtesy of the Lil Eff Affikan Cump'ny)

This photograph captures some of **Georgetown County Fire-EMS Station # 5** finest fire fighters! **Jeff Bialeka** – EMT/Fire Fighter, **Lt. Dale Hewitt** and **David Cunningham** – Medic. **(Courtesy of the Lil Eff Affikan Cump'ny)**

The Sampit – North Santee Cucumber Market (Shed) was located on Powell Road in front of **New Hope Union Methodist Church**. **Leroy Gasque** was the first **Manager**, **Joe Nathan Knowlin** and **Effson Bryant** (Beans) were two of the meticulous employees. **(Courtesy of the Lil Eff Affikan Cump'ny)**

These "official law men or popo" are **Deputy Sheriff Leroy Gasque, Sr.** (October 30, 1935 – July 14, 2004) and Grandson, **Deputy Sheriff Daniel Defoe Bryant** (January 15, 1971 – March 13, 2008) of Sampit. **(Courtesy of Daniel D. Bryant)**

Duty Daniel Defoe (Danny) **Bryant** of Sampit is among the graduates at the **Police Academy**, Columbia, South Carolina. **(Courtesy of the Lil Eff Affikan Cump'ny)**

This crisp black-and-white photo image is **Daniel Defoe Bryant** from Sampit, SC. (January 15, 1971 – March 13, 2008). **(Courtesy of the Lil Eff Affikan Cump'ny)**

De (The) Gasque Family (Pressley and Louise Gasque) 290 -301

De (The) Caper's Family
De (The) Gasque Road
Elder Willie Gasque
Bishop John Clifton Gasque
Confederate Pension Application – John Gasque
John Wesley Gasque, Jr. - Carrie Lee Wilson Gasque
Andrews Gasque – Florine Knowlin Gasque

These three generational families belong to **Pressley** (March 31, 1942 – May 3, 2004), **Janie Louise, Darlene, Jacqueline, Pressley Jr.** and baby **Clarissa Gasque**.
(Courtesy of Louise Gasque)

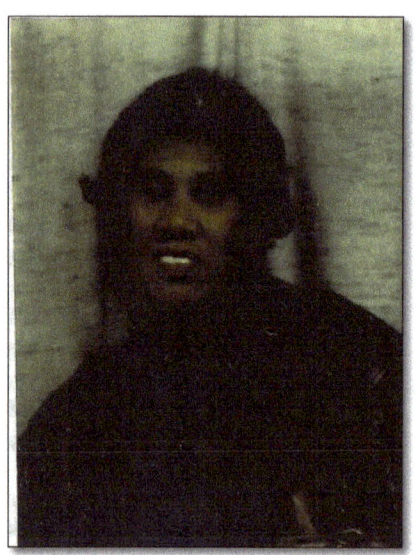 

Here is **Alafair Knowlin Beasley Drayton** (August 5, 1924 – March 11, 1999) and her son **Larry Beasley**. Alafair was the daughter of **Harriston** and **Jane Clemons Knowlin**. **Alafair** was a thoroughly mother committed to the care of her family members and others from the community. **Janie Louise Gasque** is her dear daughter.
(Courtesy of Louise Gasque)

Pressley, Louise Gasque and **Family** engaging in table talk before an "um um good" meal.
(Courtesy of Louise Gasque)

These four little girls "having fun" together are **Mary Gasque, Darlene Darby, Jacqueline Gasque** and **Gloria Grant.** (Left to right) **(Courtesy of the Lil Eff Affikan Cump'ny)**

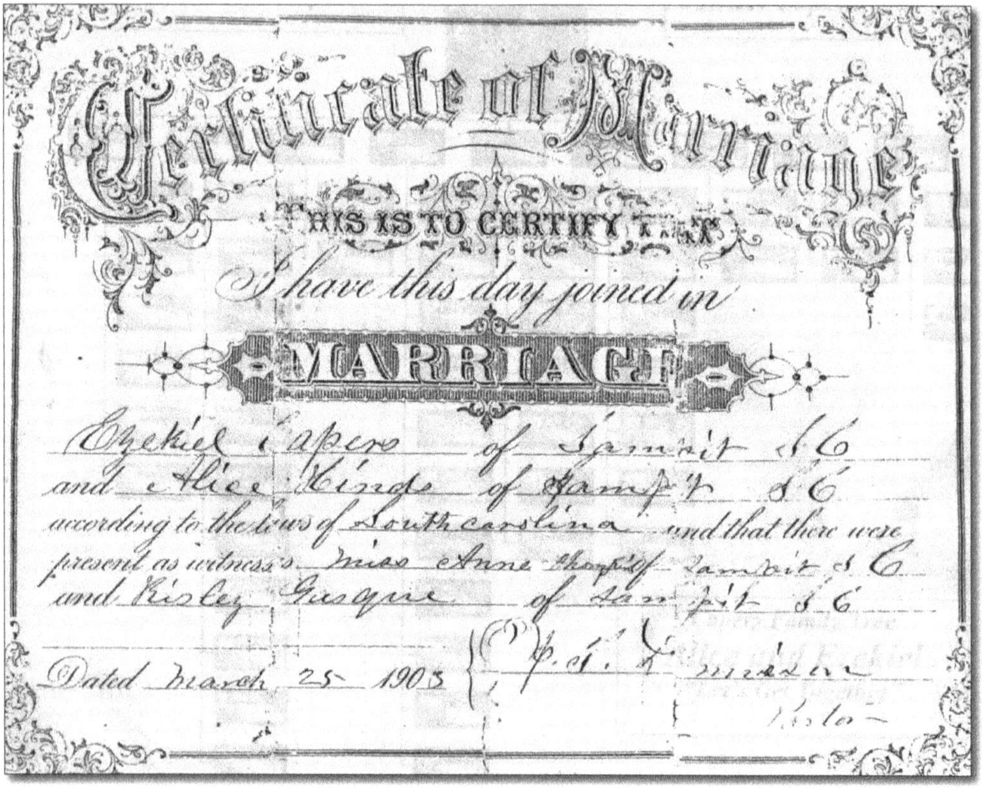

Certificate of Marriage
This is to certify that
I have this day joined in
MARRIAGE
Ezekiel Capers of Sampit SC
and Alice Hinds of Sampit SC
according to the laws of South Carolina and that there were
present as witness Miss Anne Thomp of Sampit SC
and Kisley Gasque of Sampit SC
Dated March 25 1903

Certificate of Marriage: This is to certify: I have this day joined in marriage **Ezekiel Capers** of Sampit, SC and **Alice Hinds** of Sampit, SC according to the laws of South Carolina and that there were present as witnesses **Anne Thompson** of Sampit, SC and **Kisley Gasque** of Sampit, SC. Dated March 25, 1903 **Reverend L.M. Dennison.** **(Courtesy of Lillie Mae Lewis)**

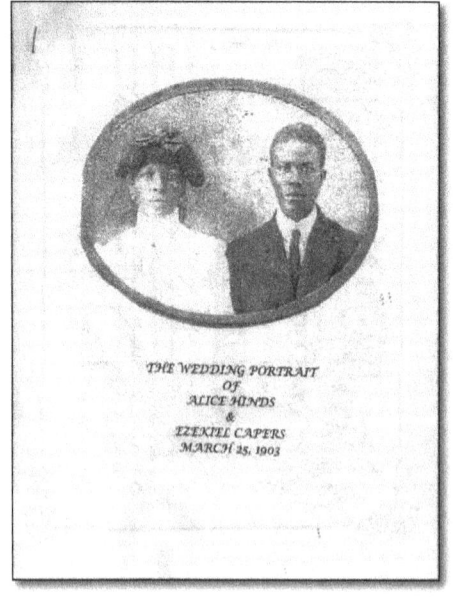

This creative personalized Wedding Program shows the "Tying of the Knot" portrait of **Alice Hinds** (May 8, 1887 – May 24, 1973) and **Ezekiel Capers (1898 – November 11, 1935)** on March 25, 1903. **(Courtesy of Lillie Mae Lewis)**

The **Caper's Family** posing for a family photographs at the **Bryant, Stafford and Caper's Family Reunion** in **2008** on the grounds of **St. Paul A.M.E. Church. (Courtesy of the Lil Eff Affikan Cump'ny)**

This beautiful historical family blanket showing Mother **Alice Hinds** Caper with daughter, Lillie Mae Caper was displayed at **The Caper's Fifth Family Reunion** in 2014. This blanket was given to Lillie Mae Lewis – the Matriarch of the Caper's Family. At right is **Lillie Mae Lewis** with that expressible bubbly smile. **(Courtesy of Lillie Mae Lewis)**

David Britton, Martha Gasque (Courtesy of Martha Gasque Holmes)

De Gasque Road. The Gasque Road, a short lane just six tenths of a mile long, in a quiet section of Sampit, serves as a home for nearly 70 school children and generations of families who have lived here since for years. The road has been a test site for just about every kind of surface known to modern transportation engineers. "The old road is over a hundred years old," Britton said as he walked along it. "We've been asking to have it paved for the last 10 years. The county has tried all sorts of things to make it more passable, but nothing seemed to work for long.

First, the road earned rocking. "But the rocks work their way to the side and eventually be lost." Britton said.

In 1994 came another experiment, slagging, which put down pieces of broken up concrete form other roads and projects. "As the concrete was crushed form cars driving over it, it started releasing dust." Britton said. "The stuff was so thick, some kids and senior citizens along the road started having respiratory problems.

Residents along the road, led by the active Sampit Community Organization, went back to the county to report the latest problems. Their perseverance was rewarded in 1996, when the county was able to set aside some of its limited C-funds money gathered from the state gas tax for Gasque Road paving.

"We were able to realize some cost savings by paving the road ourselves, using county staff" said Ray Funnye, County Director of Public Works. "This was a first for us, and it went really well. We projected a cost of $100,000 for the paving, and it looks like we'll come in under budget.

Funnye said the numbers aren't quite complete yet because there is still some minor finessing to be done on site, checking all drainage outlets and regarding along the sides of the road. These soulful **twin** sisters above are **Mary** and **Martha Gasque,** the daughters of **John Wesley** and **Carrie Lee Wilson Gasque.** (Courtesy of Martha Gasque Holmes)

This is the spacious wooden home and shed that belongs to **John Wesley** and **Carrie Lee Wilson Gasque** located off the Gasque Road. In the picture standing on the lawn is John Wesley Gasque and son, Larry Gasque. **(Courtesy of Larry Gasque)**

Wesley Gasque (March 1, 1970) and his wife, **Sarah Jane Gasque** (June 20, 1908 – November 16, 1984) were stalwart, staunch and entrusted members of Saint Paul AME Church, Sampit. **Daisy, Joann (Carrie), Rena, Geneva, Andrew, John Wesley, Thomas, Nathan, Willie, John C.** and **Raymond Gasque** are their children. **(Courtesy of Elder Willie Gasque)**

This "went back" picture are **Elder Willie Gasque**, **Daisy Bell Gasque Smith** (August 1, 1926 – April 11, 2004), **John Wesley Gasque, Jr**. (April 21, 1930 – June 28, 2012), **Andrew Gasque, Sr.** (April 16, 1928 – October 12, 2013), **Nathan** (January 1, 1936 - December 26, 2013) and **Bishop John Gasque** (January 15 1934 – February 11, 2016). **(Courtesy of Elder Willie Gasque)**

This "all in the family" portrait is **Andrews Gasque Sr.** (April 16, 1928 – October 12, 2013) and **Florine Knowlin Gasque**. (July 4, 1935 – January 7, 2013) sitting down with their extended family. **(Courtesy of Glover Gasque, Jr.)**

Bishop John Clifton Gasque (nicknamed JC) was born January 15 1934 in Sampit, South Carolina. He is the seventh of thirteen children born to the **John Wesley** and **Sara Jane Davis Gasque**. It is said that he was named after a distant relative by the name of **John Gasque** who served as a cook in the Civil War.

As a child, he attended and was baptized at St. Paul A.M.E. Church, Sampit, South Carolina, and the family church. His family was probably some of the foundering members of the church. Throughout the church history, his family members, parents and siblings were very active members and officers at St. Paul. Today the family is still very engrossed in the ministry and mission at St. Paul A.M.E.

Bishop Gasque grew up in a devoted home with Godly principles. He was converted at an early age and served at St. Paul AME Church, where he worked diligently as a young leader in the Sunday School and church choir. He started speaking for the Lord before age 10 and continued until his death.

He attended the public schools in Georgetown County, graduated with honors from Rosemary High School, Andrews, SC. After high school he volunteered in the Marine Corp and served for eight (8) years. Throughout his military careers he travelled extensively to places such as Germany, Japan, Korea, Hawaii, and California. One of the ships he travelled on was ship wrecked for hours in the Mediterranean Sea and they were later rescued.

Bishop Gasque attended Allen University, Columbia, SC where he earned a BS in Psychology and later attended Dickerson Theological Seminary at Allen University. After graduating from Seminary he served as assistant to Dr. W. D. Dent for two years. He taught at Laurens District 55 High School and was employed by Laurens County Sheriff Department.

In 1942 at the age of eight he was called to preach the gospel. It was said that as a young lad he used to preach up and down rows while plowing the family mule, Kate. In 1957 at the age of twenty-three he was licensed to preach the Word of God under **Pastor George Washington,** Pastor of St. Paul African Methodist Episcopal Church, Sampit, SC. He possessed a genuine source of power and a great faith in God. What was a calling that came down from God straight to his heart! He is secure in his calling because he is blessed with the grace of Jesus, washed in His blood, safe by His love and free from all sins because of Christ Jesus. He was known as a great pulpiteer, gifted preacher, keen understanding of the scriptures that attract many to his preaching.

Reverend Gasque was ordained Itinerant Deacon in 1960 at St. James A.M.E. Church, Columbia, SC, Presiding Elder was **Rev. I.O. Simmons** and **Bishop Samuel Higgins** was the Presiding Bishop. In 1960 he was also ordained Itinerant Elder at Brown Chapel A.M.E. Church, Presiding Elder was **Rev. I. O. Simmons** and **Bishop Samuel Higgins** presiding Bishop.

His first pastorate was the Mount Zion Circuit, Winnsboro, Columbia District, South Carolina in 1961 – 1962, Greater Trinity and Little White Hall A.M.E. Churches, Spartanburg District, Rev. I.O Simmons, 1963, Presiding Elder, Providence A.M.E. Church, Spartanburg District, Newberry District, Rev. William D. Bowman, 1971, Presiding Elder, St. Phillip A.M.E. Church, Lancaster District, Rev. A.D. Dawkins, Presiding Elder, Shiloh & Spring Field A.M.E Churches, Abbeville District, Rev. Castell Jackson, Presiding Elder, Mt. Zion & Pine Grove Circuit, Abbeville District, Rev. Castell Jackson, Presiding Elder, Calhoun Falls Circuit, Greenwood District, Rev. George T. Delvin, Presiding Elder, Popular Springs A.M.E. Church, Greenwood District, Rev. George T. Devlin, Presiding Elder.

In 1986 **Reverend Gasque** founded the **Shiloh Living Word Church**, Gray Court, South Carolina. A church planning council was held on April 12, 1986 and the church was organized.

Bishop Gasque belongs to numerous organizations: Vice President of Allen University Alumni Chapter, life member of the NAACP, Phi Beta Sigma Fraternity and Chaplain for the SC Combat Veterans.

Bishop Gasque of 2022 Eichelberger Road, Gray Court, died Thursday, February 11, 2016 at his home after a long and creative ministry. **The Celebration of Life of Bishop John Clifton Gasque** was held on Monday, February 15, 2015, 1:00 PM at Mt. Zion Missionary Baptist Church, 1448 Cain Road, Laurens, SC where **Reverend, Dr. Jefferson McDowell**, Pastor.

Pastor McDowell preached the Word of Comfort: I Fought, I Finished and Remained Faithful – 2 Corinthians 4: 6 – 7. Committal, Benediction & Interment with Military Honors was held at Forest Lawn Cemetery, Laurens, SC. Rev. Kelly Spann II, Senior Pastor of St. Paul AME Church, Sampit, SC officiated.

Bishop Gasque leaves to cherish his memories a loving wife of fifty two years, **Mrs. Amelia J. Gasque,** one daughter, **Pamela Gasque Parks**, three grandchildren, Christian, John II, Esadora, and five great grandchildren, one brother, Reverend Dr. Willie E. Gasque, Augusta, Ga., three sisters, Rena Sessions, Geneva Gasque, New York City, NY, Joanna Gasque, Sampit.

This pastoral scene is the **Dickerson Theological Seminary Ministerial Group** at Allen University, Columbia, SC. **Reverend John Gasque,** the revered cleric from Sampit is the second minister standing from left to right. **(Courtesy of the Lil Eff Affikan Cump'ny)**

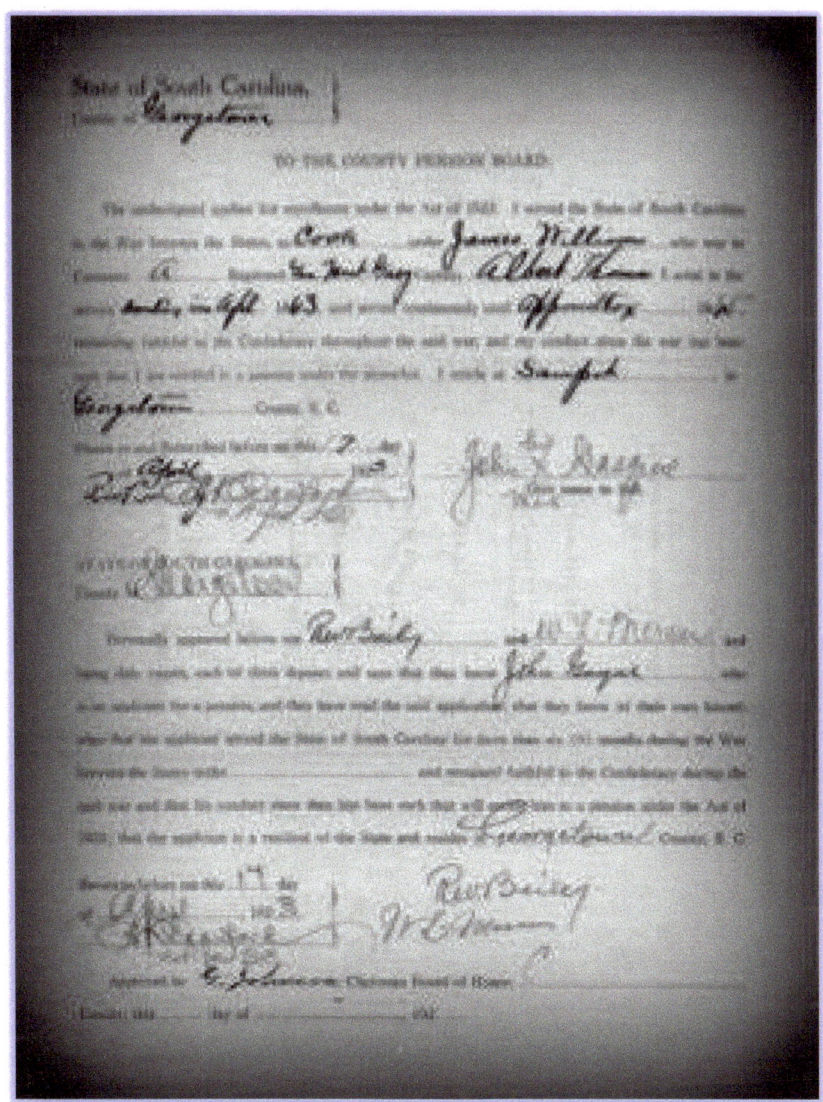

Confederate Pension Application for John Gasque
John Gasque - Cook Under James Williams

Act No. 63, 1923 SC. Acts allowed African Americans who had served as least six months as cooks, servants, or attendants to apply for a pension. Then in 1924, apparently because there were too many applications, the act was amended to eliminate all laborers, teamsters, and non-South Carolinians by extending eligibility only to South Carolina residents who had served the state for at least six months as "body servants or male camp cooks."

It is said by **Ross Stafford** that **Reverend John Gasque** was named after his great great grandfather **John Gasque** who served as a cook in the American Civil War.
(Courtesy of the Lil Eff Affikan Cump'ny)

Willie Gasque nicknamed "**Bill**" is the son of **John Wesley Gasque, Sr.** and **Sarah Jane Davis Gasque**. He has eleven brothers and five sisters.

He received his pre-kindergarten and kindergarten education from Saint Paul AME Church, next to the St. Paul AME Church. He attended elementary school at Sampit Elementary School; Junior and High School at Rosemary, in Andrews, South Carolina.

Willie was drafted in the United States Army in January 1964 and did his basic training at Fort Jackson in Columbia, South Carolina. He completed his advanced training in 1964 at Fort Lewis, Washington and completed his 1st draft in January 1964, Fort Lewis. Then he took a break in service until 1977. He then enlisted in the United States Army in 1967 at Fort Hampton, New York. His assignment took him to Europe and he received "Orders For War" and went to Vietnam in 1968.

Following many tours of duty, **Willie** was: Instructor @ Basic Combat Training Committee Group, Fort Jackson Victory Academy, Fort Campbell NCOA, Kentucky, Fort Lee, Virginia (US Army Readiness Group). He attended the following military schools; Air Assault School, Jungle Warfare Training, First Sergeant Academy, Senior NCO Commander and Staff, MATA Senior NCO, NCO Academy, M16 A1 Instructor and BTMS.

He received the following awards: Meritorious Service Medal, Army Commendation Medal, Army Achievement Medal, Good Conduct Medal (8th Award), National Defense Medal, Vietnam Service Medal, Air Assault Badge, Overseas Service Ribbon, Republic of Vietnam Campaign Medal, Republic of Vietnam Cross, Unit Citation with Palm, Army Occupation Medal, Army Service Ribbon, Combat Infantry Badge, Expert Infantry Badge, and Non-Commissioned Officer Professional Development Ribbon.

He retired with honor in January 1990. On April 7, 1980, he received his calling into the ministry at Greater Faith Temple Church of God in Christ, Clarksville, Tennessee. He was baptized with the Holy Ghost on April 7, 1980. He preached his first sermon on March 15, 1981. Other church Evangelic Temple COGIC, Clarksville, Tenn., Good Shepherd Holiness Church, Columbia, S.C., Community Memorial COGIC, Columbia, S.C., Bibleway House of Prayer, Baumholder, Germany, Greater Faith Temple COGIC, Fort Lee, Virginia, God in Christ Ministries, Glovanville, South Carolina, Shiloh Living Word, Gray Court, South Carolina where his brother, Dr. John C. Gasque, Overseer. **(Courtesy of Elder Willie Gasque)**

(Left to right) **Violet, Sarah, Mary, Larry, Levern, Mickie, Michael** and **Mary Gasque** are the children of **John W**. and **Carrie Lee Wilson Gasque**.
(Courtesy of Larry Gasque)

This neatly dressed couple is **Carrie Lee Wilson Gasque** (August 9, 1935 – February 7, 1998) and **John Wesley Gasque, Jr.** (April 21, 1930 – June 28, 2012). Carrie Lee and John Wesley were united in holy matrimony on May 21, 1951, sixty-five (65) years ago. At right are **Larry** and **Veronica Stafford Gasque** - married on at St. Paul A.M.E. Church on April 29, 1978. **Melissa, Shayla** and **Larry Gasque Jr**. are their children.
(Courtesy of Larry Gasque)

Sampit Christmas Parade

Charles Louise Waye, Sr. — Vernell Stafford Waye
De (The) Scribe with Sam Pitt (Sampit) Roots
De (The) Sam Pitt (Sampit) Action Groups
De (The) Neighbor Clean Up Group
Harold Trappier
Roy Knowling Sr. — Mattie N. Knowling
Mrs. Vergie Tennison

This entertaining scene shows **Charles Louise Waye, Sr.** (January 3, 1930 – December 21, 2010), the founder of Sampit Christmas Parade. Sampit's first annual Christmas Parade was in 1983. Starting with the idea that the children of Sampit did not all get to enjoy the major town's parade, he decided that the community should celebrate their own parade! And thus the dream became a reality, with the assistance of his partner, **James Smith**. Thirty-three years later the Parade has now become a local tradition of fun in Sampit, creativity, and great pride! **Charlie** served as grand marshal on Saturday, 8 December 2007, the 25th annual Sampit Christmas parade. **(Courtesy of the Lil Eff Affikan Cump'ny)**

This defining and unforgettable image is the **Wedding Day** picture of **Charlie Waye** and **Vernell Stafford Waye** on **December 25, 1957**. **Gladys Bryant** served as **Flower Girl** and **Willie Drayton, Jr. (Billy)** was the **Ring Bearer**.
(Courtesy of Gladys Bryant Scott)

This is **Rollin Bryant** decked out in his **Santa'** hat, pulling a Christmas Parade float with his John Deer Tractor during the Christmas Sampit Parade.
(Courtesy of the Lil Eff Affikan Cump'ny)

This artistic float shows **Reverend Reggie Grant** as the jolly old **Santa Claus** and **Patricia Trappier** as **Mrs. Santa Claus** during the **Sampit Christmas Parade** in 2014. The Sampit Christmas Parade still remained a source of entertainment, cultural pride, heritage, and amusement for African Americans that live in Sampit.
(Courtesy of the Lil Eff Affikan Cump'ny)

This showbiz family is **Charles, Vernell, Nathaniel, Tom, Alexandra** and **Theresa Waye** at the **Bryant – Stafford Family Reunion Dinner** at the Pawleys Plantation Golf and Country Club. **(Courtesy of the Lil Eff Affikan Cump'ny)**

Three generations look a like are **Jasmine (Daughter/Granddaughter), Lula Mae (Daughter/Mother),** and **Vernell (Mother/Grandmother)** posing in this sacred scene after worship service at St. Paul African Methodist Episcopal Church, Sampit. **(Courtesy of the Lil Eff Affikan Cump'ny)**

A SCRIBE WITH SAMPIT ROOTS By L. N'zinga Strickland a.k.a. Lula Mae (Stafford)

"I've been a published journalist for about twenty years and during that time I have had the opportunity to travel to various points of the world and write about my experiences for many publications. I have had the opportunity to meet some of the most remarkable people, I feel, in the universe. My work has also appeared in one of the first travel anthologies by Black women writers that included the illustrious **Dr. Maya Angelou** and **Alice Walker**. It has been an incredible journey for me, an incredible blessing and an incredible opportunity. And my writing skills, alone, took me there.

And it all began in my childhood village, in Sampit Elementary School. I'm in my early fifties now but then I was a happy second grader under the tutelage of the magnificent instructor, **Mrs. Vivian Moses** of Georgetown. I so enjoyed being in her second-grade class and the sheer joy of learning to write and always being encouraged by my loving teacher and mentor. Anyhow, that's where it all started, in my village home.

Years since I have traveled to Brazil, Africa, the Caribbean and Mexico as a travel writer. At first after meeting people on the touristy route and giving my sponsors stories they wanted about the scenery and hotels, I started to become involved with the people of the countries and less with the beach scenes and grew close to the those living there and their culture.

Amazingly, I came to realize how much it was like mine. I met a lot of people, but the majority I bonded with was people of African descent, like me. And their ways of being and life styles reminded me of my Sampit roots, in all their simplicities, kindnesses and compassion. That's the way I was raised and it kept me in good stead as a traveling writer.

I still work as a journalist now here in New York and have massive portfolios and plans to write a book about my adventures one day; hopefully, to encourage others. A beautiful occurrence has arisen for me also because of my writing career. And that's because both my

grown children have blossomed into astute, capable and published writers! For the rest of my life I will be grateful for being born a daughter of Sampit, South Carolina and the love that nurtured me there.

Lula also is the executive editor of "**The Franklin Sun - The Premier Source** for the Bryant-Stafford Family" which she started in January 2004. The family website is named in honor of her **Uncle Franklin Stafford**, the son of **Thomas** and **Bessie Bryant Stafford**. **(Courtesy of Lula Strickland)**

We honor and salute the May 8th birthday of the Honorable **Franklin Stafford**. He was born in Sampit May 8th, 1945 and departed this life May 17, 2003. He was one of eight children of the late **Thomas** and **Bessie Bryant Stafford**. (Siblings: **Vernell, Cleo, Suziah, Randolph, Joseph Hudson, Jimmy,** and **Edison**. **Franklin** was married for thirty - five years to his beloved wife **JM** and they are the proud parents of two sons. This newsletter, the **Franklin Sun**, was founded in 2004 in honor of Franklin by his loving niece, **Lula**. As many of you know, Franklin was a very prominent and celebrated businessman in two major corporations in Massachusetts for over three decades. In addition to his lifelong work on behalf of his own family, he was also a force in community service (North & South) touching the lives of countless young people and supplying them many opportunities through his corporate and personal status.

I personally remember, as a child, the members of the St. Paul congregation helping to back their communal son, **Franklin**, to go off to college (Johnson C. Smith University) and the great pride and love that our family and neighbors displayed towards him. Of course, he went on to unbelievable heights of success, yet always gave back to the community he came from and gave whatever assistance he could to family and others. Franklin was proud to be a son of Sampit, proud of his personal family, and proud of all of us! **Franklin**

Her daughter, **Jazz** is the Junior editor, son, **Khalid** is the technical consultant and **Kofi** is consultant and logo designer. This gripping photogenic setting above is **Khalid**, wife **Sachiko** and their son, **Noah Strickland**.

These Stafford Five are Thomas, Edison, Randolph, Jimmy and Franklin Stafford are the sons of Thomas and Bessie Bryant Stafford. **(Courtesy of the Lil Eff Affikan Cump'ny)**

These Sampit Action' executives are Mary T. Duncan, Gertrude Davis, Bernice J. Bryant and Louise Gasque

The Sampit Action Groups always have been active in community developments. The Sampit Action Group was instrumental in planning of the annual Christmas parade. The original parade route started from **David Smith's Store** and ends at the **Sampit Park**, one mile away. In 1992 the following served on the **Sampit Action Group**: **Charlie Waye, Sr., President; Betty Stafford, Secretary; Bernice Bryant, Treasurer;** and members: **Jerome Bryant, Milford Darby, James Smith, Sr., Bernice, Mary T. Duncan, Lila B. Prout, Harold Trappier, Leroy Trappier, Louise Gasque, Abe Bryant, Lillie Mae, Ben Stafford, Jr., Mannie Duncan, Joan Brown,** and **Gertrude Davis. (Courtesy of the Lil Eff Affikan Cump'ny)**

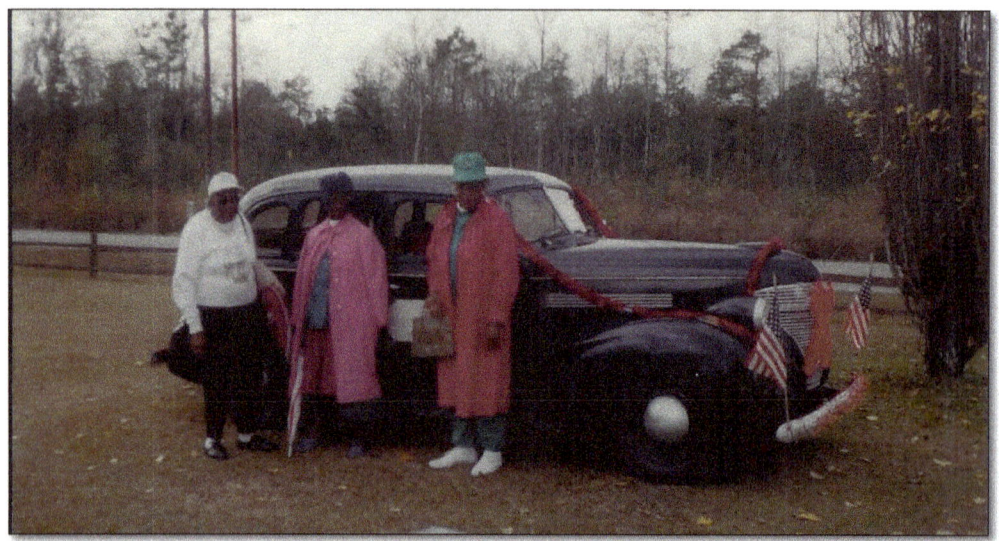

One of the earliest rural automobile owners in the Sampit community was Ross Stafford, who bought this **1939 Chevelot** for $100 in the mid-1940s. These four "Golden Girls" are **Amelia Trappier, Rosa Darby, Lena Gasque** (standing) and **Francis Davis** (sitting) are kicking it at this 1939 **Chevelot. (Courtesy of James Smith Sr.)**

The Neighborhood Clean Up Group was organized in 2002 in Sampit with ten (10) members. The purpose of the established organization was in three folds: To clean up, too beautiful and to protect the neighborhoods of Sampit. The founding members met on the 4th Monday of the month at the Sampit Community Center from 6:30 - 8:30. Its first elected president was **Harold Trappier**, Sampit, SC.
(Courtesy of the Lil Eff Affikan Cump'ny)

The officers of **The Neighborhood Clean Up Group** are elected every December. The monthly dues were $ 2.00 per month. Some of the organization's accomplishments; complete face lift of Harold Drive, Sampit Community signs, Crime watch and litter signs, and participated in a drugs march with emphasis on the "condition of the community" with Sheriff Cribbs. The group was very instrumental in bringing Duty Sheriff Robert Patterson as an active person in the community where he is responsible for its protection.

This famed family picture is **Harold, Annie Cooper Trappier** and **Children**

(Courtesy of Harold Trappier)

In 2002, **Mattie N. Knowling,** Selma, Alabama was elected President of **The Neighborhood Clean Up Group**. She is married to **Roy Knowling** who moved back to **Sampit** in 2001 after spending years in New Jersey. After moving back home, the couples became community activists and members of St. Paul A.M.E. Church where they worked on the Usher Board and in other church organizations.

In 2003, two years after moving to Sampit, they established the "**Trudie Knowling Scholarship Fund,** named in honor of Roy Knowling's beloved Mother, Trudie. " The purpose of the scholarship was to assist neighborhood children with funding of books for school/college. Every year they would host a community wide barbeque cookout at their home to raise funds for the scholarship. Tickets are sold in advance. At the cookout tickets are sold for raffling of gifts. Foods such as barbeque chicken, hot dogs, hamburgers, potatoes salad, popcorns, and tea, are sold.
(Courtesy of Roy Knowling)

This picture encapsulates the warm family setting of Roy, Mattie Knowling and children.
(Courtesy of Roy Knowling)

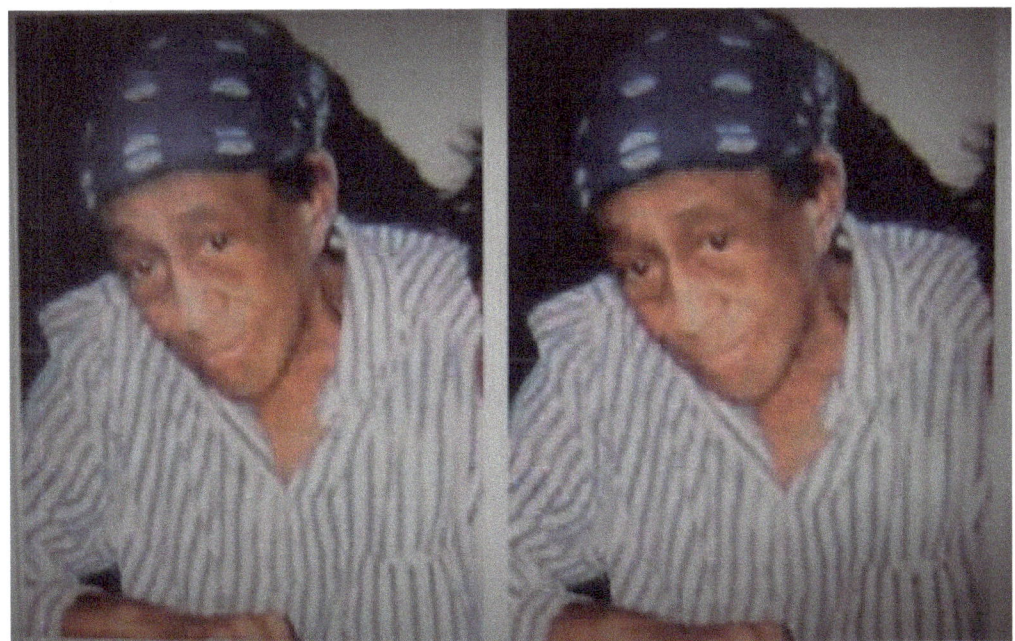

These "back in the day" doubled shot picture are **Susie Norwood**, the Mother of Mattie Knowling. **(Courtesy of Mattie Knowling)**

This sporty and stately gentleman is **Lee Norwood**, Father of Mattie Knowling. **(Courtesy of Mattie Knowling)**

This "up-close and personal moment" is the offspring of Hogan and Trudy H. Knowling - Mary, Margaret, Demetra, Thomas, Roy and Larry Knowling.
(Courtesy of Roy Knowling)

From the family archives picture file of Roy Knowling are his beautiful mother, **Trudy Holmes Knowling** (August 24, 1917 – June 29, 1958) and much-loved sister, **Mary Knowling Humphrey. (Courtesy of Roy Knowling)**

In January 2004, **Mattie** Knowling also helped in organizing the **"Sheriff's Neighborhood Walk"** to make known to law officers the crimes that take place in Sampit. Georgetown County Sheriff Lane Cribb participated in the walk along with other community leaders. In 2005, the group changed its organizational name to the "**Sampit Community Watch Group**." The Watch Group which now has over thirty active members. On Saturday, 27 September 2008, the Sampit Community Watch Group sponsored their annual picnic at the Sampit Park. Members or the organization proudly wore their blue and gold T-shirts to the picnic "**Sampit Community Watch Group**" inscribed on them. They helped in serving the foods to the 150 in attendance.

The group objective was to bring the Sampit Community together in a time of fun, playing games and enjoying the food. Some of the foods served were hot dogs with chili, hamburgers, potato chips, fried fish, and red rice. **President Mattie Knowling** says this is the second year for the community picnic. Some of the other activities at the Sampit Parks were booths set up for voter registration and selling Senator Obama's T-shirts for $ 10.00.
(Courtesy of the Lil Eff Affikan Cump'ny)

In the photo above is **County Auditor Linda Mock** who was seeking re-election on Election Day in November came to the picnic. **Sampit Community Watch Group** is still very active in the community, each week cleaning up trash beside the road and cleaning the community. The group takes pride in their community by keeping it clean and giving back to the community. Today the organization has over forty active members. Mattie Knowling, Roy Knowling and James Smith, Sr. (from left to right – pictures 4, 5 and 6) pictured above is from Sampit. **(Courtesy of Roy Knowling)**

This embraceable group picture belongs to **Roy** and **Mattie Knowling's** Family.
(Courtesy of Roy Knowling)

Palmetto Pride hosted its annual Adopt-A-Highway awards luncheon on April 16, 2015 at Stone River in West Columbia, SC. Groups from around the state gathered to receive awards for volunteer litter pickup efforts.

The **Sampit Community Watch Group** (District 5) received this award "2015 Adopt-A-Highway – County Group of the Year."

Courtesy of Roy Knowling)

One of the dearest friends of my Mother, **Bernice Jackson Bryant** was **Vergie Tennison** from Georgetown, South Carolina. Family members and friends called her **Ms. Vergie.** This title signified her special respect that she had for my Mom. Mom loved her dearly! She made many visits to her home and always brought my Mom a special gift. Mom loved stuffed bears and Ms. Vergie often brought her one. She always remembered my Mother on Mother's Day and often brought the largest bouquet of flowers. They often shared in church fellowship at Annual Usher's Strut. The Usher's Strut program was an annual event at churches where usher board visited other church groups, and struts down the isles of the church with their special music and movement. She often would visit her at home or in the hospital. Ms. Vergie was the face behind the voice at WLMC radio 1470 AM here in Georgetown. She is the daughter of **Mrs. Dieanna H. Alston** and the late **Mr. Robert L. Alston**. She is one of six siblings who are known as the "**Banana Bunch**" because of their close family ties.

Ms. Vergie has a very interesting background. She graduated from Howard High School in 1967 and lived in New York for 27 years before moving back home to help with her mom. While in New York she graduated from Royal Business School and received her secretarial certificates from Burrough of Manhattan Community College. She started her career as a telephone operator, but later became manager of 15 other employees in the Accounts Payable Department at New York Telephone. She also did the weather report for New York Telephone. Her church work included being a member of St. Stephen Community AME Church in Harlem, New York, where she was vice chairman of the Board of Stewards, vice-president of the Joint Usher Board and the Intermediate Female Usher Board, president of the Willie Lee Freeman Scholarship Fund Committee that gave graduating seniors and first and second year college students $2,000 to the college of their choice, secretary of the Board of Stewards, treasurer of the Lay organization and a member of the Usher Board. She says ushering is her first love, and still ushers at her present church, Mt. Olive African Methodist Episcopal Church. **Ms. Vergie's** work at the radio station is her ministry. She says she's getting the message out through the music. "There are all kinds of preachers and teachers. You don't have to always do it from behind the sacred desk of the pulpit. She plays the music to fit the people who are listening. From 6 to 9 am every morning **Ms. Vergie** and **Station Manager Vanessa Greene** alternate weekly for the "Joy in the Morning" program. **Ms. Vergie** serves as the Palmetto Conference Lay Organization President. **(Courtesy of the Lil Eff Affikan Cump'ny)**

This sophisticated lady is **Mrs. Vergie Tennison,** Lay President of the Georgetown District (Palmetto Conference) of the AME Church. **(Courtesy of the Lil Eff Affikan Cump'ny)**

This cultured and fashionable lady is **Mrs. Vergie Tennison** at the **Retirement Dinner** for **Bishop Richard Franklin Norris** and **Mother Mary Ann Norris,** Charleston, SC. **(Courtesy of the Lil Eff Affikan Cump'ny)**

11th Annual Richard Allen Awards – UNCF Masquerade Scholarship Luncheon

Allen University hosts its 11th **Annual Richard Allen Awards Gala** benefiting **UNCF** on February 13, 2016 at the Columbia Marriott in Columbia, South Carolina. **(Courtesy of the Lil Eff Affikan Cump'ny)**

Who is this mask lady? The masked lady is **Mrs. Vergie Tennison** masquerading at the 11th Annual Richard Allen Awards – UNCF Masquerade Scholarship Luncheon, Columbia, SC. **(Courtesy of the Lil Eff Affikan Cump'ny)**

De (The) Sam Pitt (Sampit) Park 319 - 322

De (The) Sam Pitt (Sampit) - Lookout Tower (Fire Lookout Tower)
De (The) Hang Man Tree
De (The) Georgetown Recycle Center

A beautiful 10 acres park - **De (The) Sampit Park** - Georgetown Department of Public Services shows the park sign and the Georgetown Water Tower in the background. The park is a popular day-use by residents of the Sampit community for exercising, walking, family cookouts, community events, playing sports and where the annually Sampit Parade ends. **(Courtesy of the Lil Eff Affikan Cump'ny)**

The Sampit Lookout Tower (Fire Lookout Tower) located off **Highway 17** was used for years by the **South Carolina Forestry Service** to detect forest fire in the woody and piney area in Sampit and surrounding communities. It is said that one of the Forestry Ranger was able to spot a fire in the area for miles from this lookout tower – then call into the Forestry Service to give directions to the fire.
(Courtesy of the Lil Eff Affikan Cump'ny)

De (The) Sampit Recycle Center

The Georgetown County Recycle Center - Sampit was opened in 1994, located at 2569 Saints Delight Road. The Recycle Center is used to collect residential waste, such as trash, metal, etc.

Prior to the opening of the **Sampit Recycle Center**, residential waste was dropped off at the Ball Diamond and placed in four large green trash containers owned by Georgetown County. Most of the times, the containers were filled and running over due to the large amount of trash being taken there. When the trash containers became filled, then the members would place their trash in large pile right beside the containers.

The garage disposal trucks would come by and empty the containers at least once or twice a week. When the trucks didn't show up the palled trash left a bad stench or bad order. Before the County placed large trash containers at the Ball Diamond, member normally would dump or place their trash on a spot of land behind their homes. Normally, the paper products would be placed in large tar barrels and burned.

Today, the **Sampit Recycle Center** is opened six days per week and only closed on Sundays. The Center is tightly controlled and operated under a manager system by an employee from the Georgetown Recycle Center. As you enter the property of the Recycle Center posted signs direct you where to put your residential waste. On the property, you will find about ten or twelve recycle containers, each one with a different type of waste. You have to place your residential waste in the proper container.

(Courtesy of the Lil Eff Affikan Cump'ny)

De (The) Hanging Tree. Terrorized! Petrified! Scary! Creepy! Intimidating! Nerve-racking! Shock! Unbelievable! Breathless! These are some of the terminologies that came from the mouth of my father as he drove his **1964 Ford Galaxy 500** by the **Hang Man Tree** or **Hanging Tree** in Sampit. This famous or infamous tree called by the residents that lived close to the tree was where many hate crimes (lynching) were perpetuated against many slaves and freemen. The Hang Tree is a tall stately cypress tree with limbs that reached over the road is located on the Saint Delight Road (Highway 17A) a few miles South of Lambert Town. The long limbs were used for hanging or lynching of many blacks and some white citizens.

Long time residents of Sampit stated that the **Hang Man Tree** or the **Hanging Tree** was known to be a very popular place for hanging or lynching especially to celebrate **4th July**.

When as a child, my Father, Eff always drove by the tree but never once stopped. He called it unholy grounds where the lives and bloods of many Negroes were shared. He always told us tales that his parents told him about slaves and free Negroes being hung there for years. The tree was also used as a "**whipping-post**" for "**unruly Negro (blacks)** defined by the white landowners. It was said that nightriders who policed the Sampit plantations often times harassed and threatening free blacks and slaves by saying "we are going to string you up!" This was a form of "scare tactic" to keep them in their rightful place.

A **public hanging** or **lynching** was not a pretty sight! As in most lynching, the white newspaper (Georgetown Times) and the public expressed its solidarity in the name of white supremacy and ignored any information that contradicted the people's verdict. One historian described the lynching scene "carnival-like, if not euphoric, in their demeanor, whites gathered by the thousands to watch lynching, often dressed in their Sunday best clothing.

One man described the process of lynching at the **Hanging Tree** of Sampit: Some one had the long rope ready and placed the noose over his head, throwing the end of the rope over the limb, another man drove a horse and wagon in place and they forced the young man to climb up and stand in the wagon bed and then several men pulled on the long rope as the horse dashed away with the wagon, lifting the young man clear and snapping his neck.

How many were lynched at the old "**Hang Man**" tree is unknown. It was said that some of the plantation owners recorded the slave names and kept them in their personal family histories. None of the records has been released up to this day. Historical records shows that over 5000 Black Americans were murdered in the South through lynching and other means after the Civil War which makes it undeniable that lynching were rampart everywhere—even in Horry and Georgetown Countries.
(Courtesy of the Lil Eff Affikan Cump'ny)

Effson Chester Bryant (Lil Eff) captured this priceless moment of embracing siblings Brewington Eff Bryant (Brew) and Zilcia Elizabeth Bryant (Zilcie Bear) holding hands at **Incirlik Air Base, Turkey** in 2000.
(Courtesy of the Lil Eff Affikan Cump'ny)

De Effson Chester Bryant

Effson Chester Bryant (Beans/Lil Eff) is a self-taught photographer, storyteller, historian, genealogist, writer and military veteran. He is "Straight Outta Sampit", South Carolina and descendant of the slaves on the **Thomas Boone's Plantation,** formerly Sam Pitt, nowadays, Sampit.

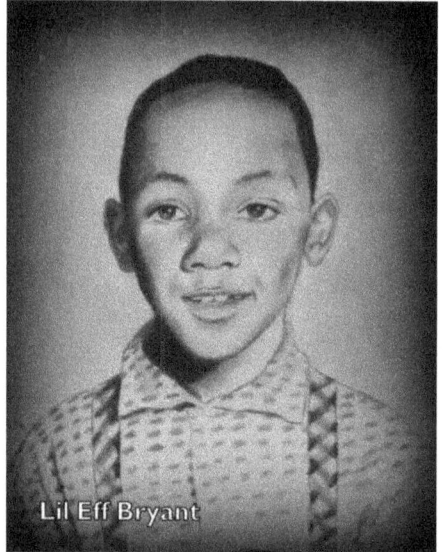

Lil Eff Bryant

Effson is the son of **Eff Bryant** of Sampit and **Bernice Jackson Bryant** of Georgetown, South Carolina. His mother called him "**Lil Eff**" and family members and friends nickname him **"Beans".**

He is a graduate of Sampit Elementary School, Sampit, South Carolina, Andrews High, Andrews, South Carolina, Allen University, Columbia, South Carolina, the Interdenominational Theological Center, Atlanta, Georgia, The Association for Clinical Pastoral Education, Inc. (CPE) and several military schools.

Effson is an Ordained Itinerant Elder (Elduh) in the African (Affikan) Methodist (Met'dis) Episcopal (Piskubble) Church (Chu'ch) since 1983, serving numerous churches in South Carolina, Louisiana and Texas. He is the Senior Pastor of Youngs Chapel African Methodist Episcopal Church, Irmo, South Carolina since 2013.

He served in the United States Air Force Chaplaincy Corps for 29 years, 7 months and 5 days. He has travelled extensively and deployed to over twenty (25) different countries. Today, he is a Staff Chaplain at William Jennings Bryan Dorn Veterans Administration Medical Center, Columbia, South Carolina since 2013.

Effson is a member of the Omega Psi Phi Fraternity, South Carolina Historical Society, National Trust for Historic Preservation, South Carolina African American Heritage Commission, Disabled American Veteran (DAV), The American Legion, National Veterans Administration (VA) Black Chaplain Association, Henry McNeal Turner African Methodist Episcopal (AME) Chaplain Association, Allen University Alumni Association and The National Association for the Advancement of Colored People (NAACP).

Effson has published the following books:

Precious Memories "Oh, How They Linger" A Walk Through the Tombstones Of Sampit – North Santee (African American Communities) – Part I – (2013)

Precious Memories "Oh, How They Linger" A Walk Through the Tombstones Of Sampit – North Santee (African American Communities) - Part II – (2017)

Libbin' (Living) In De (The) Billige (Village) - Sam Pitt (Sampit, Sampeet) (2017)

He is the owner of **"De (The) Lil Eff Affikan (African) Cump'ny (Company)** and one of the foundering members of the **"De Sam Pitt Kinfolkz Club"** in Columbia, South Carolina.

(Courtesy of the Lil Eff Affikan Cump'ny)

INDEX

A Caring Heart Hospice 27
Acknowledgements 3
Adams, John (Bishop) 223
Adams, John Hurst (Bishop) Gym 163, 184
Adamson, Diana E. 242
African Methodist Episcopal Church 49th Quadrennial Session 274
Aikens, Jordyn Ashley 152
Aikens, Justin 152
Aikens, Tara 152
Alcorn Middle School 49
Allenites 209
Allen, Barbara G. 253
Allen, Richard (Bishop) 43, 182
Allen University, Columbia, SC 182, 183, 195
Allen University, Columbia, SC Board of Trustees 187
Allen University, Columbia, SC Homecoming 2015 207
Allen University Concert Choir 212
Allen University Mu Sigma Chapter (Omega Psi Phi Fraternity) 198
Allen University, Columbia, SC National Register of Historical Places 183
Allen University Yellow Jackets vs. South Carolina Gamecocks Basketball Exhibition 212
Allen University, Columbia, SC Student Center 184
Alpha Holiness Church 22
Alston, Dieanna H. 309
Alston, Raymond 180
Alston, 309
Alston, William (Reverend) 271
Amedisys 271
An "Unveiling Ceremony" 254
Anderson, Ina 145
Anderson, Federico 145

Anderson, Francine 157
Anderson, Phillip C. 202, 203
Anderson, R.B. 41
Anderson, Sandra Aull 203
Annual Richard Allen Awards Gala 311
Armstrong, Bertha Franklin 69
Armstrong, Julia 171
Armstrong, Silas 69
Arnett, B. W. (Bishop) 190
Arnett Hall 190
Assembly Church of Kingstree 32
Atlanta Coast Life Insurance Company 118
Atlanta Coast Lumber Company 44
Aycock, E. Kenneth (Dr.) 28
Babe Creations, Anointed Quilts 3, 50, 51
Baker, Alton 146
Baker, Alvin 146, 147
Baker, Clayton 146, 147
Baker, Clyde 146, 147
Baker, Cornelius 146, 147
Baker, Earl 146, 147
Baker, Elbert 146, 147
Baker, Fred 146, 147
Baker, Hercules 146, 147
Baker, Jade 146
Baker, Jason 146
Baker, Kariconious 146, 147
Baker, Occureda 146, 147
Baker, Regena 146
Baker, Runnette 146, 147
Baker, Ruth Wragg 146, 147
Baker, Thomas, Jr. 146, 147
Baker, Thomas Sr. 146
Baker, Twilar 146, 147
Baker, Wanda 146, 147
Baker Welding Company 146
Ball Diamond 68
Barrineau Laundry 105
Beasley, Larry 284

B. B. Bourne and Company 22
B. B. Smith's Grocery Store 74
B. B. Smith Washer 74
Becca's Gifts & Craft Shop 150
Bell, Agnes 65
Bell, Dietra C. (Reverend) 265
Bell, F. A. (Dr.) 27, 35
Bell, Ki Asti 126
Bell, Kim 126
Bell, Krishona 126
Ben Green's Courier 105
Berry, Addie Bynum (Midwife) 27
Berry, Charlie Sr. (Deacon) 27, 171
Berry, Charlie Jr. 171
Berry, Clyde 171
Berry, Darrell 171
Berry, Laura Trappier 171
Berry, Lucille Ward 171
Berry, Sincera 171
Berry, Stacy 171
Berry, Thomas 171
Bessellieu, Geraldine M. 242
Bethel African Methodist Episcopal Church, Georgetown 273
Bethel Station Train Depot 11
Beverage Depot 111
Bialeka, Jeff (EMT/Fire Fighter) 280
Biden, Joe (Vice President of the United States of America) 276
Big Gate (Thomas & Bessie Bryant Stafford) 54
Bishop Richard Allen Stamp 217
Bishop Preston Warren Williams II Student Residence Hall 196
Bitter Fruit 51
Black Church Are Still Burning Memorial 195
Blandon, S.D. 223
Boatwrights Ezekiel O. 29, 30, 222
Boatwright, Laura Burgess 29, 30, 222
Bolden, Mattie 114

Bolden, William 114
Bolton, Lillie Mae 77
Bolton, Pierce 77
Bones, Edna Ward 111
Bones, Francis Arthur 109, 222
Bones, Nancy Nichols 109
Bone's Radiation Shop 109
Bone's Radiation Shop 109
Bones, Ricky 111
Bones, Roy 111
Bones, Weldon 222
Bones, W. T. 109
Bourne, Adlai 20
Bourne, Amelia 20
Bourne, Benjamin Oscar "BB" 20, 21, 71
Bourne, Benjamin (Pa Bourne) 20
Bourne & Company of Sampit 21
Bourne, Edwin 20
Bourne, Gertrude 20
Bourne, Marian 20
Bourne, Marian Levy 20
Bourne, Oscar 20
Bowen, Henry (Dr.) 268
Bristow, Beulah 65
Britton, David 279
Britton, Essie Graham 242, 243
Britton, Karen 242, 243
Britton, Torrence Jr. 242, 243
Britton, Torrence Sr. 242, 243
Brockington, Sulie Becton 233
Brown, Harold Jean 253
Brown, Joann 142
Brown, Phillip 21
Brown, Sam 41
Brewington, Florie B. Legand 40
Brewington, Levan "Van" (Reverend) 40
Brewington, Lucille B Grant 40
Brewington, Maggie 40
Brewington, Minnie Scott 40
Britton, David 271, 288

Britton, Essie Mae Graham 242
Britton, Lessie Mae Darby 101
Britton Neck Section 33
Brown, Aldeen 89
Brown, Barbara 250
Brown, Benjamin "Little Ben" 143
Brown, Benjamin Sr. 138, 140
Brown, Bernard (Reverend) 230
Brown, Billy 175
Brown Brother from Florence, SC 176
Brown, Cynthia V. (Reverend) 140
Brown Chapel Baptist Church 114
Brown, Daisy Bryant 138, 140
Brown, Delories 89
Brown, Dorothy 89
Brown, Edward (Principal) 142, 143, 144
Brown, Enid 9
Brown, Evon 89
Brown, George 175
Brown, Gwen 271
Brown, Harold Jean 253
Brown, Jane 89
Brown, Joanne Cooper 142, 145
Brown, Joe (Big Brother) 198
Brown, Leroy 89
Brown, Mary 259
Brown, Phillip 21
Brown, Robert Buster 143
Brown, Verletta 89
Brown, William B. (Reverend) 170
Bryant, Barbara Brown 82, 89, 127, 256
Bryant, Bianca 84, 92, 93
Bryant, Bernice Jackson (Bern) 6, 13, 14, 73, 144, 231, 302
Bryant, Bernice Jackson (Bern) Rocking Chairs 5, 58
Bryant, Brewington Eff 316
Bryant, Christopher 58
Bryant, Daniel 94
Bryant, Daniel Defoe (Danny) 6, 14, 281, 282

Bryant, Diana 131
Bryant, Eff 6, 13, 14, 33, 73
Bryant, Eff (Bible) 73
Bryant, Eff (Certificate of Retirement) 73
Bryant, Eff & Bernice Fambly (Family) 6
Bryant, Effson Chester (Reverend) 2, 6, 7, 10, 117, 134, 198, 201, 206, 265 277, 281
Bryant, Effson Chester (Chaplain, Major, USAF) 10
Bryant, Elizabeth Johnson 58
Bryant, Elizabeth Richardson 57
Bryant, Esther 239
Bryant, Everline 94, 95
Bryant, Frazell 94, 95
Bryant, Geneva 234
Bryant, Gladys 6, 7, 297
Bryant, Harrison 7, 129, 131, 132, 133
Bryant, Hester Drayton 14, 227 238, 239
Bryant, Hughie Benjamin (Huey) 6, 129, 134, 237, 246
Bryant, Hughie (Whuie) 58
Bryant, I'Yanna 131
Bryant, Jack 6
Bryant, Janet Gethers 129, 133, 134
Bryant, Jerome 82, 88, 90, 127
Bryant, Jerome Patrick 84, 91, 93
Bryant, Jill 6
Bryant, Joe 14, 238, 239
Bryant, Joe Louis (Big Joe) 173
Bryant, Joseph 208, 238, 239
Bryant, Justice 131
Bryant, Kenneth 94
Bryant, Kimberly Houston 91
Bryant, Lauretta 82. 88
Bryant, Leroy 245
Bryant, Leveron 94
Bryant, Lou Emma (GoGo) 6, 13
Bryant, Lula Louise Smith 57,
Bryant, Marcus 129, 131, 133

Bryant, Martha Pittman 82, 83, 84, 85, 86, 87, 88
Bryant, Ollin Jr. 94, 95
Bryant, Ollin Sr. 83, 94, 95
Bryant, Pattie 239.
Bryant, Patricia 58, 82, 88
Bryant, Patrice 84, 90, 92, 93
Bryant, Paul 58, 94
Bryant, Queen Elizabeth Thomas 2
Bryant, Rebecca 94, 95
Bryant, Rebecca Stafford 57, 94
Bryant Road Sign 82
Bryant, Robert 57
Bryant, Robert (Bob) 83
Bryant, Robert (Bobby) 239
Bryant, Rollin 83, 84, 85, 86, 87, 88, 298
Bryant, Rosetta 82, 88
Bryant, Sadie 94
Bryant, Samuel 22
Bryant, Samuel 223
Bryant, Samuel (Sammy) 239
Bryant, Sarah Bell (Teacher) 232
Bryant, Wesley 57, 94, 198
Bryant, Wesley (Old Home) 57
Bryant, Wesley Michael (Wes) 6, 14, 57, 134
Bryant, Zilcia Elizabeth 2, 134, 316
Bryant, Zilcia Elizabeth (Airman) 10
Bryant's Electric 82
Bryant Family (Hand-drawing Stretch) 12
Bryant's Grocery Store 57
Bryant's Stained Glass Window 87
Burns, Edward 204
Burns, Rodella (Reverend) 204
Butler, H. B. Jr. (Reverend) 273
Buttone, Charlesann H. 253
Bullock, Christian 145
Bullock, Dalita 145
Bullock, Floyd 141, 145
Bullock, James 145
Bullock, Heather 146

Bullock, Thedra Thompson 145
Bynum, Esell 27
Bynum, Mary June 27
Callebero, Olga 271
Campbell, Jabez Pitt (Bishop)
Campbell, Jon T. (Secretary of State)
Capers, Alice Hinds 286, 287
Capers, Ezekiel 286
Capers' Family Photograph 287
Captivating Columbia District Office 168
Carr, A. T. (Reverend) 273
Carrere, Hillary 9
Cast Iron Frying Pan with Drawing 26
Centennial Encyclopedia of the AME Church 43
Chandler, Albert 180
Chapelle Hall Auditorium 199
Charlton, Ron 279
Cherry Hill Missionary Baptist Church 248
Chevrolet 1956 Bel-Air 37
Chevrolet 1948 (Fleet Master) 32
Chosen Sisters 174
Clark, Catherine Sue 140, 141
Clark, Eric 176
Clark, George 140
Clark, Gus 140
Clark, Rita 140
Clark, Rosita 140
Clark, Susan Brown (Nurse) 140, 143
Clements, Cornellus 223
Clyburn, James E. (Congressman) 270, 275
Coffield, Jestine 261
Cohen, Benjamin 22
Cokley, Ada Edith Brown (Mother) 247
Cokley, Ann 247
Cokley, Frank 247
Cokley, Bakir Allyne 249
Cokley, Cindy Graham 249
Cokley, D'Oscar 249
Cokley, Henry Jr. 247
Cokley, Henry Sr. 247

Cokley, James (Dr.) 248, 249
Cokley, Jami Davina 249
Cokley, Janie 247
Cokley, Johnny 246
Cokley, Vera (Teacher) 247
Cole, Bruce (Dr.) 218
Cole, Lady June (President) 216, 217
Coleman, Frank 198
Coleman, Kristen Michelle 163, 165, 166
Coleman, Melvin (Reverend) 163, 164 165
Coleman, Rosalyn Grant (Reverend) 163, 164, 165. 166, 167
Collins, Betty (Nurse) 269
Collins, Herbert M. "Chip" 21
Conyers, Belinda Wilson 151, 153
Conyers, Jaylen 151
Conyers, Serena 151
Conyers, Terryus 151
Conyers, Tianna 151
Cook, Bernard 210
Coon Town 233
Cooper, Adrea 176
Cooper, Annie Cooper 113
Cooper, Carrie Lee Myers 280
Cooper, Carolos 80
Cooper, Elizabeth 180
Cooper, Emma Darby 102
Cooper, Ernest (Reverend) 29, 30
Cooper, Hattie Smith 228, 231
Cooper, Janie (Dr.) 271
Cooper, J.D. 113
Cooper, Jeffery 80
Cooper, Jermaine 180
Cooper, Jessie (Fire Marshall) 280
Cooper, Joe 80
Cooper, Joe Louis 234
Cooper, John 80
Cooper, Johnny 80
Cooper, Jonathan 180
Cooper, Joseph 80

Cooper, Joseph 113
Cooper, Juanita 101
Cooper, Kathy Knowlin 280
Cooper, Katrina Leeann Cooper 180
Cooper, Lai 180
Cooper, Lee Jay 180
Cooper, Leon 180
Cooper, Leon Jr. 180
Cooper, Lillie Mae Duncan 113
Cooper, Louedith 180
Cooper, Marion (JC) 113
Cooper, Marion Jr. 113
Cooper, Mary 113
Cooper, Michelle 180
Cooper, Nathaniel 80, 280
Cooper, Oscar James 198
Cooper, Robert 176
Cooper, Rosalyn 80
Cooper, Sampson D. 242
Cooper, Shirvey 113
Cooper, Solomon 113
Cooper, Sylvia 80
Cooper, Thomas (Sunny) 173
Cooper, Thomasina 80
Cooper, Vervitine 113
Cooper, Virginia Lambert 29, 30
Coppin Hall Historical Restoration 2002
Cornerstone 185
Corley, Lillie 65
Craven County 17
Cribb, Cammie 35
Cribb, Lloyd 35
Cribb, Nell Morris 35, 36
Cribb, Vickie 35
Cumbee, Shirley 246
Cumberland African Methodist Episcopal Church 223
Cunningham, B.C. 168
Cunningham, David (Medic) 280
Daniel, Alfred (Medical Director) 271
Daniel, Takia 153

Darby, Alfred (Reverend) 46
Darby, David Benjamin 102
Darby, Darlene 101, 285
Darby, Freddie 153
Darby, Kenneth 101
Darby, Milford 72, 101
Darby, Rosa 231, 302
Darby & Son Trucking Company 101
David Smith's Grocery & Laundry 66
David Smith's Logging Company 68
Davis, Archie Sr. 22
Davis, Bertha 97
Davis, Enid 9
Davis, Francis Smalls (Midwife) 28, 302
Davis, Gertrude 245, 302
Davis, Hallot 33
Davis, Herman 33
Davis, Iesha Amanda Scott 9
Davis, Janice 7
Davis, Jason 9
Davis, Ronald Charles II 9
Deas, Clemnite 79
Deas, Dianna 79
Deas, Daniel 89
Deas, Emma 89
Deas, Essie Duncan 76
Deas, Henry Jr. 79
Deas, Henry Sr. 72, 78
Deas' Logging Company 78
Deas, Lou Pearl 79
Deas' Shop 79
Deas, Thomas 79
Deas. Thomas James 78
Deas, Walter 78
Deas, Weldon 79
Delta Sigma Theta Sorority 92
Demphis Wragg Logging Company 235
Dennison, L.M. (Reverend) 286
Denwordy, While 269
Diabetes CORE Group 271

Dickerson Theological Seminary Ministerial Group 292
Disnee Day Care 154
D. J. Lord JAZZ 129, 132
Dobby, March 22
Dorsey, Nicholas 58
Dorsey, Sue Elizabeth Bryant 55, 58
Dozier, A.B. 242
Dozier, Naomi M. 242
Drayton, Alafair Knowlin Beasley 284
Drayton, Emma "Monk" Ravennel 238
Drayton, Lashawn 124, 125
Drayton, Lucille Bryant 122, 123, 124, 226, 250
Drayton, Marquise 126
Drayton, Odell (Dell) 123, 127
Drayton, Rebecca (Becca) 123
Drayton, Rodney 124, 125
Drayton, Sandy W. (Presiding Elder) 157, 205, 218
Drayton, Shirley Frasier 123, 124, 125
Drayton, Thomas Earl (Reverend) 238, 279
Drayton, Vincent 122, 123, 127, 176
Drayton, Willie Edward Drayton Jr. 123, 124, 125, 297
Drayton, Willie Edward Drayton Sr. 122, 123
Drayton's Auto Salvage 122
Dudley Beauty College 56
Dudley, Eunice M. 56
Dudley, Joe L. (Dr.) 56
Dumm, Jim 253
Duncan, 176
Duncan, Annie Mae Cooper 101, 102
Duncan, Arthur 106
Duncan, Arthur Lee 106
Duncan, Clevie 106
Duncan, Henry 106
Duncan, Herman 101, 102
Duncan, Jeniqua (Dr.) 271

Duncan, Joe 106
Duncan, Junior Lee 106
Duncan, Leroy (Baby) 102, 226
Duncan, Mark 176
Duncan, Mary 106, 232
Duncan, Mary T. 170, 302
Duncan, Norine 226
Duncan, Peggy 106
Duncan, Rosa Grant 106
Edgar Cleveland Morris' Store 33
Edward, Thomas W. Jr. 279
Elliott, Almenar Mercer 227, 232
Elliott, Benny K. 253
Elmore, Kathleen 261
Elmore, Marva Tompkins 269
Emanuel African Methodist Episcopal Church (Emanuel Nine) 215
Emanuel African Methodist Episcopal Church, Columbia 145
Evans, Joe (Reverend) 245
Ervin, Betty Bryant (Reverend) 246
Ervin, William Conyers Jr. (Reverend) 191, 192, 193, 227
Ervin, William Conyers III (Reverend) 246
Eve's Southern Café 136
Bachelor of Arts Degree 191, 246
Eve' Southern Café 136
Farrell, Terry L. 279
Felder, Lewis 171
Felder, Peter (Director of the Allen University Concert Choir) 221
Facine, Marie 271
First Assembly of God Church, Kingstree 32
First Pentecostal Church, Kingstree 32
Flowers, George (Dr.) 188
Flowers, Phil 47
Footman, Dianna Deas 269
Founder's Day Celebration 2016 216
Four Gospel Jubilee of Sampit 173

Frank the Cook 21
Francis, Kim 136
Frasier, Arthur 234
Frasier, Ben 30
Frasier, Bernice Lousie 228, 230, 231
Frasier, Christine 70
Frasier, Ida Evans 245
Frasier, Johnny Lee 70
Frasier, Marie R. 230
Frasier, Mary Alice 70
Frasier, Mary Funnye 70
Frasier, Ollie 125
Frasier, Shirley 246
Frasier, Thomas 173
Freeman, Anna 157
Friendfield Plantation 274
Friendship United Methodist Church 34, 35
Fulmore, Ralph 201
Fulmore, Sandra 201
Fun Day at Sampit Elementary School 257
Funnie, Kedric 221
Funnye, John (Funnye) 173
Furerson, Joseph 223
Gadsen, Charles "Chuck" 253
Garrett, Nimai 210, 219
Gary, Ambrose (Reverend) 61
Gary, Rose Lee Peguese 61
Gasque Road 288
Gasque, Andrew 289, 290
Gasque, Carrie Lee Wilson 289, 295
Gasque, Clarissa 284, 285
Gasque, Daisy 289
Gasque, Darlene 284, 285
Gasque, Florine Knowlin 290
Gasque, Geneva 289
Gasque, Grover Jr. 56
Gasque, Grover Sr. 56
Gasque, Leroy Sr. (Deputy Sheriff) 281
Gasque, Jacqueline 284, 285
Gasque, Janie Louise 284, 302

Gasque, Jenette 56
Gasque, Joan (Carrie) 289
Gasque, John 22
Gasque, John Clifton (Bishop) 289, 290, 291, 292
Gasque, John (Confederate Pension Application) 293
Gasque, John Wesley (Tillie) 173, 229, 289, 290, 295
Gasque, Julius 22
Gasque, June 22
Gasque, Kiziah 286
Gasque, Larry 295
Gasque, Larry Jr. 295
Gasque, Lena White 52, 302
Gasque, Leroy (Roy) 173
Gasque, Levern 295
Gasque, Martha 288
Gasque, Mary 288, 295
Gasque, Mary 239, 285
Gasque, Melissa 7,295
Gasque, Michael 295
Gasque, Mickie 295
Gasque, Nathan 289, 290
Gasque, Pressley Jr. 284, 285
Gasque, Pressley Sr. 226, 284, 285
Gasque, Raymond 289
Gasque, Rena 289
Gasque, Rutha Mae 234
Gasque, Sarah 295
Gasque, Sarah Jane 289
Gasque, Shayla 295
Gasque, Thomas 289
Gasque, Troy 27, 52, 251
Gasque, Veronica Stafford 295
Gasque, Violet 295
Gasque, Wesley 289
Gasque, Willie (Elder) 289, 290, 294
Gasque, William 22, 37
Gasque's Barber Shop 56
Gause, Doris Olivia Cooper 30, 31

Gause, Raymond 31, 202
Gaymon, Rufus (Reverend) 202
Geer, George R. 253
Georgetown Country Fire-EMS Station #5 279
Georgetown Country Recycle Center 314
Georgetown Plantation Police Badge 24
Georgetown 16
Georgetown Hospital System 271
Georgetown Times 24
Georgetown Sheriff Department 271
Georgia Railroad Fright Depot 9
Gethers, Betty 130
Gethers, Carol 130
Gethers, Carrie 130
Gethers, Doretha 130
Gethers, Richard 130
Gethers, Ruth Mae 130
Gerald, Frances Drayton 127
Gerald, Melvin 127
German, KarCelia Brown 142
Gibson 256
Gipson, Emma 198
Giles, Roxie Sanders (Nurse) 148
Gilliam, Gerry Lee 198, 200, 208
Gilliard, Krishona 126
Gilliard, Reather 250
Gillard, Sandra D. 271
Gilman, Judy (Secretary) 271
Gilyard, Christopher 226
Glen Stafford's Residential Electrical Business 116
Goff, Novel Sr. (Reverend) 188, 189
Grady, Z. L. (Bishop) 188
Graham, James 242
Graham, Martha 242, 246
Grand Opening & Ribbon Cutting Event 271
Grant, Angela Elizabeth 47
Grant, Anne 246

Grant, Bernie Elizabeth Frasier (Reverend) 128
Grant, Craig 84
Grant, Deborah 163, 164
Grant, Dell 163, 164
Grant, Dorothy Smith 71
Grant, Elizabeth 28
Grant, Florence White 107
Grant, Franklin 163, 164
Grant, Franklin 68
Grant, Glendale 67
Grant, Glennie 71
Grant, Gloria 285
Grant, Henrietta Brown Colleton 89
Grant, Henry R. 128
Grant, Isaiah 86
Grant, Jacquelyn (Dr.) 163, 164
Grant, Jefferson 23
Grant, Jefferson Jr. 255
Grant, Jen 255
Grant, Joey A. 67
Grant, John 82
Grant, John Jr. 84
Grant, Joseph J. (Reverend) 41, 163, 164
Grant, Joseph 163, 164
Grant, Lillie Bell 231
Grant, Lillie Mae Ward 163, 164
Grant, Lucius Sr. 128
Grant, Mannie 100
Grant, Manny Leo "Fudd" 106
Grant, Mary Alice 67
Grant, Patricia Ann 163, 164
Grant, Patricia Bryant 82
Grant, Ra' 255
Grant, Reggie (Reverend) 298
Grant, Wayne 255
Grant, Willard 107
Grant, William 176
Grant, Willie 226
Grate, Adrian 153

Grate, Ben 253
Gray, Laddie 145
Gray, Levora Thompson 145
Grayson, Alfred 44
Grayson, Angeline Greene 48, 49
Grayson, Be'auka 46
Grayson, David 45
Grayson, David Lee (Elder) 44
Grayson, Delphine Sellers 48, 49
Grayson, Elizabeth 44
Grayson, Elizabeth Singleton 47, 48, 49
Grayson, Henry 44
Grayson, Idelle 44
Grayson, Joanna 44
Grayson, Joanna Hamilton 44, 45
Grayson, Joe Lee 44
Grayson, Julius 22
Grayson, Loretta "Babe" 48, 49, 50, 161
Grayson, Marcetia 48, 49
Grayson, Mary J. Benson 48, 49
Grayson, Matthew 44
Grayson, Maxine 44
Grayson, Mildred 44
Grayson, Patricia Mathis 48, 49
Grayson, Phenie Ladson 45
Grayson, Richard Jr. 48, 49
Grayson, Richard Sr. 44, 46, 48, 49
Grayson, Rose 44
Grayson, Sammy 44
Grayson, Wesley 44, 45
Grayson, Yvonne 48, 49
Greater Gethsemane Baptist Church 27
Greater Joiner Temple 50
Green, Augustus Jr. 60
Green, Augustus Sr. 60
Green, A. Z. 223
Green, Ida Holmes 59, 60, 231
Green, James 254
Green, James Sr. 176
Green, Kevin 254
Green, Doris 61

Green, G. 223
Green, Ida Mae 61
Green, Lidia White Hanna 81
Green, Marie Brown 89
Green, Mary 22
Green, Maude Ernestine Gary 61
Green, Saby (Reverend) 22
Green, Samuel (Reverend) 61
Green, Samuel "SJ" 61
Green, Stussant A. 223
Green, William 88, 89, 90
Green, William (Honor Flight) 90
Green, William Sr. (Reverend) 59, 60
Green, William Sr. & Ida Holmes) Home 61
Green's Grocery Store 59
Greene, Benjamin E. 105
Greene, Charlena (Teacher) 226
Greene, Doris 193, 242
Greene, Hazel 226
Greene, Margaret Holmes 105
Greene, T.O. (Bishop) 191
Greene, Vanessa 309
Ground Breaking for Fire Station (No. 5) 279
Gullah (Geechie) 12
Gullah Museum & Gift Shop 158, 160, 161
Gun Shop 110
Hadden, Gwendolyn O. 191
Habersham, Thomas (Reverend) 61
Hall, Charles 141
Hall, Laura Thompson 145
Hand Cranked Telephone 27
Hand Pump (St. Paul AME Church School) 225
Hanging Tree 315
Hardee, Mildred (Nurse) 268
Harrison, Debra 259
Hawthorne, Clarke R. 168
Hayes, Sheryal 246
Hemingway, Arthur 176

Hemingway, H. Edsel 279
Hemingway, Jeremiah 219
Hemingway, Willie (Reverend) 176
Henry R. Grant's Plumbing & Repair Service 128
Herbert, John 223
Herman, Janet 261
Herriott, Joe E. 271
Hewitt, Dale (Lt) 280
Heyward, junior 229
Higgins, Eugenia DeCosta (Mother) 192
Higgins, Samuel R. (Bishop) 191, 192
Holmes, Audrey 153
Holmes, Carry 153
Holmes, Cassandra 153
Holmes, Cecil 58
Holmes, Claudetta 153
Holmes, Darren L. 253
Holmes, Edwin 96, 97
Holmes Electrical Building & Contractor 96
Holmes, Emma Davis 96
Holmes, Evone 153
Holmes, Daniel 153
Holmes, Gabriel 153
Holmes, Henry Jr. 176
Holmes, Ida Knowlin 105, 235
Holmes, James Arthur 168
Holmes, Joyce Cox 271
Holmes, Levi Sr. 153
Holmes, Lizzie 153
Holmes, Mary 153
Holmes, Martha 153
Holmes, Meshana 153
Holmes, Minnie 153
Holmes, Nell 153
Holmes, Peggy 153
Holmes, Samuel 105, 235
Holmes, Samuel James 96, 120, 226
Holmes, Thomas 22

Holmes, Tisby Bryant 55, 58
Holmes, Vanessa 153
Holmes, Yolanda (Dr.) 96, 97
Honor Flight Network 90
Hood, David 279
Howard, B.C. 41
House, Julia 157
House, William 157
Huell, Barbara 114
Hughes, Carl B. 242
Hughes, Margaret 252
Hughes, Sampson (Principal) 236
Hughes, Tom 63
Hughie, Mary 242
Humes, Theresa 246
Humphrey, Frank 22
Humphrey, Mary Knowling 306
Interdenominational Theological Center 265, 266
International Paper Company 63, 72, 73
Iszard, Annie Cooper 112
Iszard, Lamar 112
James, Edward 188
James, Frederick Calhoun (Bishop) 187, 188, 189
James, Leroy (Reverend) 201
James, Rose Lawrence 201
James, Rosa Lee Gray 188
James Square Shopping Center 187
James, Theresa (Mother) 187, 189
Jayroe, James Porter "JP" 228
Jenkins, Melvin (Reverend) 7
Jenks, Bari 9
Jenks, Leo 9
Jimmy's Place 53
Joe Cooper's Logging Company 80
John Duncan and the Singing Stars 176
John Hurst Adams Gym 184
Johnson, Charles (Chair) 271
Johnson, Clifton 116, 121
Johnson, Ella Mae Davis 116, 121

Johnson, Ethel Mae 121
Johnson, Etta 107
Johnson, Isreal 121
Johnson, Mary 121
Johnson, Rovina 121
Johnson, Vivian 121
Jones, Connie Robinson 272
Jones, George G. (Father of Rosemary School) 233
Jones, Mac Charles (Reverend) 195
Jones, Melody Bille 201
Jordan, Felix (Reverend) 140
Joseph, Lizar 24
Joy, LaKisha 255
J. S. Flipper Library 183
Kappa Alpha Psi 209
Keith Builders & Home Improvement 128
Keith's Grocery Store 62
Keith, Charles 22
Keith, Clarence 22
Keith, Clarence Jr. 128
Keith, Edith Sanders 62, 65
Keith, Edith Sanders (91st Birthday) 64
Keith, Gertrude 62, 63, 64, 149
Keith, H. 223
Keith, Helen 62
Keith, Herbert 62
Keith, Inez 62
Keith, Lila 62
Keith, Nathaniel 63, 149
Keith, Nathaniel Lee 62
Keith, Robert 62
Keith, Sara Myers 154
Keith, Vermel 62
Kennedy, Robert 205
Kennedy, Willie Jr. 120
Kinloch, Louise H. 242
Knowlin, Amos 100
Knowlin, Blondell 178
Knowlin Brothers of Sampit 177
Knowlin, Charles 177, 178, 179

Knowlin, Denise 178
Knowlin, Dorothy 100
Knowlin, Dorothy 174
Knowlin, Elizabeth 100
Knowlin, Elizabeth 239
Knowlin, Eve 136
Knowlin, Florence 100
Knowlin, Floyd Allen (Bishop) 56, 114, 177, 178
Knowlin, Gale 178
Knowlin, Gertrude 177
Knowlin, Gideon 194
Knowlin, Harriston 284
Knowlin, Hassie 100
Knowlin, Ida 177
Knowlin, Jake 174
Knowlin, Janie Louise 284
Knowlin, Jerome Lavern "Hunk" 194
Knowlin, Jimmy 100
Knowlin, Joe Nathan 281
Knowlin, John 178
Knowlin, John R. 177
Knowlin, Juanita 100
Knowlin, Leroy 100
Knowlin, Linnie Grant 100, 231
Knowlin, Lizzie Bell Duncan 177
Knowlin, Luther 100, 174
Knowlin, Magnolia 100
Knowlin, Magdelene 239
Knowlin, Mannie 100
Knowlin, Margaret 174
Knowlin, Myrtle 178
Knowlin, Patricia 178
Knowlin, Peter 38
Knowlin, Robell Duncan 178
Knowlin, Robert Lee 80
Knowlin, Ruth 174
Knowlin, Sarah 38, 194
Knowlin, Sarah 178
Knowlin, Wilma 174
Knowlin's Singers from Jamaica Long Island, New York 174
Knowling, Demetra 306
Knowling, Larry 306
Knowling, Margaret 306
Knowling, Mary 306
Knowling, Mattie 304, 307, 308
Knowling, Roy 304, 306, 307, 308
Knowling, Thomas 306
Knowling, Trudy Holmes 306
Knox, Brookes Larnell 153
Lab Corp 271
Labostrie, Erin 9
Ladies of Sampit Elementary School Place 261
Ladson, Dorothy L. 234
Lamar's Fish & Chip 112
Lambert, Rufus 27
Lance, Thomas S. (Reverend) 114
La'Trece, Savanda 153
Law, Terry B. 170
Levi J. Coppin Hall 185
Lewis, C. (Reverend) 223
Lewis, Clarence 176
Lewis, Lille Mae 286, 287
Libbin' in de Billige – Sam Pitt 13
Lighthouse of Jesus Christ Church 56
Linda's Gifts & Crafts Shop
Lindsey, Linda Wright 264
Linnie Knowlin's Transportation 100
Liquor Store 110
Livington, Mazine 255
Love, Amos 198
Luncheon Wragg Brick Work 81
Lula the Nurse 20
Luster, Donald (Reverend) 98
Mac, Tall Bigdaddy 153
Maceo Lodge No. 55 F.A.M. 41
Mack, Dorothy Burgess Thompson 240, 261

Mack, Sabrina Mack (Principal) 255, 259, 260
Male Leadership Empowerment Symposium 206
Mance, R.W. (Reverend) 273
Manick, Cassandra Holmes 153
Mansfield Plantation 24
Mansfield Plantation Slave Chapel 24
Maps of South Carolina Parishes 18
Marshall, Albert 22
Maunie J. White & Son 115
May Day Spring Festival 257
Mays, Benjamin E. (Dr.) 263
McCants, Gwendolyn 234
McCants, S. P. 223
McConnell, Kate D. 35, 222
McConnell, Jannie 271
McCray, Jasper 255
McCrea, Dalvon 153
McDonald, Leroy (Staff Sergeant) 262
McDonald, Veronica Scott 262
McGainey, Annie Sanders 149
McGill, John Yancey (State Citizen) 228
McKnight, Alfair 108
McKnight, Alvina D. 242
McKnight, Annie D. 170
McKnight, Bexter 108
McKnight, Charlena 108
McKnight, Charlie Mae 108
McKnight, Clarice 108
McKnight, Doward 108
McKnight & Frasier Funeral Home 75, 77
McKnight & Frasier Funeral Home (Dedication Ceremony) 77
McKnight, Jannie Mae Berry 108, 171
McKnight, Jon 108
McKnight, Leon 108
McKnight, Mary Cooper 75, 77
McKnight Professional Gardening & Cleaning Service 108
McKnight, Richard 75
McKnight, Ricky Joe 108
McKnight, RJ 108
McKnight, Sylvester 108
McKnight, Wallace J. Jr. 76
McKnight, Wallace III 76
McKnight, Wallace J. Sr. (Reverend) 75, 76
Board of Trustee 76
Motor Vehicle Building 76
McKnight, Venus 108
McManus, Gilmore 242
Means, Arnetha Smith 240, 242
Means, Ellis Calvin Jr. 240, 242
Means, Ellis Calvin III 240
Meeting Place 167
Michelle Obama Family History Quilt 159
Miller, Leona Myers 154, 271
Miller, Monroe 202
Miller, Wilhelmenia Elizabeth 203
Miller, Tabitha 145
Minnie Tax Service 116
Miss Nell's Tour – The Real South Tour 36
Mitchell, Jeffery (Elder) 265
Mixon, J.F. 73
Mock, James M. Jr. 279
Mock, Linda (Country Auditor) 307
Mom Almee 20
Morant, Johnny 279
Morning Glory Cemetery, Inc. 75
Morris, Ann 34
Morris, Clifton 34
Morris, Dan 34
Morris, Dosia Trisvan Anderson 34
Morris, Edgar Cleveland 33, 34
Morris, Francis 34
Morris, Herbert 34
Morris, Ida Bell 34
Morris, Jack 34
Morris, Lucille 34
Morris, Marie 34

Morris, Nell 34, 153
Morris, Rufus 34
Moss, Elizabeth 259
Moultrie, Brian 126
Moultrie, John 126
Moultrie, Tom 72
Moyd, Curtis 180
Moyd, Darryl 180
Moyd, Derrick 180
Mt. Zion African Methodist Episcopal Church 126
Mt. Zion African Methodist Episcopal Church School 250
Muldrow, Emma 198
Mu Sigma Fraternity – Omega Psi Phi 208
Myers, E. P. 41
Myers, George II 154
Myers, George III 154
Myers, Isiah 154
Myers, Jeffrey 22
Myers, John 101, 127
Myers, Leila 154
Myers, Thomas L. 240
National Honor Society at Rosemary High School 237
Native Sampas Indians 16
Neighborhood Clean Up Group 303
Nelson, Alvin 246
Nelson, Barbara (Reverend) 81
Nelson, Willie J. (Presiding Elder) 168
New Hope Union Methodist Episcopal Church 22, 80
New Hope Chapter #343 170
Newman, Benita 210
Newman, Willie 201, 210
Nine-Miles Curve 12, 39
Nine-Mile Curve Fire Station 279
Nixon, Danny 246
Ntsangani, Noluthando 165, 166
No. 1 Store 35
No. 2 Store 27, 29
Norris, Richard Franklin (Bishop) 163
North Santee Senior Citizen Center 250
Norwood, Lee 305
Norwood, Susie 305
Notary Public Certificates 43
Nowling, Robert Jr. 22
Nowling, Robert Sr. 22
Oak Grove Grammar School 11, 35, 222, 224
Oak Grove Colored School 11, 224
Obama, Barack Hussein (44th President of the United States of America) 272, 273, 276
Obama, Barack (Democratic Nominee for the President of the United Sates of America 275, 277
Obama, Michelle Lavaughn Robinson (First Lady of the United States of America) 272, 273, 274, 276
Obama, Michelle Lavaughn Robinson (Michelle Obama History Quilt) 159
Odom, David L. 242
Old Card Road 11
Old Exchange & Provost Durgean 24
Old Kilsock Train 21
Olivet Church, Fayetteville, GA 7
Omega Phi Fraternity 198
Omega Psi Phi Fraternity (Mu Sigma Chapter) Display 199
Original Truetone Singers of Andrews, SC 180
Orr, Francena Frasier (Reverend) 230
Out Door Toilet (St. Paul AME Church School) 225
Palin, Sarah (Governor) 276
Paradise Park, Silver Spring, Florida 226
Parrott, Allen W. (Reverend) 205
Patterson, Sunni (Officiant) 9
Payne Institute Marker, Hodges, SC 182

Pediatric Waiting Room (In Memory of Mr. Thomas J. Robinson) 272
Perry, Chandler 152
Peterson, Jill (Dr.) 269
Phi Beta Sigma 309
Pinckney, Clementa (Reverend) 202, 205
Pinckney, Eliana 215
Pinckney, Felitcha Cumbee 258
Pinckney, Jennifer 202, 215
Pinckney, Malana 215
Pinckney, Myra 271
Pinckney, Roberta H. (CEO) 271
Pittman, Almeter 83
Pittman, Annie Laura 82, 83
Pittman, Dora 83
Pittman, Ollie 83
Pittman, Rome 85
Pittman, Rosa Gray 85
Point, Samantha W. 255
Police Academy, Columbia SC 282
Porter, James 228
Postell, Joseph (Presiding Elder) 202
Pressley, Alberta 241
Pressley, Cloria McKnight 241
Pressley, Louise 241
Pressley, Onetha 241
Pressley, Mary 241
Pressley, Natine 241
Pressley, Samuel 241
Prince, Brenda 246
Prince Frederick Parish 11
Prince George's Parish Church Winyah Parish 11
Prioleau, Angela 254
Prioleau, Crystal 254
Prioleau, Della 254
Prioleau, Edmund 251
Prioleau, James Edmund (Reverend) 251, 254, 271
Prioleau, James Edmund III 254

Prioleau, Maria W. 251
Prioleau, Rebecca Vernette Williams 252, 254
Prout, Earl Edwin 94, 95
Prout, Lila Mae Bryant 94, 127
Pugh, Lisa 255
Pushia, Suzaanna 246
Quarter Century Society, Inc. 73
Quiet Storm Electronics 129
Queen's Beauty & Hair Care 56
Racial Crop and Systah 51
Ragin, M. Charmaine (Presiding Elder) 205
Ramon's Brownie Pills 31
Rapley, Wanda (Reverend) 166
Ray, Aisha 84, 86
Ray, Christopher 82, 86
Ray, Jeremiah 8
Ray, Lauretta 82, 86
Ray, Robert 82, 86
Reed, Mac (Fire Chief Georgetown Country) 279, 280
Reid, Frank Madison Sr. (Bishop) 191
Reown, Lila Keith 237
Reown, Luther N. 237
Reown, Oliver L. 237
Reynolds, Jerrod (Dr.) 271
Rhue, S. 223
Rhue, Tryphena 246
Rice, Sydney 261
Richardson, Judy (Presiding Elder) 205
Richardson, Ruthledge 57
Richardson, Phoeble Davis 57
Richburg, Ella Gadsden 204
Richburg, Tiffany 204
Riley, Richard W. (Governor) 43
Rish, Brandon 145
Rish, Brandon Jr. 145
Rish, LaTonya 145

Rising Sons and Daughters Lodge Hall 171
Roberts, Walter 29
Robinson, Mary 273
Robinson, Chilwill 255
Robinson, Frasier 253, 273
Robinson, Frasier Sr. 159
Robinson, Jessie 240, 241
Robinson, Jim 273
Robinson, Marline 165, 166
Robinson, Rosa Lee Pressley (Teacher) 240, 241, 242
Robinson, Rosella Cohen 253
Robinson, Thomas J. (Principal) 253, 272
Rodgers, Jerome 99, 123, 127
Rodgers, Nina 99, 127
Rodrigues, Andres J. (J.D) 156, 157, 158, 160
Rodrigues, Beatrice 157
Rodrigues, Janette 157
Rodrigues, Vermell "Bunny" Smith 155, 156, 157, 158, 159
Rosemary Alumni Annual Holiday Banquet 246
Rosemary High School 233
Rosemary High School Graduation Class of 1964 244
Rosemary High School Graduation Class of 1970 246
Rosemary Station 11
Ross Stafford Business Office 39
Ross Stafford Conference Room 42
Ross Stafford's Logging Business 39
Roy & Mattie Knowling's Family 308
Rudolph, Helen P. 279
Ruffin, Twyla 133
Rufus Lambert's Store 27
Rutledge, William 180
Sabb, Leroy 201, 211
Sabb, Venus 201, 210, 211
Sajak, Tatt 255
Sampas (Sampit) Indians 11, 17

Sampit 12, 17, 18
Sampit Action Groups 302
Sampit Bridge 17
Sampit Christmas Parade 298
Sampit Community Watch Group 307, 308
Sampit Elementary School 251, 253
Sampit Elementary School 4th Grade Class 255
Sampit Elementary School 5th Grade Class 256
Sampit Elementary School Library Medical Center Staff 259
Sampit Elementary School Waiting Area 258
Sampit Elementary School "Welcome to Sampit Elementary School 259
Sampit Senior Citizens Center 227, 228, 231
Sampit Senior Citizens Center Ribbon Cutting Ceremony 228, 229
Sampit Headstart Graduation Class 232
Sampit Headstart Program 231, 231
Sampit Logging Company 71
Sampit Lookout Tower 313
Sampit Masonic Lodge #429 170
Sampit Monument 103
Sampit – North Santee Cucumber Market (Shed) 281
Sampit Park 313
Sam Pitt 11
Sampit River 17
Sampit Township 12
Sampit United Methodist Church 34
Sanders, Annie 148, 149, 226
Sanders, Bernice 63
Sanders, Creola Grant 62, 67
Sanders, Dodie 63
Sanders, Elizabeth 148
Sanders, Ethel 234
Sanders, Ezekiel 63
Sanders, Francis Grant 63, 148

Sanders, Franklin "Bigwheelz Sanders" 56
Sanders, James   149
Sanders, Jim 63
Sanders, Lillian 63
Sanders, Quacoo 22
Sanders, Rock Humphrey 63
Sanders, Rosa 63
Sanders, Sam (Reverend) 62
Sanders, Shirley 148, 149
Sanders, Teresa 63
Sanders, Thomas O. 148
Sanders, Thomas L. 148, 149
Sanders, Thomasena 234
Sanders, Tom 63
Sanders, Tonney 255
Saultus, Henry 24
SC Governor's Office of Aging 271
Scott 256
Scott, Alphonso N. (Reverend) 262, 265
Scott, Benjamin 262, 263
Scott, Decmist Inez 65
Scott, Donnell 153
Scott, Evelyn 262, 263
Scott, Gladys Bryant 7, 8, 134
Scott, Iesha Amanda 7, 9, 134
Scott, Laurietta 262
Scott, Leroy 262
Scott, Martha   246
Scott, Maudest Rhue 253, 255, 271
Scott, Pompey (Scotty) 7, 134
Scott, Veronica   262
Scribe With Sampit Roots 300
Selph, Annie 86
Sessions, David E. 242
Seventh Episcopal District Messenger 192
Seward, Lee M. (Presiding Elder) 168
Shackleford, Stace Marie 153
Sherald, Ethel Buttone 264
Sherald, John L.   264

Sheriff, Hilla (MD) 28
Simmon, Robbin 223
Simmons, Annie G. 202, 215
Singleton, Caroline V. 250
Singleton, Henry "Hackless"
Singleton, March (Reverend) 22, 223
Singleton, Maria Kennedy (Danny) 47
Singleton, Tajuanda 255
Slave Auctions Sign, Charleston 24
Slave Chapel (Mansfield Plantation) 24
Small, Ethel Bolden (Nurse) 114
Small, Samuel R. 114
Smalls, Elijah 28
Smalls, Ethel G. 242
Smalls, Joanna Grant 28
Smalls, Marion 201
Smith, Anna Simmons 157
Smith, Beulah Harris   98
Smith, Buster 153
Smith, Carl 234
Smith, Charles 72
Smith, Cleo Stafford 98, 127
Smith, Daisy Bell Gasque 290
Smith, David Samuel 66, 72
Smith, David Samuel (Reverend) 66
Smith, Dominique Middleton 67
Smith, Ellen Timmons   74
Smith, Edward "Hamp" 157
Smith, Freddie 234
Smith General Merchandise & Store 110
Smith, Harry 157
Smith, Holt Lindbergh 110
Smith, Jacob 173
Smith, James E. Jr. 98
Smith, James E. Sr. 98, 144, 307
Smith, Jesse Edward (Principal) 233
Smith, Joe Deal 35, 222
Smith, John Benjamin 74
Smith, Linda 98
Smith, Luke 153
Smith, Mable Bryant 98

Smith, Mary Grayson 153
Smith, Mary 246
Smith, Mary Bertha Duncan 66
Smith, Pauline William 66, 226, 231
Smith, Queen 234
Smith, Richard 100
Smith, Rodney 157
Smith, Rosa Bell 231
Smith, Rose 153
Smith, Sherman Omar 67
Smith, Shirley 67
Smith, Solomon 98
Smith, Stanley 153
Smith, William 22
Smith, William 157
Smith, William (Presiding Elder) 168
Smith, Wilma Spann 67
Smith, Verna Lee Powell 110
Smith, Vernon 68
Smith, York 22
Smitty's Lawnmower Repair Shop 98
Snipes, Acy William 237, 242
Snipes, Rachel (Valedictorian) 237
Solomon, Stephanie 145
South Carolina Board of Education (Midwife Retirement Certificate) 28
Southern Six Singers 176
Spann, Kelly II 86, 127 (Reverend)
Spann, Silas (Reverend) 210
Spears, John H. 253
St. James-Santee Family Health Center 268, 270
St. Paul AME Church 27, 225
St. Paul AME Church School 13, 225
St. Peter Baptist Church 27
Stokes, Sherry (Finance Supervisor) 271
Strickland, Darci (WLTX 19 News Anchor) 202
Stafford, Allen 104
Stafford, Ben 37

Stafford, Ben 116, 119
Stafford, Ben Jr. 119
Stafford, Bessie Bryant 55, 98, 234
Stafford, Cleo 53, 226
Stafford, Damien 116
Stafford, Debra Johnson 116
Stafford, Edison 54, 153, 27, 301
Stafford, Emma Brewington 37, 42, 177, 226, 241, 242
Stafford, Eshmeil 37
Stafford, Francis 38
Stafford, Francis Sanders 37
Stafford, Franklin 53, 54, 234, 301
Stafford, Freddie 7, 119
Stafford, Geneva 119
Stafford, Glen Levi 116, 117
Stafford, Gwendolyn 104, 246
Stafford, Janie 104
Stafford, Jimmy 53. 127, 301
Stafford, Joe Nathan 104
Stafford, Johnny Lee 120
Stafford, Josephine 104
Stafford, Josiah 116, 149
Stafford, Kiziah Gasque 37
Stafford, London 22
Stafford, London I 37
Stafford, London II 37, 38
Stafford, Lorenza 104
Stafford, Lynn 176
Stafford, Marie 104
Stafford, Martha Hawkins 103
Stafford, Mary 117
Stafford, Mary Funnye 116, 119, 231
Stafford, Milton 103
Stafford, Minnie 116, 119
Stafford, Moody, Jr. 33, 72, 103
Stafford, Moody Sr. 103
Stafford, Queen Elizabeth Smalls 56
Stafford, Perry 104
Stafford, Randolph 53, 226, 244
Stafford, Rebecca Gatson 37

Stafford, Regina Darby 37
Stafford, Rosa Lee 116, 119, 234
Stafford, Ross 33, 37, 38, 41, 42, 72, 125, 251
Stafford, Rufus 117, 119
Stafford, Sarah 37
Stafford, Sarah 119, 120
Stafford, Stiruffen 37
Stafford, Suziah 226, 234
Stafford, Thomas (Drawing of Modest Home) 54
Stafford, Thomas, 37, 53, 55, 301
Stafford, Thomas 98, 234
Stafford, Tommy 119
Stafford, Turner 37
Stafford, Vernecia 104
Stafford, Vernell 53, 226
Stafford, William 118, 119
Stafford, William 37, 120
Strickland, Darci 204
Strickland, Jasmine 299
Strickland, Khalid 300, 301
Strickland, Lula Mae 299, 300
Strickland, Noah 301
Strickland, Sachiko 301
Sullivan, Adrienne LaTres 249
Sullivan Island Historical Sign 23
Sumpter, Betty Lou 157
Sunset Inn Club 106
Susan K. Komen Foundation 271
Sutton, Antwon M. (Principal) 49
Sutton, Harry 49
Swanson, David 24
Swatzel, Tom L. 279
Swayzer, Loretta 134, 135
Swayzer, Lou Emma Bryant (Specialist) 10
Swayzer, George 134, 135
Swinton, Tony 22
Systah 51
Table of Contents (Inflummashum) Information 4

Taylor, Joan (Dr.) 269
Taylor, Wayne P. 253
Tennison, Vergie 309, 310, 311
Thanksgiving Day 2015 (Huey and Janet Bryant's House) 133
The Centennial Encyclopedia of the AME Church 43
The Georgetown Times 24
The Franklin Sun 300
The Neighborhood Clean Up Group 303
The Store 20
The Shop 38, 53
Thomas, Angela 204
Thomas, J. E. (Secretary) 191
Thomas, Robert 204, 220
Thomas, Robert E. (Reverend)
Thompson, Addie 251
Thompson, Almeta Sanders 28
Thompson, Anne 286
Thompson, Daisy Brown 137, 139, 141, 144, 143
Thompson, Doris 137
Thompson, Edgar 137
Thompson, Etta 242
Thompson, Francis 137, 139, 141, 145
Thompson, Harold 28
Thompson, Hurbert 137
Thompson, James 137, 139, 141, 144, 145
Thompson, Joseph Garvin (Principal) 87, 187, 233, 234, 242, 244
Thompson, LaTonya 137, 139, 141
Thompson, Laura 137, 139, 141
Thompson, Laura Ella Lorick 137, 138
Thompson, Leah Shepherd 251
Thompson, Levora 137, 139
Thompson, Lila 137
Thompson, Maggie Ann 137
Thompson, Olive Lee 137
Thompson, Pearl 137
Thompson, Richard 137
Thompson, Richard Carroll 145

Thompson, Ricky 137
Thompson, Roosevelt 28
Thompson, Sarah 137
Thompson, Thaddeus L. (Principal) 251, 254, 271
Thompson, Thedra 137, 139, 141
Thompson, Torrence 251
Thompson, William Jefferson 137, 138
Thompson, W.S. 41
Thornton, James Jr. 76
Thornton, Walletta Joyce McKnight 76
Tigler, Elizabeth Brown 170
Tika Motel, Myrtle Beach 100
Tilton, A.J. 222
Tindal, Mamie A. 242
Tompkins, Ester Mae 269
Tompkins, Henry 22
Trappier, Alexander 22
Trappier, Amelia 231, 302
Trappier, Annie Pearl Cooper 303
Trappier, Bernida Washington (Secretary) 236
Trappier, Elex 223
Trappier, Francis Bells (Trap) 80, 173
Trappier, Harold 303
Trappier, Isaac 171
Trappier, Lillie 171
Trappier, Mary Gasque 269
Trappier, Patricia 298
Trappier, Prestena 171
Trappier, Ronson 171
Tricia's Beauty Salon 82
Trudie Knowling Scholarship Fund 302
Tucker, Alberta 174
Tucker, Mary Bryant 238
Tucker, Martha 174
Tucker, Rose Mae 174
Turpentine 22
Vantage Wood Burning Cooking Stove 52
Vashawn 255
Village Road 35

Wallace J. McKnight Christian Education Building 42
Ward, Gus T. 73
Ward, Joseph 176
Washington, Bernie 68, 71
Washington, Bertha 38
Washington, Constance 203
Washington DC Dermatology 97
Washington, Samuel 22
Washington, Anitra 255
Washington, Benjamin 152
Washington, Bertha 38
Washington, Mrs. George 226
Washington, Gregory 152
Washington, Jada Simone 152
Washington, Marcus 152
Washington, Myra 152
Washington, W. J. 41
Washington, Phillip (Reverend) 203, 205
Washington, Rebecca 246
Washington, Sara Wilson 152, 239
Washington, Tara 152
Watts, Walter 29
Waterways Map of Georgetown County 16
Waye, Alexandra 299
Waye, Charles Louise Sr. 297, 299
Waye, Nathaniel 299
Waye, Theresa 299
Waye, Tom 299
Waye, Vernell Stafford 297, 299
Whites 29
White, Albertha 115
White, Andrew 52
White, Benjamin 115
White, Beulah 115
Wright, David 264
White, Florie 250
Wright, George Ronald (LDDR) 264
White, Gerald 255

White, Herbert Jr. 115
White, Herbert Sr. 115
White, Isiah 115
White, James 115
White, James 52
White, Joe 115
White, Lila 115
White, Lular Wilson 52
White, Mary C. 115
White, Maunie Jr. 115
White Maunie Sr. 115
White, Michelle 255
White, Roberta 115
White, Rosa Bell 115
White, Sallie Grant 52
Whitmore, Jackie 214
Wineglass, Mary Green 246
Williams, Abraham 22
Williams, Daisy 66
Williams, Henry Zachariah 252
Williams, Julia 157
Williams, Preston Warren II (Bishop) 163
Williams, Preston Warren II (Bishop) Student Residence Hall 196
Williams, Rosette Dennison 252
Williams, Sollie 66
Williams, Wilma Delores Web (Wilma Delores Webb Williams Student Residence Hall) 197
Wilson, A'ja (University of South Carolina Gamecocks Women's Basketball Team 214
Wilson, Althea 260
Wilson, Hessie Armstrong 68, 69
Wilson, Hestina 69
Wilson, Carrie Moyd 68, 69
Wilson, Christine 70
Wilson, Donnie 69
Wilson, Edward 68, 71
Wilson, Evelyn 152

Wilson, Floyd (Reverend) 69
Wilson, Grady Sr. (Mr. Grady) 150, 151, 173, 229, 231
Wilson, Herbert 271
Wilson, IRissa 70
Wilson, Jacqueline 69
Wilson, Jimmie 69
Wilson, Kareem 260
Wilson, Krystal 70
Wilson, Mack 223
Wilson, Miranda Princess 153
Wilson, Rebecca Holmes (Evangelist) 150, 151
Wilson, Roosevelt 69
Wilson, Solomon (Pee Wee) 69
Wilson, Sylvia 69
Wilson, Teddy 69, 260
Wilson, VeTarya 70
Wilson, William 68
Wilson, Willie 69, 70
Woodbury, James 233
Wragg, Alfrenita 23
Wragg, Audrey 81
Wragg, Cardell Rhue 81
Wragg, Curtis 235
Wragg, David 224, 228, 279
Wragg, Demphis 72, 235
Wragg, Geraldine 235
Wragg, J. 223
Wragg, Javaughn 235
Wragg, Jefferson 81
Wragg, John Demphis Jr. 235
Wragg, Leonard 81
Wragg, Luechen Jr. 81
Wragg, Luechen Sr. 81
Wragg, Luechen Sr. (Luechen Wragg Brick Work) 81
Wragg, Lue Jean 81
Wragg, Mark 81
Wragg, Monique 81
Wragg. Samuel 228

Wragg, Samuel Sr. 81, 235
Wragg, Sarah Holmes 235
Wragg, Valerie 235
Wragg, Verleria 81
Wragg, Wannetta 246
Wragg, Wilhelmina White 81
Wright, Claudia Sherald 264
Wright, George 264
Wright, Joseph 271
Wright, Richard Robert Jr. (Reverend) 43
Young, Archer 186
Young, Charles (Dr.) 186
Young, Charlotte 186
Youngs Chapel AME Church 65
Young, Christopher 186
Young, Nathaniel 252
Zion Baptist Church, Columbia 248, 249

Libbin' (Living) **I**n **D**e (The) **B**illige (Village)

Sam **P**itt (Sampit, Sampeet)

Lil Eff

www.ingramcontent.com/pod-product-compliance
Lightning Source LLC
Chambersburg PA
CBHW061810290426
44110CB00026B/2839